Give a Manor Take a Manor

The Rise and Decline of a Medieval Manor

By Murray Johnston

Published by New Generation Publishing in 2019

ISBN
Paperback: 978-1-78955-688-9
Hardback: 978-1-78955-689-6

www.newgeneration-publishing.com

 New Generation Publishing

Dedicated to Andrew Eden,
and the many lords of ancient Watford,
who have come and gone before.

And the lands of Watford parish, which forever grow older but never change,
the people come and go, but lands remain and never move;
Like a great jig-saw puzzle, matching piece to piece has been a pleasure,
and for what remains, the search continues.

Contents

Table of Figures

Acknowledgements

Numerous sources have been explored to provide the foundation for this work. These days, excellent material is commonly available on the internet. Sources mined extensively include:

http://www.medievalgenealogy.org.uk, https://archive.org, http://www.british-history.ac.uk.

Also, my research visited the extensive archives and invaluable original material of: The Bodleian Libraries of the University of Oxford, the British Library, the College of Arms, TNA of London, and especially NRO in Northamptonshire. The NRO's Ormonde Kilkenny collection deserves a special mention. My thanks to the very helpful staff of them all.

For two now aged works: First, the book by Sydenham Hervey, written just over a century ago, which sets an excellent example of research on a parish – *Ladbroke and its Owners* – and which also provided considerable useful information relevant to this Watford story. Second, the work of historian John Bridges 300 years ago must be recognized. Notwithstanding corrections in this work to a few of his statements, a modern reader of Bridges cannot help but be humbled by his enormous accomplishment. He did all his research manually; certainly without anything as convenient as the modern internet.

My appreciation for many Latin translations goes to Diana Spelman, an historical researcher based in Norwich, and for certain IPMs, to palaeographer Hilary Marshall of the London area. This work would have been somewhat incomplete without such invaluable assistance. Any errors made in bringing their work to this book is proof that I am merely human.

Thank you to many for all the help and advice. Not least of all, Dan White, 'reeve' of Watford whose enthusiasm for Watford history is inspiring, my appreciation for his boundless generosity. And the many farmers of Watford today for their willingness to dig into the past, including Adams, Frost, Gilbert, Incley, and Payne. Also to Priscilla Carney, whose determination to find the origins of Agnes de Ardern pinpointed Guthmund and his son, Herald de Ardern. And of course to the one at home who tolerated, encouraged and advised at key times throughout this endeavour, thank you!

With appreciation to the Heritage Lottery Fund for their support of Watford Church.

July 2019.

Glossary

Certain terms commonly used in Medieval times are unfamiliar today. The following introduces a selection of these terms; some have a greater description in the text.

Appurtenances: The rights that attach to a virgate or yardland of land, i.e. to access and use more than the arable ground of a virgate or yardland, especially pasture and meadow.

Alienate: The act of disposing, selling or otherwise conveying title to land from one person to the next often requiring the authority of a license from the king or other lord.

Carucate: A measure of arable land varying in area according to productive value, originally the land area a team of eight oxen could plough in a season. Equal to four yardlands or virgates.

Currency: One pound sterling (£), originally a pound weight of silver, was divided into 20 shillings (s) or 240 pennies (d). The alternate currency was the mark, worth two-thirds of a pound, or 13 shillings and 4 pence, or 160 pennies. A noble was half a mark, or 6s 8d.

Demesne, Villeinage, Free Tenancies: The most common three categories of rights of individuals working on or occupying land within a manor; the demesne was land held directly by the lord, villeins paid rent to the lord for use of certain lands, and free tenants occupied land and owed homage and service to the lord.

Enfeoff: To give someone freehold property or land in exchange for their pledged service.

Fine: The fee or tax paid to the king or his court for a formal record of a final concord transferring title to land, or for some other favour, ruling, license, or grant.

Held: Used in the context of an individual who 'held' land or other related assets, meaning the individual had the right to occupy and use the land.

Hide: See Carucate.

Indenture: Medieval form of the modern contract. An agreement executed in two or more copies with edges correspondingly indented, or cut across in wavy lines, as a means of identification by matching the several copies.

Inquisition, IPM (Inquisition Post Mortem): An enquiry instituted by the Crown to investigate and advise the Crown on rulings regarding matters such as inheritance of land after the death of someone who held land.

Intail, in tail, entail: To restrict the inheritance of property to one's lineal descendants.

Knight's Fee: The amount of land required to support the service a knight owed to the Crown, and comprised a number of hides or carucates according to assessed value.

Late or Lately: Meaning 'previously' or 'formerly', for example, 'Maud late wife of John'.

Livery: The ceremonial procedure at common law of conveying freehold land to a grantee.

Messuage: A dwelling house or homestead together with its attached outbuildings and the land of the dwelling and that immediately surrounds it.

Moiety: Usually the half part, for example, the moiety of a knight's fee.

Relief (of a knight's fee): An amount paid to the king (or an overlord or baron) to re-establish or re-license an heir to possess the manor lands previously held by his predecessor.

Render: To pay or provide, for example, to render 3 shillings rent, or render the service of ploughing a field.

Respite: To delay, for example to give respite for performing homage until next July.

Rolls: Records commonly of the Crown written onto parchment, often rolled into a tube for storage; hence the Fine Rolls, Close Rolls,

Patent Rolls, Pipe Rolls (of the Exchequer), Charter Rolls, and others, each recording different kinds of rulings or decisions.

Scutage: A fine or fee paid by a knight to the Crown in lieu of the knight serving in the army. Pronounced *skyoo-tij*.

Seisin: The valid possession of land by freehold.

Service: The medieval obligation owed by a tenant to a lord in return for the right to hold or use land granted by the lord to the tenant.

Town: An identified area within a parish, often but not always the whole parish, in farming areas usually associated with common farming methods within the town, and not necessarily indicating a village or group of dwellings in the modern sense.

Virgate: Usually, one fourth the area of a hide or carucate. The term 'virgate' was used in earlier, Latin, documents.

Yardland: See Virgate. The term 'yardland' was used in later, English, documents.

Modern Map, Locating Watford, Northamptonshire

Figure 1: Map[1] Northamptonshire, East Midlands & South East England

The Parish Lands

Figure 2: Watford Parish, Northamptonshire

Give a Manor Take a Manor

PART 1: The First Watford Manor

Richard de Clare Crosses with the Conqueror

Edward the Confessor, King of England, left no clear heir when he died in January 1066. The only English claimant to the monarchy was Harold Godwinson who was crowned in the same month. He immediately faced complications – two others wanted the throne. Hardrada, the king of Norway, was the first to pursue his claim. He and his Viking force invaded the north of England in September of 1066. King Harold, a skilled general, hurried north with his army to protect his crown and defeated Hardrada in a surprise attack near York.

While the king was busy fighting in the north, the other contender to the English throne, Duke William of Normandy, readied his invasion fleet on the coast of France. William claimed King Edward had promised him the throne, so he firmly believed he was the chosen successor. The Duke's army landed on England's south coast near Hastings on almost the same day as Harold's victory in the north of England. Harold and his battle-weary army hastily returned south. Less than three weeks after his victory in the north, Harold's tired army of perhaps 7,000 faced the forces of Duke William in the south. The location, later named Battle, was a few miles from Hastings. The Duke's army was greater in number than Harold's and arguably better equipped with horsemen and archers. Throughout the day of October 14, the battle raged. William's men finally weakened Harold's defences with a feigned flight manoeuvre. Many of Harold's leaders were killed, with Harold himself dead from an arrow through his eye, according to some narrators. Duke William was crowned King of England in December 1066.

Those who helped the Duke in the defeat of King Harold were richly rewarded. As was common practice by the victor in a conflict, William stripped lands from Harold's supporters and granted them to his favourites. Richard fitz Gilbert, count of Eu and Brionne in Normandy, was one of three dozen elite knights who accompanied the Duke of Normandy to lead the swift conquest of England in 1066.

The existing network of parishes across England formed the framework for the king's land grants. Larger parcels of land within a parish came to be called manors. However, a 'grant' was not free of obligation. According to Norman custom, in return for the right to 'hold' and use the king's lands in the future, recipients owed the king the

Figure 3: Arms of de Clare

'service of a knight's fee'. Initially, such service was performed as a soldier, or knight, in the king's army for a fixed period of time whenever called upon by the king. Richard fitz Gilbert was given many manors and parcels of lands mainly in Suffolk, Essex, Surrey, and Kent. One of the most important was the town of Clare in Suffolk, which prompted him to take the name *Richard de Clare* and adopt a coat of arms presenting a gold shield with red chevrons (see[2] Figure 3).

Twenty years after his conquest of England, King William decided to find out exactly what lands he owned, what they were worth, and to whom he had 'given' them. He sent his surveyors across the country and had their findings recorded in the Domesday Book. In turn, the Book became the basis for the king's taxes on those who held the manors and lands by right of knight's fee. The Survey is now a great source of knowledge of times nearly a thousand years past.

Gilbert, Richard de Clare's second son, had grown to be a young man in his early 20s by the time of the king's Domesday Survey of 1086. Richard's many land holdings were recorded in the Survey. At the time, Richard was in the process of retiring and before the Survey was taken, he handed over his Northamptonshire lands to Gilbert. Gilbert had not yet adopted the name 'de Clare', new to his father at the time of the Survey. Instead, he was given an alias 'the cook', which distinguished him from other Gilberts (e.g. Gilbert de Gant). He appears in Domesday as *Gisleberti cocus*, or 'Gilbert the cook' (see[3] Figure 4). The lands of Gilbert the cook in 1086 comprised two manors and two minor land holdings, all in Northamptonshire.

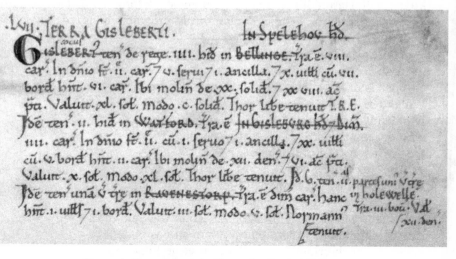

Figure 4: Excerpt from the Domesday Book, 1086

One of Gilbert's manors was the parish of Watford in Guilsborough Hundred. The surveyors recorded that Watford supported four ploughs – used on arable land for growing crops. The land was valued at only two hides. Half of the ploughs and two serfs were based on the lord's own land. The other two ploughs were worked by 20 tenants – each rented a small piece of land from the lord and often worked for him as well. Five peasants also toiled on the tenants' land. The lord of Watford had a mill which earned 12d per year in cash income from the tenants. Other than the arable land, there was 6 acres of meadow, which was never classified with arable land. Before the Conquest, when held by Thor, the manor was valued at 10s per year. Now, in 1086, Watford was worth 40s annually, which was relatively little and probably reflected the low value of two hides.

Richard de Clare died four years after the Great Survey. While his elder son was given lands in the family's ancestral homeland of Normandy, Richard's younger son, Gilbert, inherited the de Clare estates in England. He was now Gilbert de Clare and one of his many lands was the manor of Watford, held of the king by service due to the king of one knight's fee.

After a rich and eventful life, Gilbert de Clare died about 1117, leaving his wife Adeliza de Clermont and eight children. His eldest son inherited most of the de Clare lands and titles. Gilbert's third son, Baldwin, married Adelina de Rollos, niece of Baron William of Brunne and inherited the Northamptonshire lands, including the manor of Watford.

The Barony of Brunne had been created by the Conqueror's youngest son, now King Henry I, and given to a favourite, William de Rollos. A barony included several manors or fiefdoms of lands. The lord of each manor within the barony owed homage and service to the baron for his knight's fee. In turn the baron owed homage and service to the king for all the manors and knight's fees within the barony. The Barony of Brunne soon became a part of the Watford story.

King Henry I called for the next survey[4] of Northamptonshire, the 'hydarium', around 1120-25. The entry for Watford reads, *In Watford iiii hides de feodo Baldewini filii Gilberti* – Baldwin son of Gilbert holds the 4 hides of Watford by knight's fee.

The certification of 4 hides might suggest an increase in reported area of Watford, apparently figured out between Domesday and the time of King Henry I. Some say Silsworth and Murcott were added to Gilbert's 2 hides at Domesday to make the 4 hides of Baldwin de Clare. But the measure of 'hides' represented a base for tax assessments, not a specific acreage. There was no generally accepted standard for the size of a hide applied universally over the centuries. One method of measure[5] was based on a hide (or carucate) of 160 acres, therefore a virgate (or yardland) at four to the hide contained 40 acres, and four hides, or 640 acres, could represent a knight's fee.

There is no doubt that Watford supported one knight's fee, whether 2 or 4 hides. Neither Silsworth nor Murcott was named as part of any holding in the Great Survey. Parishes next to Watford such as Buckby, West Haddon, and Crick saw no reduction of assessed size after 1086, so no land area was 'moved' from another parish to Watford. King Henry's assessors must have arrived at the obvious conclusion that a fee of two hides greatly understated the taxable value of Watford parish – much to the Treasury's delight.

𝕬gnes's Legacy

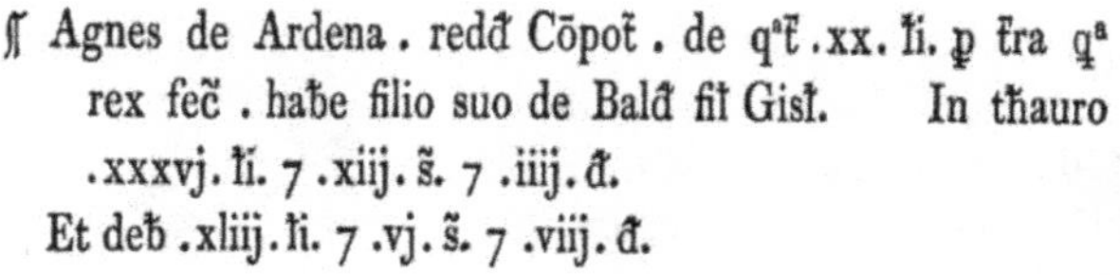

¶ Agnes de Ardena . redd̄ Cōpot̄ . de qᵗ̄ .xx. l̄i. p t̄ra qᵃ
rex feč . habe filio suo de Bald̄ fil Gist.   In t̄hauro
.xxxvj. l̄i. 7 .xiij. s̄. 7 .iiij. d̄.
Et deb .xliij. l̄i. 7 .vj. s̄. 7 .viij. d̄.

Figure 5: Grant of Land, Pipe Rolls 1129-1130

*Agnes of Arden renders account of £80 for land which
the king caused her son to hold of Baldwin son of
Gilbert.
In the treasury £36 13s 4d.
And owed £43 6s 8d.*

Figure 6: King Henry I

Late in the time of King Henry I (see[6] Figure 6), the families of de Clare, de Rollos, and de Ardern find common ground at Watford. Baron William de Rollos was recently deceased, so the king took the opportunity to re-grant the Barony to one of his favourites. That was Baldwin, son of Gilbert de Clare. At the same time, the king granted the manor of Watford to the family of Ardern, to be held of the Barony of Brunne. And the year marked the beginning of five centuries of continuous and sometimes untidy possession of the lands that Agnes entrusted to her Ardern descendants.

The Arderns first entered Watford in the 31st year of King Henry, or 1130. The occasion was recorded in the Pipe Rolls, sometimes known as the Great Rolls of the Exchequer, under **NORHAMTESCIRA**, or Northamptonshire (see[7] Figure 5).

This was a substantial grant of land – an £80 fine is too high for a minor matter. Plainly, the lady Agnes of Ardern carried sufficient influence or reputation with the king, whether in her own right or as the widow of someone with that status. While the grant did not name a parish, there can be little doubt the grant included the Watford manor.

The king appears to have granted Agnes more than Watford – explaining why no single parish was named – that is, potentially the several holdings of Baldwin fitz Gilbert in Northamptonshire. Agnes was able to make a substantial payment immediately, again indicating the Lady was not poor. The odd amounts paid and owed in Sterling had a base in the alternate currency – the mark. Thus, Agnes accounted for a fine of 120 marks in total, paid 55 immediately, and owed 65 marks for settlement at a later date.

At the same time as the Arderns were granted lands, Baldwin fitz Gilbert de Clare paid into the king's treasury the large fine of just over £300. With that payment, he and his wife Adelina, the niece of William de Rollos, were granted the Barony of Brunne, previously held by William. So the king addressed two concerns; Agnes and her family gained Watford and other lands, but the same lands remained within Baldwin's Barony.

Although the king granted Watford to Agnes and her son, they did not hold the lands *in capite*, meaning held directly of, or by grant from, the king. Instead, the Arderns were to hold Watford of Baldwin de Clare and therefore owe service to the Barony, not the king. For more than 60 years the Ardern lands and manor of Watford would be held under the umbrella of the Barony of Brunne. As long as Watford remained within the Barony, the Ardern possession would remain somewhat overshadowed by the Baron.

Agnes was married twice and by her first marriage as Ardern she had two sons, Alexander and Eustace. She paid the fine of 120 marks to protect the rights of Alexander. He was not of full age in 1130 and therefore did not have the right to hold the lands of Watford in his own name. Nonetheless, by this grant and fine, Agnes secured the right for herself and Alexander when he came of age to hold the manor lands by service of one knight's fee.

The Arderns were descendants of a Warwickshire family with close connections to the Earls of Mercia and who took their name from the Forest of Arden. Turchil de Ardern of Warwick was one of the very few natural English Saxon lords permitted by the Conqueror to hold lands in England after 1066. Whether with foresight or by an old animosity, Turchil did not support King Harold in the battle against Duke William, which won him favour with the new King. As his reward, in 1086 Turchil held more than 52 lordships within county Warwick, including Bickenhill.

Eustace de Ardern was the other of Agnes's sons. Henry de Ardern, the grandson and eventual heir of Turchil, came to hold the lands of Bickenhill among others. He granted his daughter the services of his relative, *Eustachii de Arderne de Bychenhulla*, which meant Eustace should give anything due from the knight's fee of Bickenhill to his daughter, not to Henry. While Eustace became *de Bickenhill* by name and hold the manor of Bickenhill in Warwickshire, his brother Alexander was destined to hold the manor of Watford in Northamptonshire.

Agnes was one of the generation after Turchil and his brothers Guthmund and Kettelborn. She appears to be either a daughter or daughter-in-law of one of the three brothers, most likely Guthmund. The generations following Agnes on both sides of her family remained connected to the principal line of the Arderns.

Once established in Watford, the Arderns marked their presence with the arms[8] of *Ardern of Watford* (see[9] Figure 7). The arms may be formally blazoned[10] as: *Ermine a Fess checky Or and Azure on a Chief Azure two Mullets Or pierced Gules*. These arms are obviously taken from the arms of Ardern of Rodburne (see Figure 51) presenting eight black ermine (a symbol of a fur) with a blue and gold checkerboard strip across the base. Watford added only the blue chief (band across the top) featuring two gold stars with red centres. The Arderns of Rodburne

Figure 7: Arms of Ardern de Watford

were descendants of Turchil of Warwick. The shared Arms further indicate the Arderns of Watford descend from the same Warwickshire family as Turchil. However, while many of Turchil's family stuck to the Rodburne style of arms, the Watford descendants adhered to two arms – the Rodburne blazon and at the same time another coat of arms, quite different.

After the lady Agnes married for the second time, she did not lose her links to the noble family of Ardern. Her second husband was Hugh de Keynes (or Caynes, Cahaignes),[11] and their children retained his name. Hugh was another who paid fines in 1130 – a total of £20 for the farm of Silverstone and income from certain Forest lands.

Hugh generously gave Dodford manor to Luffield Priory, located at the border between Buckinghamshire and Northamptonshire. The prior named the lady Agnes of Ardern in his defence against William de Caynes, grandson of Hugh's nephew. William was trying to recover the right to present clergy for appointment (the 'advowson') to the church of Dodford, because he knew the appointment represented an income:

> Hugo de Caynes, lord of Selueston and Dodeford and keeper of the forest
> of Witlewode, in the time of King Henry son of [King] William the
> bastard, which Hugh took to wife lady Agnes of Arderne and built the

castle de Bosco, the same Hugh gave the church of Dodeford with appurtenances to the church of Luffield, confirmed by his charter.

William's claim annoyed the prior, because the gift of Dodford had been confirmed by Hugh's son and his nephew. When Richard de Chaynes, Hugh's son, confirmed the gift about 1160–1163, one of the witnesses to the deed was Agnes's son, *Alexander de Ardena*.

In 1135 King Henry I died and only a year later so did Baldwin's eldest brother, who left sons to take over as Lord of Clare while Baldwin continued as Baron of Brunne. In contrast, King Henry left no heir. With the support of the English church and barons, the deceased king's nephew Stephen took the throne, shoving aside Henry's preferred candidate, his daughter Matilda. She had married the future Duke of Normandy and faced opposition from the Anglo-Norman barons. The period known as 'The Anarchy' followed, a civil war marking Stephen's entire reign. Baldwin took the side of King Stephen.

As a 'man of the highest rank', Baldwin de Clare delivered a speech to the king's army before participating in the first Battle of Lincoln in 1141. A kinsman bearing the de Clare chevrons on his shield can be seen on the far right of the scene (see[12] Figure 8). The Battle was one of several with Stephen and his barons lined up against those loyal to the Empress Matilda, her half-brother, and the king of Scotland. Despite Baldwin's stirring speech, Stephen's forces lost the battle. Baldwin received many wounds and with King Stephen and other lieutenants, was captured. Fortunately, both regained their freedom in an exchange of prisoners. Stephen resumed his briefly interrupted reign.

Baron Baldwin de Clare had several daughters, one of whom was Emma. She married Hugo Wac, a recent arrival in England from Normandy. After Baldwin died about 1154, the king granted the Barony of Brunne to Hugo. Once again the king favoured a son-in-law to hold the Barony, and Watford's new Baron was Hugo Wac.

Figure 8: Baldwin fitz Gilbert (left) delivers a speech, 1141

Eighty years after Domesday, King Henry II called for the barons across England to report their land holdings. Henry II was the son of

Matilda, so in the end, King Henry I would have been happy to see his grandson as monarch, even though Stephen's reign of 19 years had skipped his daughter, Matilda. As requested, the barons documented their holdings and the basis for them, which were summarised in what came to be called The Red Book of the Exchequer of 1166. Hugo Wac of Lincolnshire, the Baron of Brunne, wrote one of these charters[13] in which he reported just over 10 knight's fees, including Watford:

> To beloved Henry King of the English, Hugo Wac greetings and faithful service.
>
> Sir William de Coleville holds of the Barony which I hold of you 2 knight's fees, namely Roland de Creton one fee, and Alexander de Watford one fee; and so much I gave to him [Coleville] of my lordship of Brunne that from it he owes me the service of ¼ of a knight's fee.
>
> ... [then mentions another 5 ⅝ fees: two of Ernald de Bosco, two of Renald de Tanet, one of Helius de Kingsdon, and later mentions in Herts three 'poor' part fees – two of a quarter fee and one of an eighth] ...
>
> When King Henry enfeoffed William de Rolles, then William de Rolles gave Osmund de Wasperi one fee of his demesne, which William, his son, holds of me.
>
> And Baldwin fil Gilbert – after King Henry gave to him the lordship of Brunne for his services – he gave to Robert fil Gubold one fee for service, which his son holds of me. And to a certain pincerna of his, Gerold of Deping, he gave half a knight's fee of his lordship of Deping, which the same Gerold holds of me.
>
> My Lord, thou wishest to know by what service I hold my Barony of you. This is the service with which my predecessors with their bodies served King Henry, who gave the land to them, and I owe the same service of my body to you. ... My Lord, this charter behoves to be fully performed, and if you desire to inquire further I will notify to you as my Lord. Farewell.

Hugo Wac's charter confirmed his Barony not only held the fee of Watford but also that each of de Rolles and Baldwin had been baron before him. He also clarified that the barony could only be granted by the king, and therefore could not be inherited. The Red Book of 1166 includes another entry[14] in Gloucestershire – confirming Hugo's lands had been taken over by Baldwin: *Hugo Wac, of land that Baldwin son of Gilbert held, 1 knight's fee.* Hugo Wac made the required payment to the exchequer for his ten and one-eighth knight's fees in 1167-8. He somehow seems to have avoided any such payment for the Barony in 1171-2. Hugo died about 1176 and his son, Baldwin Wac, was granted the barony.

Eustace I: The Struggle for Recognition

Alexander's family name as declared in 1166, *de Watford,* came from the parish where he lived, which was a common custom at the time. The eldest son of each of the next four[15] generations was named Eustace, after Alexander's brother. In turn, each Eustace used either the traditional *de Ardern* or the adopted *de Watford* for his family name.

The handover of the manor to Alexander's son likely happened by the early 1170s when Eustace's name begins to appear. However, the evidence, or lack thereof, suggests Eustace never gained the king's recognition of his right to hold the Watford manor within the Barony of Brunne.

In his first known appearance, Eustace de Watford was one of the witnesses chosen by Maud, the Countess of Clare, to witness her gift of land (see[16] Figure 9) in Northamptonshire. If Alexander had been alive, then as lord of the manor he would have been the more likely witness. To confirm her grant Maud added her seal to the deed, which pictures two women holding a bird. Only after Maud's husband died in 1173 did she have the authority to give her lands without her husband's involvement. The first and seventh witnesses to the countess's deed were *Rob. fil Sewini vicecom. de Northton* and *Heustac de Wadford.* Robert son of Sawin was indeed sheriff of Northamptonshire from 1170–1174. So Eustace de Watford added his name as witness about 1174.

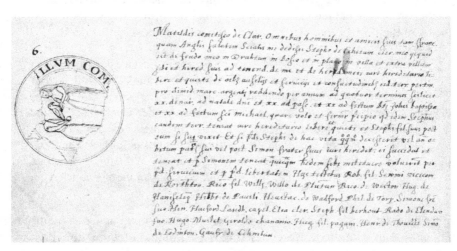

Figure 9: Grant and Seal of Countess of Clare, c 1174; copied c 1620

Sir Philip de Davyntre was a well-known knight of Northamptonshire and a Sheriff of neighbouring counties between 1166 and 1168. He was a friend and neighbour of Eustace de Watford – the chief tenant of a large part of Murcott township. Eustace's manor spread across the three towns making up Watford Parish, one being Murcott. About the mid 1170s, Philip made a gift of lands in various parishes of Northamptonshire and like the Countess, chose *Eustachius de Ardene* to be one of the witnesses to his deed. Philip and Eustace acted as witness for each other's deeds, and Philip soon returned the favour in an important deed that increased Eustace's land holdings and brought an addition to the de Watford family.

Back then, the possession of land was akin to the gold standard. Only the very few were fortunate enough to hold any land at all. Most peasants lived only to work on the land for their lord. Or as a kind of middle class, chosen tenants paid rent to the lord for the right to use a defined area while they and/or peasants worked the ploughs and planted crops on the tenancies. Land provided income and status. One could be sure there was an important motivation any time someone gave land or was given land. Even more, securing proof of possession of the land was of paramount importance.

When looking to increase the family land holdings, Eustace used the opportunity to find his eldest son a suitable wife. Eustace de Ardern was given a large parcel of land outside Watford that remained with the family long into the future … with strings attached. By chance, the deed[17] also confirmed that Alexander was the father of the first Eustace – there were no church records of births, deaths and marriage so long ago. As to general timing, this gift was made in the lifetime of the first Eustace – because he was named as beneficiary *and* the son of Alexander – at a guess, in the mid 1170s. Sir Philip de Davintre witnessed this deed.

> Feoffment by Roger son of William de Essebi to Eustace de Arderna son of Alexander for his homage and service and for 7 marks and 40d, of four virgates of land in Essebi, with three cotters (borderis) in the said town, to wit the cottages (bordellam) which Hawisia, Walter Cook (cocus), and Tustanus Cook (cocus) held; rent 16s. Fragment of seal (a bird). Witnesses: Philipp de Davintre, William de Oxend[on], Richard de Quenton, Adam de Essebi, Richard de Arderne, William de Arderne, Simon son of Philip, Robert his brother, Simon Malore and four others (named).

For centuries the four virgates in Esseby, later known as Cold Ashby in Guilsborough Hundred, were held as a ¼ knight's fee by the heir of Watford. When a significant part of a manor was split off and given to someone, the manor lord ensured that part of his obligation to the king for his knight's fee was also passed on. In this case, the parties agreed that the four virgates represented a quarter of a knight's fee, so Eustace owed a quarter of any related cost faced by whoever held the knight's fee of Cold Ashby, as well as 16s rent per year.

The Hawisia named in the deed married Eustace II and her marriage settlement was the lands in Esseby. All parties understood that once Eustace I was no longer manor lord, the lands and the income from them would pass to Eustace II and his wife for their support.

Gifts such as these involved the donor writing a deed or charter stating what land was given, by whom, to whom and under what conditions. Often no date was included – which can be frustrating – but much can be learned by a taking a close look at the witnesses to the deeds. Signatures were virtually never added at this time and did not become common practice until centuries later, although a seal was often attached to the deed. Nonetheless, both sides of the deal made very sure reliable men or women were standing by to witness what was happening and be ready to confirm the event should anyone raise any doubt long into the future. The important matter to record in writing was the gift itself, adding certainty with witness's names. If someone presented one of these deeds or charters as proof of his right to hold land, the fact that the gift was recorded in writing and that well-known individuals stood witness might be sufficient to remove any doubt. Where doubt might exist, an original deed could be presented to a new authority such as the king for confirmation by a process known as *inspeximus*. There was no consistent repository for deeds such as these; sometimes a copy was provided to one of many branches of the government, other times not. William de Esseby's deed, with his seal, was provided to and kept by the king's Exchequer.

Eustace's manor remained in the shadow of the Barony of Brunne and therefore to some extent subject to the whims of the Baron. Eustace wanted to ensure he and his descendants retained possession of the manor. He realised that his tenure depended at least to some extent on the Baron, and so he set about taking Watford out of the Barony to be held direct of the king, or *in capite*. As was common at the time – one or two hundred years after the Conquest – manor lords gave lands within their fief to the abbeys and priories of the Church throughout the country. Such gifts provided income in the form of rent paid to the abbeys and monasteries to support their occupants. This avoided any need for the Pope in Rome or the monarch of the realm to find them money from his own treasury.

Expecting to gain wide recognition, particularly from the king, Eustace gave[18] Watford Church to St James Abbey, near Northampton. His charter, which names Eustace as *de Erderna*, spelt out the gift and listed the witnesses. To add certainty, and the assurance his family was onside with the gift, Eustace recruited two of his sons as witnesses, one of whom was a cleric. Two generations later another de Watford son, also named William, took the example and likewise became a man of the cloth. Five witnesses to the gift of the church also appear on the Cold Ashby deed, including Sir Philip, suggesting both documents were written at about the same time – potentially, say, 1176.

> A charter, whereby Eustace de Erderna gave the church of Watford to the church of St. James of Northampton and the canons there in frank almoin for his own soul and the souls of his sons and his father and mother and wife; witnesses, Henry de Haddona, Philip de Davyntre, Richard de Erderna and William the clerk his brother, Simon son of Philip de Davyntre, Robert son of Philip, Thomas de Haddona, Philip his brother, Henry the squire of Philip, Humphrey de Hameslap, Michael Piel, Robert the Abbot's servant, Ralph Porter.

Watford gave much more than merely the bricks and mortar of the church to the Abbey. St James had been first established about 1105 by William Peverell, a favourite of William the Conqueror. An overview[19] of lands held by St James Abbey at the time of Dissolution includes: *'Watford and Silsworth: diverse rents and farms; Farmer of the rectory of Watford; Tithes in Silsworth.'* In fact, Watford's many gifts were the highest in annual value to St James other than gifts by Northampton town. Not hard to believe Eustace de Watford wished to impress someone with his generosity.

Watford's gifts to St James included farmland in both Watford and Silsworth, whose tenants paid rents to the Abbey. The farms included a precisely measured 66 ½ acres in Watford, and another gift was the mill sitting on a farm in the north east of Watford town. Besides land, the Abbey was given the tithes generated from all the farmland in Silsworth. Tithes, usually one-tenth of crops, produce or other profits, were an important source of income for the Rector of the church and upkeep of the church itself. In this case, while tithes arising in Watford and Murcott continued to the credit of the Rectory of Watford, the tithes from Silsworth were sent direct to St James Abbey.

Another entry in the St James register, confirming the gift of the church by the family several generations later, reads: *Eustace son of Eustace de Ardern for the soul of his wife Beatrice & his father Eustace confirms the abovesaid deed.* The 'abovesaid' deed was the gift of Watford church, as detailed earlier. The confirmation conveniently names the wife of Eustace III, not previously known. Too many times one Eustace was named as the son of another Eustace, making a challenging task of figuring out which Eustace was which.

Most abbeys and monasteries held their lands *in capite*, i.e. of the king, or of a high-ranking baron at least. This Abbey was unusual because its lands were held in *frank almoin*, the spiritual tenure by which a religious institution held land with a general duty to pray for the donor. Eustace did indeed make the gift of Watford Church with this in mind; he clearly said the gift was in frank almoin, desiring the canons of the Abbey to pray for his parents, his sons (of which he had many), and for himself and his wife. What's more, it may not have been possible for Eustace to give lands *in capite*, because he did not hold them *in capite*.

Fortunately, at least a few official records naming Eustace de Watford were dated. His presence in Watford is acknowledged in 1176 and 1177 when he made two agreements[20] with the king – one for a fine of 40 marks and the other for 10 marks – both recorded in the Pipe Rolls.

A forty-mark fine was levied by the king's *Forest* – relatively heavy for an unspecified infringement. The Forest was a medieval court set up by Henry II (see[21] Figure 10) with authority over forest laws, hunting grounds and the like, although there are examples of actions going further. Eustace paid 20 marks immediately, and the king's treasurers added: *And he owes 20 marks*. A year later Eustace remitted the second 20 marks, winning the comment: *And he is acquitted*. Clearly, in 1176 the king's Forest acknowledged Eustace as 'of Watford'.

Figure 10: King Henry II

The second fine of 10 marks was imposed in 1177. This was a 'new plea' to the Justices for the Crown and Common Pleas: Eustace de Watford renders account of 10 marks for licence to agree with Baldwin Wac. In the treasury 5 marks. And he owes 5 marks. Later the shortfall was addressed: the sheriff renders account of 5 marks of Eustace de Watford for license to agree with Baldwin Wac. In the treasury delivered. So Eustace paid a 'fine', or fee, to obtain the required 'license', or blessing, of the king for his agreement with Baldwin Wac. Unfortunately, the nature of the agreement is not specified, but is open to speculation. One such requirement could be for Baldwin, the new Baron of Brunne, to give permission for Eustace to give away the church of Watford.

Alternatively, the king's license might have been required for the grant of a bride or groom in marriage. Baldwin Wac had experience with this notion. Whether from kindness or arrogance, he paid two large fines in 1176 and 1177. The first was because he took it upon himself to give permission for a woman to marry. Often a noblewoman could marry only when decided by someone who had the right to grant or deny the permission. In this case it was the king himself who held the right. The second and greater fine again concerned a marriage involving the Wac family, but also the related inheritance of lands.

Another priory to benefit from Watford was St Andrews in Northampton, founded about 1084. The registry of St Andrews reports[22] a gift: *Alan de Watford, four virgates of land in Silsworth* although as usual, without a date. Alan made his gift[23] *with the assent of Alex(ander) his brother,* with witnesses Philip de Daventry, Simon Basset, and two others. Philip had been the Sheriff of nearby counties, and Simon Basset was equally prominent, serving as the Sheriff of Rutland from 1178-1179. The trail is clear in that Eustace's first two sons were named Eustace and Alexander after his uncle and father. Then a younger son, Alan, tapped one of those elder brothers to add support to his gift. Later records indicate the rental income to St Andrews from the 4 virgates in Silsworth was 16s per year.

Eustace II: Watford into the Limelight

The second Eustace took over the lordship of Watford as a young man in his late 20s. His tenure was long and covered the reign of three kings. In his time, he successfully wrestled the Watford manor away from the obscurity of the Barony of Brunne to become a prominent knight's fee in Northamptonshire held direct of the king. As a consequence, at that time the king's treasury began collecting payments for Watford direct from Eustace of Watford.

Unlike the uncertainty surrounding his father's inheritance, the transition of the Watford manor to Eustace II is clearer from a series of entries in the Pipe Rolls documenting three different agreements with the king. Each is traceable from the initial fine, followed by payments made, until finally 'quit'. Two are of consequence.

With the first, recorded in 1183 under the name de Watford, Eustace pays 20 marks for a plea agreement with the king of an unspecified nature. The second in 1184, as de Ardene, involved a fee of 5 marks for *morte d'ancestor.* This was the king's confirmation of an inheritance Eustace had lost following the death of an ancestor. Taken together, the agreements suggest the lands of the Watford fee formerly held by the first Eustace and before him by Alexander, both now deceased, were confirmed by the king to Eustace de Watford II.

While the king recognised Eustace's occupancy of the Watford manor, the lands and knight's fee nonetheless continued under the Barony of

Brunne. Eustace still had more work to do. On his side at least he had the prior of St James. But he needed more. At some point in the next two decades the final push likely took the form of a cash payment to either or both of the Crown and the Baron. Both tended to need money to cover high spending. As a result, the de Watford family went into substantial debt during the time of Eustace II.

At the very end of the 12th century, Eustace de Watford II appears twice in efforts to sort out his interests in land. In one case, William fitz Adam sued Eustace for possession of two virgates of land in Watford, which he said descended to him from an ancestor. Eustace countered with the accusation that William was a bastard and therefore ineligible to inherit. A Bishop decided that William was indeed legitimate. With that, Eustace failed to turn up at court to press his case, and so lost possession of the land to William.

The other case concerned Eustace's land in Welford, some ten miles northeast of Watford. Like Cold Ashby, this was another of Eustace's significant holdings outside the parish of Watford. Looking back to the time of the Hydarium around 1120-25, there was a holding in Welford, consisting of 1 ½ hides, then held of the fee of Baldwin Fitz Gilbert de Clare. These lands appear to have been granted to Agnes de Ardern and her descendants in 1130 along with the manor of Watford. Now, Eustace de Ardern granted his one-half knight's fee in Welford to Richard Luvet, forever. Richard gave Eustace 5 silver marks for the grant.

Eustace de Watford adopted a coat of arms[24] to distinguish the Watford line (see[25] Figure 11) of the family. These bear little resemblance to the arms of *Ardern of Watford* (see Figure 7) other than use of the colours blue and gold. The Watford arms were taken from Guthmund and his son Harold de Ardern of Upton, who had not adopted the Ardern arms of Turchil, Siward and the main Ardern line of Rodburne. New arms, different to existing paternal arms, were normally only granted to a newly prominent individual. The arms of Harold of Upton

Figure 11: Arms of de Watford

can be described simply as a red shield base with a gold chief (band across the top). Eustace of Watford distinguished himself by adding the label of three points transverse the chief, which indicated the arms were taken by an eldest son. These arms of de Watford appear as the fifth quartering in the sixteenth century certification of the arms of de Burneby (see Figure 33). The rise in distinction of Eustace II when gaining status as a fee held *in capite* might suggest the Arms were granted to him, although since all four of the Eustaces were eldest sons, that cannot be certain. One of the younger sons of Eustace II also adopted Harold's arms, in his case without the label of three points but with three gold crosslets in the base (see Figure 14).

Like any and all other manor lords in the kingdom, Eustace did not 'own' the lands of Watford; rather, he 'held' them. In medieval England, after the advent of William the Conqueror, no one 'owned' lands other than the king himself. However, the king granted possession of land to his favourites, often knights who had served the monarch well. In return, 'knight's service' was owed to the king, which meant the fortunate landholder could be called upon to serve in the king's army for 40 days. Or, if preferred, the grantee could pay the king a fine known as 'scutage' to avoid performing actual service in the army. The intent of scutage was to fund a substitute soldier with weapons and horse to serve in the king's force.

While this was the original purpose, with time scutage became a convenient means of taxation to gather funds for whatever purpose the king preferred. In his long reign of 35 years, Henry II collected seven scutages, his son King Richard in a busy ten years took three scutages, and Richard's younger brother John declared eleven in seventeen years. Late in the twelfth century, in the time of King Richard, something happened to cause Eustace de Watford II for the first time to meet the ongoing obligation of holding a knight's fee on his own account, rather than through the intervening Barony of Brunne.

The young prince Richard had acquired the tag *Cœur de Lion* following his fierce leadership of a siege in France. Demonstrating allegiance to his Norman ancestry, in July 1189 Richard and the King of France led an army that defeated Richard's own father, King Henry II, in the southwest of France. As one of the peace terms, Richard was named heir to the throne of England. Two days later, King Henry II died, and the new king of England was Richard I.

After he was crowned, Richard imposed scutage at 10 shillings per fee intended to fund his wars in Wales. King Richard then embarked upon several Crusades commencing with the so-called Third Crusade, financed largely from the healthy Treasury left by his father.

After victories on islands in the Mediterranean and another on its eastern shores in 1191, his allies abandoned him so Richard and his army proceeded alone. Richard won further victories but never re-conquered Jerusalem, the ultimate purpose of the Crusades. After inconclusive battles with Saladin, the leader of his opponents, Richard was ill and aware that his younger brother John was up to mischief in England. He settled with Saladin and in October 1192 set out for home. While on his way two months later Richard was captured, and after 14 months' imprisonment was released upon payment of the immense ransom of £100,000. Soon after returning home in 1194 and forgiving his brother, Richard turned his attention to the reconquest of Normandy.

Such a venture needed money, particularly after the considerable depletion of the treasury caused by paying a king's ransom. So in the 6th year of his reign, Richard demanded his first universal scutage at 20 shillings per knight's fee, with 'no exceptions', specifically to fund the King's Ransom. For whatever now obscure reason, this event triggered the first scutage recorded as paid direct into treasury by Eustace de Watford. And Eustace learned first-hand that the king's treasurers did not miss a beat when making sure every penny was accounted for.

1194: Among similar reports for others in the county, the sheriff of Northampton 'rendered account for 20s scutage of Eustachio de Watford ... In treasury ... And is quit'. Curiously, in this and other scutages in the 1190s, Baldwin Wac continued to pay scutage for his barony of ten and one-eighth fees. Any likelihood that the Exchequer collected the Watford scutage twice seems rather low. More probably, the king substituted another manor for Watford within the Barony of Brunne – apparently the parish of Somerby.

1196: Two years later, Eustace began to encounter problems making payments. This time, the scutage of 20s per fee was for King Richard's second armed expedition into Normandy. Under a heading for knights who did not hold a fee direct of the king, there is a payment into treasury of 20s from Eustacii de Watford. Then, Eustacius de Arden incurred an additional debt of 4 marks to absent himself from the second invasion of Normandy. The third scutage of 20s was also demanded in this year, so the sheriff advised the Exchequer that Eustacii de Watford had not yet paid the fee.

1197: Referring to Eustacius de Arden and Eustacio de Watford, the king's accountants noted the Watford fee owed 4 marks for absence from the second army and 20s for the third scutage. Another dimension is added to Eustace's financial status when the sheriff 'rendered account for 60s from James son of Samuel, for 30 bezants,[i] which he owed for his debts against Eustacium de Watford'. This is the first official indication the Arderns of Watford were in debt to the Jewish lenders. Debt was not uncommon among landholders. Indeed, that the de Watfords were no exception was confirmed decades later.

---

[i] A gold coin of about a sovereign, of Byzantium or Constantinople origin, brought to Europe by the Crusaders.

1198: Eustacius de Ardene finally found the resources to pay the 4 marks owed for license to escape from the second army to Normandy. He also paid 11s 9d towards the second scutage, which left a debt of 8s 3d. The exchequer evidently decided Eustace had to pay the second scutage twice – once like everyone else, and a second time together with his fine of 4 marks for not attending the Normandy invasion. In the same year, the King's Forest fined Eustachius de Watford 1 mark for keeping greyhounds; he paid 12s 4d and therefore owed 12d (or 1s). And he still owed 20s for the third scutage.

1199: King John now reigns in England. The unfortunate King Richard was dead after being accidentally hit by a crossbow bolt in France. The Red Book for 1199 – 1200 has Eustachius de Watforde holding one fee in Northamptonshire. King John decided his first scutage would be two marks (26s 8d) per fee rather than the 20s favoured by his elder brother, Richard. Eustacius de Ardenn is reminded of his debt of 8s 3d for the second scutage, and Eustacii de Watford, of 20s for King Richard's third scutage. Naturally, the new king's treasury did not overlook Eustacius de Watford's debt to the Forest of 12d. Eustacius negotiated an exemption from crossing the sea to Normandy with a payment of 40s. A comment is added in the Red Book: *He has peace of his scutage after the 40 shillings [3 marks] which we hereby record.*

1200: Unfortunately, Eustace's 'peace' applied only to the current round of scutage – he was not forgiven his debts arising from King Richard's second or third scutage. Eustace owed 20s for the third scutage, but managed to pay 10s 8d, leaving a debt of 9s 4d. Not to forget the Forest, Eustacio de Watford paid the 12d he owed into Treasury and was quit.

1201: In the third year of the reign of King John, Eustace de Arden owes 8s 3d for King Richard's second scutage, and Eustace de Watford accounts for another 9s 4d for the last king's third scutage. Thankfully, Eustace de Watford was able to pay into treasury a fine of 3 marks for 1 knight's fee and was quit. The Fine Rolls record the important entry: *Eustace de Watford has given 3 marks. He holds one knight's fee in chief.* This was the first time the Watford fee was acknowledged *in capite*, meaning held direct of the king, rather than of a barony. So the Baron of Brunne no longer held Watford.

1202–1204: Eustacio de Ardenne paid 5 marks for 1 knight's fee. And Eustacius finally paid off the 8s 3d owed for King Richard's second scutage and was quit. The Watford Arderns are not recorded making payments in the two years 1203 and 1204, when the fourth and fifth of King John's scutages were collected.

1205–1207: Eustace resumes payments. In 1205 he was quit for 2 marks of the 6th scutage. The next year sees Eustacius going into debt of 20s for the 7th, although he manages to clear this in 1207.

The Exchequer of England kept careful record of knight's fees in England to provide the basis for who should be charged scutage for what knight's fees. In the first decade of the 13th century, in the time of King John, either the Red Book or Book of Fees contain at least three of these entries, all confirming Eustace as the possessor of the fee of Watford. In each case the record is almost the same: *Eustace de Watford holds one knight's fee.*

To put the one knight's fee held by Eustace in perspective, around this time Northamptonshire alone supported about 135 knight's fees. These included the great baronies of the Abbot of Peterborough with 60 knight's fees, Richard Basset with 15 fees, the Honour of Robert Chokes with 15 fees, and the 15 later 13 fees of Robert Foliot in Northamptonshire. The county Sheriff often reported another block of 25 to 35 fees, although he did not specify them by name until 1194. Every knight's fee in the country recorded by the Exchequer was obliged to pay the scutage of, for example, 20 shillings or 1 mark per fee, whenever demanded by the king.

Eustace de Watford II followed the example set by his father and made gifts to two more abbeys of Northamptonshire.

Sulby Abbey was one of them. The Abbey, situated in the parish of Sulby next to Welford, was founded about 1155. King Edward II issued[26] '*Confirmation to the abbot and convent of Suleby of numerous private grants made to the sometime abbot of Welleford now called Suleby.*' The Register offers some detail, including: *donations in Welford and Watford by Robert de Luvet and Eustachius de Ardern, in Cold Ashby by Ralph de Silsworth.* Conveniently, Richard Luvet of Welford, previously referred to, helps date the Watford gifts. Robert de Luvet was Richard's son, so the gift was made by Eustace II about 1210. He granted[27] a virgate, a meadow and a cottage, in the manner following:

> Also grant and confirmation, which Eustace de Arderne made to the Canons, of all the land with appurtenances in Welleford, which Robert Luveth gave & granted to them. Also grant and confirmation which Eustace son of Eustace de Wathford made to the same Abbot & Canons and brothers of the said fraternity of one virgate of land with appurtenances in Wathford. Moreover, grant and confirmation, which the same Eustace son of Eustace made to the same Abbot and Canons of the meadow of the demesne of Wathford which is called Calumede, and of one cothland [cottage or cottage-land] of land in

27

Wathford, and one half acre of land in Chald-Asseby, from Ralph the smith, son of Ailmer of Suelesworth; and from all who should be born of him, with all their chattels.

Daventry Priory also received gifts from Watford. This priory was founded about 1090 and the parishes of Daventry and Watford were among 26 benefactors. One gift[28] reads: *Robert de Braybroc, former sheriff of Northampton, bought from old Eustace de Watford the meadow which is called Sanford, rendering annually to the said Eustace, two shillings.* Robert de Braybroc was sheriff for the five years 1209 – 1214 under King John. This, together with the reference to 'old' is consistent with Eustace de Watford II being the vendor of the meadow late in his life, around the same time as his gift to Sulby, about 1210.

Eustace III: The Rebel

In his later years, King John saw a transition of the Watford manor to Eustace III. His father died well-advanced in years, so Eustace III was no youngster, long since 'of age'. Although not destined to be lord of Watford for long, Eustace lived through one of the most tumultuous times in English history – the First Baron's War and the Magna Carta.

After being informed of the death of Eustace de Watford II in 1213, the king ordered[29] the sheriff of Northamptonshire to give Hawisia her dower in Eustace's lands:

> to cause Hawysia who was the wife of Eustace de Watford to have her reasonable dower of the free tenement which was of the said Eustace formerly her husband in Watford & Silvesworth ... because in the County of Chester she undertook that she will not marry without our [the king's] licence & assent.

A few weeks later, the king ordered[30] son and heir Eustace de Watford III to have the Watford manor after he paid the fine. But Eustace didn't have enough money to hand, so instead he provided acceptable security for the amount. He was granted payment terms – 10 marks in each of January, April, June and September of 1214, the calendar year following.

> Eustace de Arden has made a fine with the King for forty marks to have the lands which were of Eustace de Arden, his late father, and of which he was seised on the day he died. [Security & payment terms specified] And Eustace should have full seisin without delay, to hold the said lands with their appurtenances, and with help of his free tenants, should be acquitted of the said fine.

As usual, the precise Exchequer did not lose track of Eustace's debt. Several months after the Fine Rolls confirmed his possession of Watford, the Pipe Rolls recorded the remaining unpaid fine of 30 marks. Of that, 10 marks was paid into treasury with 20 marks outstanding. The debt of 20 marks *for holding land as enclosed in Watford* was recorded a year later, in 1215, the last and most challenging year of King John's reign. On this occasion, the debt was noted in the Northamptonshire Roll under a heading: *the debts of Aaron*. Again a reference to Watford being in debt.

The Exchequer in 1214 records 40s scutage for the king's war in Poitevan, France, due from Eustacius de Watford for his 1 knight's fee. The scribes failed to note whether the amount was received into treasury or remained unpaid. A year later, they did note: 'Eustachius de Watford renders account of 40s for 1 fee. In treasury 37s 6d. And he owes 2s 6d.' Perhaps the king's treasurers had been justifiably anxious over the failure of King John's attempted revenge against King Philip of France, leaving England lost of its Angevin possessions in France.

John de Ardern, brother of Eustace III, was disappointed to find that the 7 virgates in Watford given to him in his father's lifetime were mortgaged. His father, Eustace II, had given John's inheritance as security for a loan from the Jews of Northampton. Eustace II paid 70 shillings annually to the king's exchequer for the debt, and now the same obligation lay on John's shoulders. Unfortunately, like his father he was short of cash. Instead, John provided[31] a horse for the king's use as substitute for his father's annual payment of 70s, and so the king granted John his lands. Then, four days later, with a second and similar ruling, the king gave John receipt for the horse and confirmed he should have his 7 virgates.

14th January 1214: John de Arden has given one horse of worth at the will of the lord King, paying to have quittance for such debt ... And it is ordered by the barons of the exchequer that John should be acquitted of those 70 shillings annual rent. And the sheriff is ordered that John, without delay, by the said fine, should have full seisin of the said lands with appurtenances, which on the occasion of the said debt were in the hands of the King. Geoffrey de Mandevill is pledge for John, for the said horse, as accounted aforesaid.

18th January 1214: John de Arden has rendered to the king one horse of worth for a certain fine made with the lord King to have seven virgates of land with appurtenances in Watford, which Eustace de Watford, his late father, had stood as surety for the Jews of Northampton. And it is ordered by the Barons of the Exchequer that John should be quit of that horse of worth. Witnessed by the King at Southampton.

Only a few years later, John de Ardern gave his brother Eustace all his land in Watford. A witness to the gift was Robert de Say, who turns out to be a special favourite of the king. Eustace III may have added John's 7 virgates to the holding of his other brother, Edmund de Watford, leaving Edmund with 14 virgates. This was indeed true of Edmund's son many years later.

Eustace III and his brother timed their efforts well when obtaining the rulings needed to gain formal recognition of their landholdings, for the king was about to be seriously distracted from day-to-day events. The king's autocratic reign was already stirring the barons into action – they were not about to take heavy taxes lying down. Early in 1215, England's northern and eastern Barons roused themselves and in May congregated at Northampton and soon after renounced their feudal ties to the king.

The First Barons War commenced when the barons attacked but failed to take Northampton Castle. Nonetheless, they proceeded to successfully take London. King John was forced to attach his great seal to the Magna Carta in June 1215. But John set aside the Great Charter and the war with the barons continued. Many of the barons, including supporters such as Eustace de Watford, were cast adrift[32] by the king due to their allegiance to the rebel cause.

> The Sheriff of Northants is ordered to cause Robert de Say to have land which was of Eustace de Watford in Watford with appurtenances which the lord king granted to him for as long as it pleased him.

The Barons asked for and won the support of prince Louis, heir to King Philip of France, and the conflict morphed into a war of succession to the English throne. Louis and his force landed in England and soon took two of King John's castles – without John in them. By July of 1216, the French prince laid siege to the strongest fortress in England, Dover Castle. At the same time the French were harried by a guerrilla force of archers from southeast England. After three months without success at Dover, prince Louis made a truce and left for London. Only days later, King John died – in October 1216 – leaving his 9-year-old son, Henry III. The truce didn't last

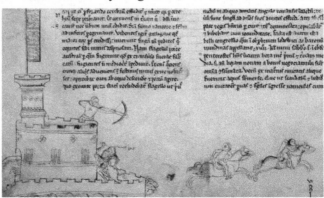

Figure 12: The Second Battle of Lincoln, May 1217

long, and the Protector of the young king quickly brought many of the Barons, including supporters such as Eustace III, around to the English king's side against the French.

In May of 1217 prince Louis suffered a major defeat at the second Battle of Lincoln (see[33] Figure 12). The forgiving attitude of the newly crowned King Henry towards the Barons and their followers was a smart tactical move. Immediately after the success at Lincoln, one of the many orders[34] issued in the name of the young king came when, like many others, Eustace returned to fealty:

> The King to Falkes de Breaute the Sheriff of Northamptonshire. Eustace de Watford has returned to our fealty & service. Therefore we order you to cause him to have seisin of all his lands in your Bailiwick which he held on the day he withdrew from the fealty & service of our father, King John. Witnessed at Stanwell, 15th day of June.

The youthful King Henry III collected a round of scutage in 1220. This time, however, the tax was not based on knight's fees, but rather on land area. The Treasury measured the area of each parish in carucates and charged the tax at two shillings per carucate. Various officials of the time said that for tax purposes a carucate ranged from 100 to 160 acres. The entry[35] relating to Watford states: *From Watford, Murcott and Silsworth, of 21 carucates, 42 shillings.*

Watford parish was measured at 21 carucates, which was the largest area and therefore highest tax in Guilsborough Hundred. The next largest parish in the Hundred was Cottesbrooke, at 18 carucates. The treasury had effectively declared the area of Watford parish to be more than 2,000 acres of, technically, arable land. Notably, Watford's rating had increased more than five-fold, from 4 to 21 carucates between the time of Henry I and Henry III, even if the tax per knight's fee had not changed by much … except for King John's efforts.

Not long before his death, Eustace III, son of the Lady Hawisia, witnessed the confirmation[36] of a gift to the Abbey of St James by Eustace IV. Eustace de Watford, son of Eustace de Watford, confirmed the gift of a cottage and 2 acres in Watford. The gift would earn Eustace the annual rent of one pound of cumin (a spice), but only after the death of the Lady Hawisia, formerly the wife of Eustace de Watford, his grandfather. Another example of several Eustaces de Watford making specific identification an adventure.

> Know that I Eustace de Watford, son of Eustace de Watford, have confirmed to the church of St James the gift which Robert Malory de Welton made to them of one cotland & 2 acres of land in Watford, paying

annually to me after the decease of the lady Hawisia formerly wife of Eustace de Watford, my grandfather, one pound of cumin &c Witnesses: Simon de Throp, Thomas de Haddon, William de Daventre Knight, Eustace son of the lady Hawisia, Eustach Gulafre &c

Eustace IV: Trusted Manor Lord of Northamptonshire

In April 1221, the next transition of the Watford fee occurred only eight years after Eustace III had taken on the lordship. Eustace IV took his place in the hierarchy of County Northampton, performing duties when called upon, although he had his share of scrapes to deal with.

The young Eustace de Watford IV gave security for relief of one knight's fee and performed homage to the king for his father's lands in Watford (see[37] Figure 13). Accordingly, the king ordered[38] Eustace to have the lands. The expression 'for relief' of one knight's fee was the king's way of saying the heir did not need to perform another great service for the king to be again rewarded by the grant of the manor. Instead, the king recognised the ancestor had already performed the service, so the king now 'relieved' the heir of the same obligation.

Figure 13: Relief of one Knight's Fee, Fine Rolls, 1221

Stamford, Northamptonshire. To the sheriff of Northamptonshire. Eustace of Watford has performed his homage for a knight's fee with appurtenances in Watford formerly of Eustace of Watford, his father, which falls to him by inheritance. Order that, having accepted security from the aforesaid Eustace for 100s. for relief, he is to cause him to have full seisin of the aforesaid knight's fee. Witness H. etc.

King Henry III or his representatives, for he was only 13 years old at the time, saw fit to impose the standard rate of 100 shillings for relief of one knight's fee, an amount determined in the time of his grandfather, King Henry II. King John, the previous king, had required 40 marks of Eustace's father eight years before – more than five times the 'standard' rate. But then, shortly after Eustace's father died, King John had been forced by the Magna Carta to return to the much lower 'standard' rate of 100 shillings. Consistent with his practice of high taxation, perhaps King John decided to use Roger of Howden's standard – that a knight's fee should be as little as 400 acres, by which basis Watford was indeed more than five times larger.

Money, or the lack of it, was an ongoing problem for the de Watfords. They had difficulty making due payments to the king's exchequer and through several generations, the family was substantially in debt. In 1242 Eustace de Watford is recorded with two debts totalling £1,263, then a very large amount. He paid 10 marks, and was told to pay down the remaining debt at the rate of 5 marks per year, a similar amount to 70s per year. In reality, at this rate the loan would have taken about 375 years to repay. As far back as 1222 the debt amounted[39] to 2,033 marks (£1,355) payable to the Jews. Nonetheless, at the same time as Eustace's substantial debt was recorded in the Pipe Rolls, he was able to pay scutage of 5 marks.

To avoid unwanted attention from the Treasury, Eustace apparently did pay at least scutage as well as the minimal amount due on his debt. Several entries relating to scutage are recorded within the period of 1235 to 1242. Each time, the record was almost the same: *From Eustace of Watford one mark for one knight's fee of the king.*

The 1250s were busy years for Eustace. He was one of many well-known manor lords in Northamptonshire to witness the gift of the church of Billing to Leicester Abbey. In 1252 he was one of four local lords asked to report back to the king concerning the castle and park of Northampton as well as four manors. The king wished to know in what operational state the previous guardian, Robert Basset, had left the castle and manors for the new guardian, William de Insula. Then Eustace and another were appointed to verify the tenants' reports of income from the king's possessions in the cities, boroughs and demesnes of the county.

Eustace's uncle John had given up his Watford lands, but he did well by marrying the heir of the Honour (or barony) of Aldford in Cheshire. He adopted his own arms (see[40] Figure 14), with the same gold chief and red base as de Watford, but with three crosslets. John de Ardern, who also used the name de Aldford, became a prominent and influential citizen not only in Cheshire, where he and his wife lived, but also more widely on behalf of the king. He is seen as early as 1237 executing a mandate to deliver the castles of Chester and Beeston according to the king's order. John's equally influential son was Walkelin de Ardern, who in a scutage of 1252 for Chester held 7 knight's fees. In 1253, he is awarded a salary from the Exchequer of £20 a year 'to maintain him in the king's service, until the king provides him in wards, escheats or a marriage to that value'.

Figure 14: Arms of Ardern of Aldford

In 1254, Walkelin de Arderne used his personal influence to benefit his cousin. He persuaded the king to grant exemption to Eustace de Watford among others from being appointed against his will to official duties such as jury service or sheriff. Taking on the role of sheriff could be a demanding appointment and was not necessarily willingly accepted. Discharging such duties brought financial obligations and other burdens. Two years later, Walkelin de Arderne again used his authority, this time as the king's marshal. In return for the inevitable fine paid to the treasury, he obtained a ruling exempting Eustace de Arderne from making himself a knight for the next three years.

These 'exemptions' did not last long. In 1258, Eustace de Watford was one of four 'knights' appointed to enquire about 'excesses, trespasses and injuries' committed in Northamptonshire. They were instructed to personally bring the result of their inquiries to Westminster. And a few months later, Eustace was formally appointed to the position of Sheriff to 'keep' the county in the form laid out by the king and his council.

Eustace was appointed as a custodial sheriff rather than a farmer sheriff, a duty he took on once again in 1264. A custodian[41] sheriff had to account for the total sum produced from the resources of the county and in return he was paid an allowance, similar to a management fee. On the other hand, a farmer sheriff committed himself to pay a fixed annual amount to the treasury from same resources and could keep any surplus for himself.

Eustace[42] was paid 50 marks for his custody of the county during his second tenure along with another 40 marks as an allowance for his tenure in the earlier period. Not until the pipe roll of 1265–66 was Eustace declared quit of the £30 he owed for the remainder of the county profit for his first tenure.

In the time between his two appointments as Sheriff, Eustace continued to serve the king. He was reimbursed £7 3s 7d spent in 1260 for repairing the prison in Northampton castle (see Figure 21), as testified by Ralph Basset, the previous keeper of the castle.

Like many others, Eustace sought out and used the weight of an order gained from the king to advance his own interests. For this, in each of three cases, he paid a half-mark fine. In 1260 and 1261, he won an order to the Sheriff of Northamptonshire for a hearing before John of Cave. In 1267, the order was for a hearing on a specific day before the Justices at the Bench.

There were also commissions directed to Eustace de Watford. In the later years of his life, only a few years before he died, he was tagged three times. He and his fellow justices were required to conduct trials of the prisoners held in the county jails within the county, rather than have them transported to Westminster for trial. This duty was not new to Eustace – he had been one of three back in 1254 called upon by Henry III to perform the same duty at the king's jail in Northampton.

'Sir Eustace, lord of Watford, knight', took back his tenement in West Haddon from the vicar of West Haddon and instead granted the land to the church and monks of Daventry. Similarly, Eustace de Watford repossessed all services due to him from land in Wyleby, Warwickshire, and chose this time to give them to the warden, associates, and sick of the hospital of St John located outside the East Gate of Oxford.

Despite his good deeds, the lord of Watford was able to find himself in trouble. In 1262 Eustace de Watford, his son-in-law William de Parles, Peter de Ardern (son of his cousin Walkelin), and another all found themselves detained in Leicester jail for the death of Gilbert de Barton. They posted bail. This incident was only shortly before major political upheaval, although appears to be more personal than political.

Some of the free tenants in Watford were very well-established citizens of the parish. These individuals were often asked to witness legal documents. Eustace wrote a charter about 1265, granting a toft called Caldewell in Watford, formerly held by Robert Lord, to Geoffrey Capel. Even though the gift was not large, the document was written and witnessed to stand the test of time. Among the witnesses were Eustace Golafre, Richard Traci and Richard Juel, all of whom, including Geoffrey Capel, were among Eustace's free tenants.

Eustace de Watford IV, as chief lord of the knight's fee of Watford, already had key tenants in Watford parish long before he died. The chief lord was, nevertheless, obliged to respect applicable laws, including the rights of his tenants. Action taken by Eustace in April of 1264, reportedly while he attended the Battle of Northampton, caused him to face a court[43] hearing concerning his second largest holding based in the 'town' of Murcott. The court ruled Eustace should pay a fine, and chewed out the tenant. The tenant occupied the Murcott lands of Philip de Daventry, grandson of Sir Philip de Daventry, held of Eustace by service of a ¼ knight's fee.

> John de Braunton says against Eustace de Watford that in the feast of the Ascension of the Lord 48 Henry III, the said Eustace came against him with force at his manor of Morecote and carried away all the goods he found there, viz corn found in his barn & he took away oxen and horses, & plundered his presses and carried away all other equipment & casks with cysaria, broke his fishpond and carried away his fish, plundered all his corn for the following autumn and occupied the said manor with all its appurtenances until the said land was recovered by the judgement of the King's court. By which it has deteriorated and he has damage to the value of £100, unlawfully & against the peace &c at the time of disturbance &c.

And Eustace comes & defends, not by force &c & not against the peace &c. And he says that there was never anything pleaded in the King's court by which the said land could have been recovered by the judgement of the court. But he says that Philip de Davintre held the land in chief of Eustace by Knight Service, that he entered the land as chief lord and keeper (warden?) of the land after the death of Philip.

And the said John comes and says that Philip of Davintre was surviving and long after was in the Isle of Ely.

And Eustace says that he was seised of the land at Easter before the said Ascension & seeks inquiry.

And John says that he was seised at the time of Ascension and seeks inquiry.

12 jurors, knights & others, on their oaths say that Eustace, where he was at Northampton, sent his men to Morcote in the third week after Easter because he feared that John would be enfeoffed in order to disinherit him. And that the goods they took there were valued at 10 marks. And that the goods were taken by Eustace's men on his order during the time of trouble within the time of the said John. Therefore, Eustace is in mercy & should pay John the 10 marks. Moreover John is in mercy for a false claim that the robbery was at Ascension when it was before that by 4 weeks.

Two generations after the First Barons War, similar events occurred in the Second Barons War of 1264–1267. This time, Simon de Montfort (see[44] Figure 15) led a group of barons in the southeast and Midlands against the rule of the king, Henry III. Again, their key complaint was excess taxation. The barons sought approval of another charter limiting taxation and the king's powers over inheritance. When that charter was set aside by King Henry III, the Second Barons War began with the Battle of Northampton in April of 1264.

Eustace de Watford[45] was among 39 knights of Northamptonshire who can be classified as Contrariants [those against the king]. With estates around Welton,

Figure 15: Simon de Montfort

Daventry, Brockhall and Watford, these Contrariants were a mere two miles away from Simon de Montfort's lands at Thorp in Norton and even closer to his property in Welton. Many, like Eustace de Watford of

Northamptonshire and Thomas de Arden of Warwickshire, held [manors] directly of the king or loyalist magnates, yet were in opposition. A large number of Northamptonshire Contrariants, such as neighbours Eustace de Watford, Robert fitz Walter of Daventry, and Philip de Daventry were present at the Battle of Northampton.

The King's army first assaulted the south gate of Northampton. His son, Prince Edward, guided troops under cover around the castle positioning him to lead a major assault on the north-west corner of St. Andrews Priory. The wall quickly collapsed and remaining defences followed. The Royalist infantry poured in to plunder and burn the town and even the churches. Immediately, the castle itself was under siege. Only three days after commencing the battle, the surviving rebels in the castle surrendered. The scholars of the new Northampton University apparently had fought hard for the rebels, but because many were the sons of influential men King Henry was persuaded not to execute them. Instead, Henry banned universities from Northampton.

Eustace de Watford, Edmund de Arderne, Thomas de Arderne, and Philip de Davyntre, all of Northamptonshire, also participated in the Battle of Lewes in May of 1264. This time, King Henry III and his supporters were resoundly defeated and for a short time, de Montfort ruled. However, a name well-familiar to the Arderns of Watford, Gilbert de Clare, a direct descendant of Gilbert the cook, re-joined the Royalist cause and after raising a large army defeated and killed de Montfort at Evesham in 1265.

One common estimate for the year of Eustace's birth is 1200, based on his inheriting Watford in 1221 at the full age of 21 years. If so, Eustace IV would have participated in those two battles at the age of 64, which appears somewhat unlikely. Perhaps the 1221 succession was of Eustace III, while that of Eustace IV around 1246 to 1254 remains undiscovered, unrecorded, or documented in rolls since lost. If not, then we might rest with the idea that the aged Eustace IV was a 'supporter' of the rebels rather than a 'combatant'.

In any case, as with the First Barons War, many of the knights came to be forgiven by the king after providing good service, for example by holding an inquisition for the king ... probably nudged along by the defeat of de Montfort. Sir Eustace was no exception.

Pardon[46] to brother Robert de Sancto Leonardo for the death of brother Thomas de Sancto Leonardo, as it appears by inquisition made by Eustace de Watford and Richard de Hanred that he killed him in self defence.

Remission[47] to Eustace de Watford, for long service, of all indignation and rancour of mind conceived towards him by the king by occasion of any trespasses charged against him in the time of the late disturbances; and pardon to him for any trespasses and excesses done by him in the said time.

Late in his life, Eustace found he had been given land in Watford by Peter de Aketon, and decided to keep the land in the family but outside the manor estate. Sir Eustace, knight, gave his three married daughters (one was unmarried) a messuage and 5 virgates of land in Watford (see[48] Figure 16). The charter was undated, but given the witnesses, and that his son-in-law William le Brun and brother Thomas were both still alive, was probably written around 1268.

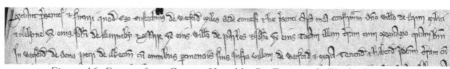

Figure 16: Extract from Grant of Land by Sir Eustace de Watford c 1268

The family's debt again caught up with the elderly Eustace in 1271. He and one of his sons-in-law were ordered to appear in front of the Justices concerning overdue payments required on debt to the Jews. The king interceded and told the court the pair should be forgiven penalties and interest on the debt for the several months around the time of the court hearing.

The Manor of Watford in 1276

Early in 1276, Sir Eustace de Watford IV died marking nearly 150 years of Ardern possession of the Watford Manor. As was common from the twelfth to sixteenth centuries, deceased persons had their land holdings evaluated at an 'inquisition'. This was an enquiry led by the king's escheator with a jury of 12 or more local residents. An escheator and jury considered only real estate, not personal estate. They figured out how much land and by what right the land was held and inherited. Based on this, fines (taxes) were imposed when the king confirmed the inheritance. The findings of the inquisition[49] were reported to the Exchequer and usually turned into an order from the king. For Eustace, the entry in the Close Rolls[50] is so detailed that the result provides unique insight into Watford manor and effectively becomes a census of the persons who lived, worked, or possessed lands in the parish at the time.

The laws and practices of succession in medieval England determined that the eldest surviving son was the inheritor of the principal land holdings of the father. If there were no sons, then the daughters all inherited equally. This applied to Eustace de Watford – he had four daughters and no sons. Regarding land, the child or children inherited their father's right to hold and benefit from the land. Therefore, each of the four daughters inherited his right to one fourth of the Watford manor and lands. The four daughters were: Athelina la Brune, the eldest daughter and a widow, Sarah, wife of John de Burneby, Joan the wife of William de Parles, and Ellen the youngest and a 'damsel' – the tag she earned for being unmarried.

The escheator reported the manor of Watford consisted of the capital messuage with manor house, 19 virgates of demesne, 35 ½ virgates of villeinage, and free tenancies, all held of the king in chief by service of one knight's fee. The expression 'held of the king in chief' meant the manor and its lands were held directly from the king, with no intervening baron. The total value of the manor was £64 8s 1d per year plus 5 virgates held by his three married children, gifted to them by Eustace and worth £4 annually. The escheator also recorded the age of the heritors, done to assure the king they were of legal age and therefore able to inherit. In this case the daughters were aged 30 'and more', which was the terminology used to communicate the individual had turned 30 at last birthday, or was at least 30 years old and quite possibly older. So the youngest, Ellen, was born about 1245 while her sisters were each progressively older.

The outcome of the inquisition was issued as a ruling in the Fine Rolls to the sheriff of Northampton who in this case was also the escheator for the county. He was to deliver to each of the daughters, the 'sisters and heirs of Eustace de Watford, tenant in chief, their portions of the inheritance of Eustace, they having done homage'. In the year immediately following the inquisition, each daughter paid a fine[51] to confirm that the inheritance from her father remained safely in her name.

John de Burnaby and Sarah his wife, Aline la Brune and Ellen de Watford, sisters of Sarah, daughters and heirs of Eustace de Watford, deceased, 20 marks, three parts of a knight's fee

Two months later: *William de Parles, 10 marks, a fourth part of a knight's fee*

The following table summarises Watford parish as held by Eustace de Watford and reported in the Close Rolls of 1276, including the land allocated to each of his daughters. An estimate of population has been added by the author – residents would have included farmers, labourers, and tradesmen of many kinds from stonemasons, smiths, carpenters, tailors, brewers, bakers and more.

Land	Land (virgates) allocated to each daughter				Total land (virgates)	Estimated population
	Athelina	Sarah	Joan	Ellen		
The Chief messuage & manor house	The Hall with courtyard, two chambers, and whatever there is to the south	The part between Athelina and Joan	The part to the north next the messuage that was Thomas de Watford's	The sheepcote with crofts and meadow under the garden as encl. by hedge	Nil	10
Demesne	4 ¾	4 ¾	4 ¾	4 ¾	19	40
Villeinage	8 ⁷/₈	8 ⁷/₈	8 ⁷/₈	8 ⁷/₈	35 ½	75
Free	7 ¼	17 ¼	15 ¼	3 ¾	43 ½	75
Totals	20 ⁷/₈	30 ⁷/₈	28 ⁷/₈	17 ³/₈	98	200

The 4 virgates situated in Esseby (Cold Ashby) held for about the prior century were excluded from the table above so that the totals represent Watford parish only. As well, according to normal practice, the escheator excluded the land area occupied by the chief messuage and a number of small holdings of free tenants and cotmen with messuages, crofts (a small plot of land near a dwelling house), tofts (a homestead with the attached arable land), cottages, and the odd acre or two.

The inquisition indicated a progression in the number of hides in the parish. There were two hides at Watford for King William's Domesday, four with Henry I, twenty-one during the reign of Henry III, and now, in the time of Edward I, nearly twenty-five hides for the Watford manor.

As was customary, Margery, Eustace's widow, was dowered with one third of the estate in order to ensure she could continue living in the style to which she was accustomed and not be turned out by the younger generation. When she died, her dower lands would be returned to her daughters.

THE DEMESNE OF WATFORD IN 1276

The demesne of a lordship was those lands attached to the manor and retained for the lord's own use. Each of 25 fields making up the 19 virgates of the demesne was carefully listed by name, plus a meadow and a spinney. The escheator painstakingly recorded the acreage of each field and allocated one quarter to each of the four sisters. A summary of the escheator's work suggests that thirteenth century Watford quantified one virgate as 20 acres. Each daughter was allocated about 95 acres, being the total of all her quarter shares, recorded in the summary as 4 ¾ virgates.

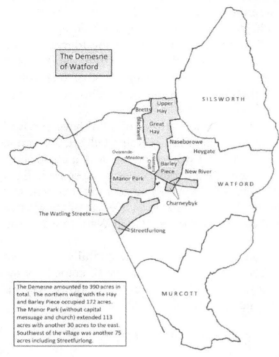

Figure 17: The Demesne of Watford

Although not listed, either by name or number, the lord had serfs to work the demesne land for him, supplementing the villeins who also worked there. At a guess of two per virgate, about forty serfs lived on the demesne.

The location of the demesne, as shown in Figure 17, is based partly on the fieldnames and acreages listed by the escheator in 1276. Some modern maps outline Watford's demesne only to the north of the manor estate. As far as it goes, this may be accurate, but cannot be complete, because that area is nowhere near 400 acres. Another area, westwards from the manor house itself, seems logical. The Close Rolls contain a few fieldnames recognizable in early modern times, and other fields can be identified either by their size in acres or according to the order in which they were listed – pretty much north-south. Examples of recognizable fieldnames include: Hayfurlong, Barlifurlong, Churnebyk, and Stretfurlong. Fields recognizable by their size, if not by name, include two at 24 and 32 acres plus the 2 acre lot 'Next Le Hay', which together represent the Upper Hay of 58 acres. Other fields, while not immediately recognisable by name, with other documents can be generally located when two descriptions such as 'in the field beyond the town' and 'in the field on this side of the Streete' are both true.

THE VILLEINAGE OF WATFORD IN 1276

Villeins were feudal tenants entirely subject to the lord or manor, to whom they paid dues and rendered services in return for use of the land. Again with great care, the escheator listed the name and holding, usually one virgate, of each villein in Watford, and to which of the four sisters he was allocated. There were 38 villeins in total, each listed by name. Each sister had eight different villeins with a virgate each, another one villein each with a half virgate, and there were two more villeins for all four sisters, one with 2 virgates and the other with 1 virgate.

Several families of villeins named in the Watford of 1276 have survived through the centuries. Those include the families of Ralph Gilbert, Richard le Palmer and Adam le Freeman. While most worked on the land, a cleric and a smithy were identified while the trade of many others was not specified. Each villein could have been single, married, or with one or more children and therefore, speculating, each household might contain an average of at least two persons. Accordingly, the population of villeins in 1276 in Watford was about 75 people, possibly more.

The escheator did not forget the grieving widow. He dutifully designated by name three specific villeins from each sister's retinue, or 12 in total, for the dower of Eustace's widow, Margery. Not by chance, the 12 dower villeins represented as close as can be to one-third of all the villeins.

FREE SERVICE TENANTS OF WATFORD IN 1276

Tenants of lands under free service owed homage and 'service' to the lord – the name did not mean their service or homage was 'free' in the modern sense. The required service could be performed in any one or more of several ways. If the service owed was a portion of a knight's fee, which only applied for the larger tracts of tenanted land, the tenant could be called upon to serve in the army in the traditional way of a knight's fee, or pay scutage to avoid the army service. Another 'service' sometimes owed, becoming more common over time, was the payment of money as an annual rent. Lastly, the 'service 'could be actual labour to be performed each year by the tenant. In Watford, two examples were:

Geoffrey de Chamberlain: For his 1 virgate, besides annual rent of 2s, 2 hens, a white loaf and six gallons of ale to the lord - he shall find a man to lift the lord's hay for a day and for another day to make cocks of the hay, and he shall plough with the lord for a day, and in autumn he shall find a man for two days, price of the whole work 14½d

Alexander Michel: For his ½ virgate, besides annual rent of 2s 6d - he shall find the lord two men for two days at his cost in autumn and on one day one man at the lord's food, and he shall plough twice a year with the lord, and shall find a man to lift the lord's hay and a man to make cocks of hay, price for the whole work 11d

The 40 free tenants of Watford, all named, were listed with their holding and allotted among the sisters. In each case the escheator listed the service due by the tenant to the lord. Although each daughter's allocation was not equal in land area, it was equal in value as measured in annual rentals, at about 26s 6d each. In addition to the farmers and cottars were tailors, smiths, millworkers, brewers, and other tradesmen. For Margery's dower, three or four of each sister's free tenants were earmarked representing one third of her annual income from free tenancies.

All in all, allowing for three of the 40 free tenants not resident in Watford, there were 37 families. With similar logic as applied with the villeins, an estimate of free tenant population of Watford might be 75 persons. Perhaps because she was the eldest sister, Athelina's free tenants included some of the most reputable; individuals who were occasionally called upon to serve as witnesses to deeds, for example. These included Richard Juel, Geoffrey Capel, and Eustace Golafre. These families and others such as the Freemans lived on in Watford for centuries.

Each of the sisters took on at least one special free tenant.

Sir William de Arderne, tenant of Athelina. He was one of the two brothers of Eustace de Watford IV. This William had 'sir' as a prefix to his name but no 'knight' as suffix – this was the common designation for clerics. If William died with no heir of his own his holding would go to the next heir, which in this case meant become part of the de Burneby manor. The one yardland and mill of Old Mill Close in the northeast of Watford town was later known as the Hindmill Closes and Meadow containing about 57 acres. The mill generated 6s 6d annual income to Sir William and he in turn paid rent of 4s and two capons to the lord.

Master William de Watford was a favoured cleric to the crown. In appreciation of his work, the king gave him gifts such as livery of a supercoat and cloak with squirrel fur and hood of deer-skin for going as messenger of the king into Spain. On another occasion, the king appointed his 'beloved and faithful Master William de Watford' as one of the justices in the court for hearing pleas of the Jews.

Edmund de Watford, tenant of Sarah de Burneby. Edmund was a cousin of, and an executor for, Eustace de Watford IV. He was the second of five successive generations with the name Edmund de Watford, who continued to hold all or most of the 14 virgates partitioned to them in 1276. These lands came into the hands of the Catesby family more than a century later. Showing obvious favour to family, Edmund's rent was only 6d per year.

Robert, son of Thomas de Watford, also tenant of Sarah de Burneby. Thomas de Watford was another brother of Eustace de Watford IV and had predeceased Eustace. Robert, his son, was the first of six generations of de Watfords holding the two virgates and other lands in Watford. These land holdings also ended up with the Catesby family about two centuries later. Rent was again set favourably at 6d.

John, son of Philip de Davyntre of Murcote, tenant of Joan de Parles. His holding of 11 virgates represented a large portion of Murcott town and came with the obligations of a ¼ knight's fee. John was the great grandson of Sir Philip de Daventre, a witness to the gift of Watford church to St James Abbey. This large de Daventry holding remained core to the Parles, Cumberford, and finally, the Spencer estates in Watford parish.

Adam de Assheby, a tenant of Ellen de Watford. Adam was tenant of 5 virgates in Esseby (Cold Ashby), which had been given several generations before to Eustace, son of Alexander de Watford, by Roger, son of William de Essebi. Ellen died without heir so this holding also ended up with the Burneby manor. Adam's service obligation to the lord was a ¼ knight's fee.

Four priories held land in Watford, although only two holdings were mentioned among the free tenancies. One was Sarah's meadow of the prior of Davyntre, rented for 2 shillings. The other was Joan's 1½ virgates of the abbot of St James by Northampton, held for the rent of 6d as well as pepper and cumin. Not listed were St James' extensive other holdings in two of the parish's towns, lands in Silsworth held of the priory of St Andrews, and the lands of the abbot of Sulby.

The towns of Watford, Silsworth and Murcott

The medieval parish of Watford contained the 'town' and village of Watford itself as well as several settlements, including the 'towns' of Silsworth and Murcott. The sites of Silsworth and Murcott are known; the former at the north of the parish and the latter in the southern extremity. A 1771 map[52] of the south of Watford parish indicates the original Murcott 'town' encompassed 680 acres when including 22 acres of the village itself. About half of Murcott was transferred from Watford parish to Long Buckby parish in the 18th century.

In medieval times, before the partition of Murcott, Watford parish contained about 3,753 acres. Silsworth extended about 914 acres, and Murcott, 680 acres leaving Watford 'town' with the remaining 2,159 acres.

While both Silsworth and Murcott have been associated with medieval settlements, only Murcott survived as a recognizable village through to the early modern period. Since the earliest of times, Silsworth is mentioned in the context of tenements, tofts, pastures and meadows, sometimes with field names. The first known mention is of Alan de Watford donating lands in Silsworth around 1180. King John mentions 'Silvesworth' in 1213 in the context of a dower for the widow of Eustace de Watford. The 1220 scutage lists all three towns: *Watford, Morcot and Sivelesworth.*

There was a settlement of sorts at Silsworth in and for some time after 1276. Modern archaeologists believe a small group of houses or dwellings existed where Silsworth Field, Middle Field and Hill Meadow join. Ralph the smith operated his smithy on an acre of land with a cottage there. Robert the son of Hugh de Silsworth lived on a virgate of land, as did Alexander, son of Alexander de Silsworth, on a croft with an acre. Robert le Freman occupied a virgate of land in Silsworth. Residents transacted in parcels of land in the 14th and 15th centuries. By the sixteenth century there is little or no evidence of a village. While enclosure had not taken much effect in Watford or Murcott by this time, all the fields of Silsworth, including the many small parcels of the Highfields, had been enclosed by about 1600.

Figure 18: Silsworth Town

The following describes Silsworth's 914 acres in several parts (see Figure 18).

In the north, there is what became known as Sharrocks pasture and meadow with 40 acres. Just south is the Highfield of 110 acres, eventually carved into about 15-20 small closes. Immediately adjacent, to the west, is Highfield Close of 90 acres, which became three fields. The Catesbys in the 16th century counted Highfield and Highfield Close together as 200 acres.

South and east is Middle Field, or the 'Great Ground', of 150 acres, mostly pasture with a small meadow. All three together at 390 acres formed the Burneby manor of Silsworth, of which 150 acres appear to be priory lands.

Just to the west is Hill Meadow and further west, the Oad Ground, the two totalling nearly 150 acres. In the southwest with 170 acres is Silsworth Field, which abuts the great Hay fields and Naseborowe of Watford 'town'. Together, these large fields appear to have been a Parles then Comberford manor, potentially including an abbey holding.

In the far south, or the South Field for want of a better name, are three large pastures, Cooksfield, Viccars and Northingworth, totalling over 200 acres, including meadows. At least the first two of these three fields were held by the Burneby manor.

The lands of Murcott, before division with Long Buckby, can be described as follows. The 11 virgates plus their appurtenances of variable size later became a fixed 284 acres – two large tracts of land and another 15 acres for part of the village. This was originally held by the de Daventry family of the Parles manor and later by the Earls Spencer for over 400 years. Another 2¼ virgates plus appurtenances was held for centuries by the Burnebys, followed by the Clerkes, then the Cartwrights in the 18th century. This holding was originally 'dispersed' in the fields of Murcott, but was probably limited at the time of the 1771 inclosures to a distinct parcel of 70 acres. At that time the remaining 300 or so acres were made up of five separate holdings[53] totalling 11¼ yardlands, for a total of nearly 25 yardlands in Murcott. Whether these 18th century holdings existed as virgates in medieval times, is unknown.

Most of the tenants in the parish were not wealthy landlords. But each man greatly valued his plot of land from which the family made a living. As often as possible, such tenancies would be passed from one generation to another and thereby became very much part of family life.

The enumerated land estate left by Eustace de Watford IV in 1276 included nearly 100 virgates of land or about 2,000 arable acres, compared to 3,750 acres in Watford parish as a whole. While at this time, the escheator chose 20 acres as the size of a virgate, the land area of one virgate varied from parish to parish, but normally did not vary in the same parish over time. Typically, virgates did not include meadows, pastures, common lands or unproductive land such as woods, lakes, spinney[ii] or marshes. Meadow and pasture was usually attached to yardlands by right or, in the vernacular then used, were the *appurtenances* to the yardlands and represented the right to graze animals in the common lands of the parish or village.

In Northamptonshire, one yardland could be as little as 12 to 14 acres or as large as 60 to 80 acres, commonly around 20 to 30.[54] This variation in size of a yardland can often be accounted for by the quality of the arable land for growing crops, because yardlands were the basis for taxation. Very good quality cropland might result in smaller yardlands. Medieval history provides several options for the size of a virgate. Late in the twelfth century (1198), one of the king's justices, Roger of Howden, recorded that for taxation purposes on a national scale a normal carucate was 100 acres. Therefore, with four virgates to the carucate, one virgate (or yardland) averaged 25 acres.

Watford appears to reflect an unusually large expanse of grounds over and above the arable lands. Also, most of the ground in the parish held by the abbeys of Northamptonshire was excluded from heritable premises or the virgates listed. All of these lands amount to an additional area of about 88% of the 100 arable virgates. Later documents refer to meadows or pastures which were large fields forming farms in their own right. Examples in Watford include Radmore, Boylond and Overend. In another twist, while at this time about half of Murcott was quantified in virgates, or arable lands, Silsworth was mainly pasture and meadow, with only exceptional mention of land in the 'town' quantified or 'held' in virgates. Those great pastures and meadows of Silsworth were not among the free tenancies of Watford parish listed in 1276.

Two other names associated with Watford parish were Catesby and Comberford. Each was an enclosed manor in the medieval sense, but neither is known to be associated with a settlement in the parish. Both of these manors of Watford are considered at length later in this work, along with the largest manor in Watford known as Burneby's manor.

[ii] Pasture is grassland for grazing livestock; meadow is land with grass grown to be cut for hay; spinny is an area of trees and bushes.

Give a Manor Take a Manor

PART 2: The Burneby Manor

Sarah de Watford and John de Burneby: 1276–1303

Following the breakup of the Watford manor in 1276, the Burneby family quickly assembled the largest holding in Watford. Three of the four parts of Sir Eustace's manor became the de Burneby holding. Sarah, the second of Sir Eustace de Watford's four daughters, married John de Burneby. He was the son and heir of lord Robert de Burneby (see Arms[55] Figure 19) and his mother was a daughter of Thurston Basset, a powerful family of Staffordshire. Sarah and John were the first of twelve lords through ten generations[iii] to hold the Burneby manor.

Figure 19: Arms of de Burneby

Preserving the right to hold land was not simple for any of the daughters. Each had to navigate her way through the laws and customs of medieval England to keep her holding. An order from the king issued in the year 1280 included the words 'upon John's death' indicating the demise of John de Burneby. The king directed the Sheriff of Northamptonshire to deliver to Sarah the Watford the lands of her inheritance. She should also have the stock and goods lying on John's lands previously taken by the Crown. The king was willing to adjourn the customary homage for the lands due by Sarah until the next parliament.

Next, Sarah ensured her son's inheritance was acknowledged by the king. In 1285 the king ordered Henry de Bray, the escheator for the region, to permit Eustace, son and heir of Sarah de Burneby, daughter and co-heiress of Eustace de Watford, to enter the lands she held in chief in Watford. The king acknowledged Sarah's right to hold the lands descended to her from her father. He granted her son, Eustace, permission to hold the lands he would inherit from her, after he paid homage to the king. Eustace made fine to hold the lands in October 1285. If he had recently turned 21, then he was born around 1263.

The sisters also transacted among themselves, necessarily ensuring all was done according to the requirements of the day. In or before 1282, Ellen granted to her sister, Sarah, a toft called 'le Cotes' enclosed between Ellen's meadow and the king's highway, together with a croft called

---

[iii] see Appendix 2.

'Kalvecroft'. The witnesses to the exchange included John de Burneby, Edmund de Watford, Thomas Rynel, and John, the son of a smith. The enrolment of this grant must have been delayed about two years, as John de Burneby had died by 1280. The sisters were careful to ensure each had as witness one of her free service tenants – Thomas Rynel was one of Sarah's, and John, son of the smith, was Ellen's. Edmund de Watford was the patriarch of a closely related de Watford family, of whom more later.

In an all-important step to secure their inheritances, by testimony of the king's treasurer, each of three daughters made fine and paid her scutage in 1287. The three were Sarah de Burneby, Ellen de Watford, and Joan de Parles. There is nothing to indicate why Athelina was not among them, although she may have lost her lands by then or she had died.

Athelina and Ellen, sisters of Sarah

The youngest sister, Ellen de Watford, who was unmarried, had a tougher time protecting her inheritance. Only two years after her father died, she found it necessary to defend her right to hold her 'purparty' of Eustace's lands. The king had taken the lands into his own hands because he believed Ellen had given away the lands without his license. However, this later proved to be false, and the lands were duly returned to her.

While some ordinary laws recognizable today existed in the thirteenth century, a touch of royal favouritism did not go amiss. One of Ellen's villeins was Walter le Palmer of Watford. Walter's son Robert, at the instance of the king's son Edmund, was pardoned for causing the deaths of Walter Ingold and Simon le Provost, both of neighbouring Crick.

Ellen risked her lands being handed over to the Crown if she died as a 'damsel' without an heir. To avoid this possibility, she obtained an order from the king in 1291. The escheator (not Henry de Bray) should permit Ellen de Watford to give Eustace de Burneby £20 yearly value of lands in Watford 'to be held of the king in chief as Ellen now holds them'. The order also instructed that Eustace should be permitted to enter and hold the lands until the next parliament, on the condition he paid homage to the king for the lands. By fine made in November 1291, Ellen's lands came to the de Burnebys in fee, held of the king in chief for one quarter of a knight's fee. In total, then, one half of the knight's fee of Watford was held by the de Burnebys.

Sarah's elder sister, Athelina, was a widow. Her husband, William le Brun, had died before 1276. At that time, her quarter share of the Watford lands returned to her own name. William was alive in 1266 to stand as surety for his troublesome brother-in-law, William de Parles. He was also alive when Athelina's father gave Lord William de Brun, knight, and his wife Athelina along with their two married sisters and brothers-in-law a messuage and land in Watford. The charter was undated, but given the witnesses was probably written around 1268 to 1270. The titles 'lord' and 'knight' indicate William had been knighted and that he was a landlord.

Athelina died without an heir, although her later life and year of decease is a bit of a mystery. The escheator for the county, Henry de Bray, took possession of her lands in October 1285 by fine, although by what right was unclear. He acted on behalf of the king and so was found to hold this quarter of the Watford lands in 1296. However, Henry de Bray was far from an honourable adjudicator. He was one of a number of high-profile officials of England's legal system who were arrested, trialled, fined, and imprisoned by the king between 1289 and 1290. He must have been a favourite, because almost immediately his lands, goods and chattels were restored to him after he made fine with the king for his trespasses. And he was allowed to continue his duties.

In Athelina's case, among others, Henry did not discharge his duties as fairly or as quickly as he might have done, because the king found it necessary to issue special instructions. In 1299 the king ordered Master Henry de Bray be granted the lands for as long as he lived, with reversion to the king on Henry's death, in return for enfeoffing the king with the lands in Watford and paying an annual rent of £20. Henry would also be pardoned of all debts, fines, and accounts which he came to owe the king while he was an escheator and bailiff or in any offices whatsoever by whatever reason he ought to be charged, and of all trespasses he may have committed against the king. As agreed, by fine Henry enfeoffed the king with 16 virgates of land, 16 acres of meadow and 19s of rent receipts in Watford and Silsworth. The king then granted exactly the same lands and income back to Henry, for life, at a rent of £20 per year.

Henry de Bray died in 1303. Upon his death, the king granted Henry's rented land as a fee-farm to Eustace de Burneby and Maud, his wife, in fee simple for the annual rent paid to the Exchequer of £20. These same lands with the same description and rental income remained with the de Burnebys for centuries, forming the 'third part of the manor of Watford'. Furthermore, the 16 virgates can be seen to be the sum of Athelina's 7 virgates of free tenancy lands and 9 of villeinage. The demesne of 4 ¾ virgates was excluded from the summary of virgates of land held, which was not unusual.

Eustace de Burneby: 1303–1343

On the same day Eustace de Burneby was granted the fee-farm lands, he enfeoffed Nicholas de Warwick with a carucate of land (four virgates) in

Watford and Silsworth and 20s 2d rent. He promptly re-enfeoffed himself and his heirs. This land was probably the demesne.

From this time, in 1303, Ellen's lands were referred to as a fee-farm and were subject to the king's discretion as to whom the rent should be paid. Successive kings took advantage of the income, and, over several centuries ordered Eustace and Maud, or the successors of Eustace and Maud, to pay the income to one or the other favoured person. Other than such grants to persons closely connected to whichever king sat on the throne, these orders were also made to chosen servants of the king. Instances of these occurred in 1318, then in 1323 to cancel the 1318 order, and again in 1405, 1472, and 1481. With another order in 1483 transferring many fee-farm rents from the former Earl of Pembroke to the Receiver General, the Watford fee-farm payments continued through the sixteenth century and into the seventeenth, until the time of George Clerke.

In the early fourteenth century, Eustace de Burneby had to live up to obligations associated with holding two parts of a knight's fee and one more part by rental. In 1307, to support his war effort against the Scots, the king claimed scutage from his fiefs, i.e. money due from those who held a knight's fee, but did not directly attend the war effort. After initially instructing Eustace to pay scutage, Eustace made his case and the king then issued an order to the treasurer and barons of the exchequer. They should acquit Eustace de Burneby, tenant in chief of his lands, of the demand made to him for scutage for the king's army of Scotland in 1305. He had already performed his service with the king's army. Edward, prince of Wales, had testified to this by his letters to the king. These matters were resolved only a few months before King Edward I died, during times of great turmoil and war between England and Scotland, involving William Wallace and Robert the Bruce among others.

Service to the king in circumstances such as war was made worthwhile to the individuals concerned. Geoffrey, son of Warin, was granted a pardon by reason of his service in Scotland for homicides in the realm and for fleeing from the church of Watford where he had taken refuge from his enemies and refused to stand trial. The pardon extended to any consequent outlawry.

Two other prominent men of Northamptonshire were granted a commission of *oyer and terminer* (to hear and determine) concerning the person who killed Richard le Taillur of Watford. The commissioners determined two months later that Ralph Waldeshef had killed Richard le Tailler in self-defence. The fortunate Ralph was released from Northampton goal with a pardon.

Eustace de Burneby appeared in chancery in March 1308 and tendered his homage (see[56] Figure 20) to the king for lands he held in Watford. Although the new king's reign had commenced when his father died in July 1307, his coronation was not until February 1308. No doubt the knights of England who owed homage hurried to renew their vows to the new king as soon as possible.

Figure 20: Ceremony pledging homage to lord

Between 1306 and 1311, Eustace's cousins, the Parles family, had been obliged to defend their ownership of a small but relevant parcel of land claimed by John de Dumer and his son, Richard. Evidently, the Dumers claimed lands lying in the Burneby fiefdom. After the dispute, Richard Dumer was given two licenses to grant lands to Eustace de Burneby. One was for a messuage and half a virgate with appurtenances in Watford, and the other was for two messuages with a virgate and three acres in Watford and Silsworth. It is not impossible that the Parles and Burneby lands under dispute with Dumer were the same grounds, and the licenses were issued to grant the lands to the manor of Watford.

Hugh Wake and two others were given a commission of oyer and terminer in a case brought by Nicholas de Warwick's four executors, one of whom was Eustace de Burneby. They charged a group of men, including Nicholas's son William, with driving away 50 oxen, 20 cows, 16 bullocks, 300 sheep, and 40 pigs, all worth £100, which were in their custody as executors.

Eustace continued to hold the king's confidence, as the year 1314 was one of several in which he was appointed sheriff of Northampton. In addition, Eustace was one of three chosen[57] by the king to serve in Northamptonshire in the capacity of conservator of the peace. They were to investigate the great outrages perpetrated by his knights and others who had committed murders, disturbances and transgressions:

> As the king understands from the loud complaint of his people, that after
> he set out upon his march to Scotland, great outrages had been committed

as well as by knights and others, who confederated together, held conventicles and other unlawful assemblies, as well by day as night, committed assaults and murders, broke the parks both of the king and his subjects, and hunted the deer, which outrages have not been duly repressed by the sheriffs and other officers and ministers of the king. The conservators are to enquire by the oath of good and lawful men concerning such disturbances and transgressions, and also all other offences against the peace. All persons against whom indictments shall be found, or who shall be notoriously suspected, are to be pursued, taken, and kept in custody by the sheriff so that they be not enlarged without the special command of the king. The *posse comitatus* is to be raised whenever necessary. The conservators are to make returns from month to month to the Council at Westminster of their proceedings, and of the names of the malefactors. The king will shortly send certain of his lieges into their county to do justice upon the offenders, and also to ascertain whether the conservators have been sufficiently diligent, and how the sheriff has conducted himself therein.

In his capacity as the Sheriff of Northamptonshire in 1314, the king ordered Eustace be paid three amounts – £53, £7, and £34 – by the bailiffs of Northampton 'to make provisions for the king's use', no doubt for one armed conflict or another.

Nearly two years later, Eustace was again one of three appointed by the king to undertake service in the county. They were to collect the fifteenth of tax in Northamptonshire, which had been granted for the hosting of the war in Scotland. The threesome should carry the money accruing therefrom direct to the Exchequer. Similarly, in another order for Northamptonshire, Eustace was charged with 'electing' an armed footman for the king's army. The footman would be paid 4d per day by the king 'for 60 days going with the king against the Scots'. King Edward II continued battling the Scots after his humiliating defeat at Bannockburn.

After another year, Eustace de Burneby and three others were appointed to act for the king to fix two problems. They should enquire into the offences and malpractices of the king's ministers and others in the counties of Leicester, Warwick, Lincoln, Rutland, and Northampton, who had taken prizes contrary to the statute of Westminster of 3 Edw I (1275). Second, the four should enquire into the use of measures in the same four counties in accordance with the Magna Carta, and they should punish the offenders and deliver measures of the standard of London for use in those counties.

Eustace de Burneby was also given commissions of oyer and terminer in 1316–18 concerning:

i.   Trespass committed against the parson of the church of Great Doddington;
ii. Complaint by John de Daventre of an assault against him in Daventre by 22 men;
iii. Complaint by the parson of Woketon of assault by six men in Northampton;
iv. Complaint by John de Wyleby against 11 and more people who entered his close at Wodecroft, cut and carried away the herbage and corn, and also assaulted him.

The busy Eustace found time to make a gift of land. He granted the prior and convent of Daventry a 'small parcel' of land situated in Daventry in 1318.

Whatever appearance Eustace maintained toward his fellow countrymen, like his ancestors, he remained short of ready cash. The Exchequer had received a demand for repayment of a large debt owed by Eustace. The king issued an order to Eustace and Sarah de Burneby on their own account and as tenants of the late Ellen de Watford's lands. Eustace and his heirs should pay 4 marks a year at the Exchequer against the £243 7s 2d of John and Sarah's debt and the £244 12s 10d of Ellen's debt. This appears to be the remainder of the de Watford debt of £1,263, recorded some 75 years before, then repayable at 5 marks yearly, since split between the four daughters. Apparently part of the outstanding debt – £488 – was payable to one individual, John de Hesilrygg. John petitioned parliament, council and the king, asking for the repayments of 4 marks to be cancelled and the sheriff be ordered to collect the whole amount from Eustace. In attempting to find favour with the king, John cited his part in the capture of Gilbert de Middleton at a revolt in the north of England, who was captured at Bannockburn. In the meantime, his lands had been ravaged. The decision was not recorded.

Eustace appears to remain in the king's favour. The sheriff of Northamptonshire was one of the many county sheriffs to receive similar orders[58] from the king in 1319. *The sheriff was to cause Eustace de Burneby to have scutage for the army in Scotland although he did not offer his due service in that army, so that his service is not found in the rolls ... for that army, it is evident to the king that Eustace did his service.*

Eustace's political allegiance – support for King Edward II – can be seen in orders given to him and two others and then countermanded. First:

[59]**March 1. Coventry**. Writ of aid for Eustace de Burneby and [two others] appointed to levy 12 men at arms in the county of [Northampton] and 1,000 footmen and to lead them to the king. Mandate for the sheriff of the county superseding any other mandate for levy of foot.

And two weeks later:

[60]**March 14. Derby.** Order superseding the order to choose twelve men-at-arms in the county of Northampton, to wit one man from each hundred, and a thousand footmen in the same county, and to cause them to be brought to the king to set out against his enemies and rebels, as the latter have fled from the king's army at Burton-on-Trent, so that their rebellion is restrained, wherefore the king wishes to spare the charge of the aforesaid men, provided that the footmen be ready to come to the king with the said Thomas, Eustace, and William in twenties, hundreds, and constabularies when summoned by the king.

The reference to Burton-on-Trent was to the Battle of Burton Bridge on 10 March 1322, fought by King Edward II against the Earl of Lancaster in the Despenser War. This was a baronial revolt against Edward led by the Marcher Lords, Roger Mortimer and Humphrey de Bohun. After the battle, Lancaster was pursued closely by the king's men and was eventually captured at the Battle of Boroughbridge on March the 16th. He was later executed on the king's order.

However, the king's superseding order of March 14 had not arrived in time:

[61]**March 19. Doncaster.** Commission to [two others and] Eustace de Burneby … reciting that … the county of Northampton granted to the king of late twelve men at arms … and 1,000 footmen … at their own costs for fortie days … for the expenses of which footmen 1,000 marks were assessed … whereof 500 marks have been paid … and a certain sum has been paid to the said footmen for their wages … and appointing the said commissioners to levy the residue of the said 1,000 marks … the king wishing that the said footmen, whom he is now permitting to return home, should come in the king's service at the king's wages, if he should wish to have them at another time …

The king's wars were not over. In the year after the Battle of Burton Bridge, an order requesting aid was issued to Eustace de Burneby and two others in Northamptonshire. They should supply 1,000 quarters of wheat and 1,000 quarters of barley for the war in Scotland. Yet another year later, Eustace and another were commissioned to array in Northamptonshire 20 hobelers and 50 archers, not to be confused with another 250 footmen to be arrayed there. The trio should lead the men to Portsmouth for embarkation to Gascony at the king's wages, all by Mid-Lent Sunday. Neglection of the duty would be at their peril, and their progress must be certified to the king by February 2nd. The king was readying for what would be a short war over his possessions in France, which he lost. The situation prompted the king to send queen Isabella on a peace-making visit to France.

Upon being required to inspect Northampton Castle (see[62] Figure 21), Eustace and an associate estimated necessary repair costs at £1,097. An old tower begun in the time of King Henry the Elder, called 'Faukestour', needed the most restoration.

Together with Robert de Daventry, tenant of the Murcott lands in Watford, Eustace de Burneby investigated and gave information to the king about the manor of Stowe. The king had taken the manor from a rebel and re-granted the lands to the archdeacon of Northampton. The two investigators reported that the former tenant had burnt several buildings, a mill and some small houses alongside the manor, so the king granted timber to the new tenant for repairs. He also promised that the archdeacon would not be forced to find armed men or armour for the king simply because he held the manor, as was normal with other manors.

The de Burneby's fee-farm first brushed with royalty in 1327. In the first year of his reign, King Edward III saw fit to grant to queen Isabella a large pension for life. Parliament recognised her services in the matter of the treaty with France and in suppressing the rebellion of the Dispensers and others. The lands assigned to her by way of dower were to be increased in value from £4,500 to 20,000 marks a year, consisting of castles, honors, manors, towns, lands, tenements, hundreds, farms and rents, to the yearly value of £8,722 4s 4d. There followed a long list of such rentals, including in the middle, £20 annually paid by Eustace de Burnaby and his heirs for a fee-farm in Watford.

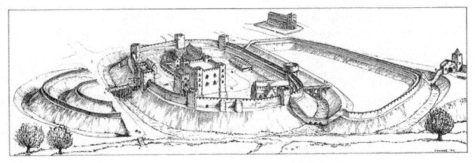

Figure 21: Northampton Castle

Queen Isabella was the mother of King Edward III and the wife of Edward II. Eleven years younger than Edward II, she lived for another 30 years after he died. Her grant was altered in some way in 1331, 1334, and 1345. Isabella, who was a daughter of one of the kings of France and the sister of another, had indeed travelled to France in 1325 and did conclude a treaty with France. But while in France with her son, the future Edward

III, she began an affair with Roger Mortimer. They returned to England in 1326 and led a small force to depose Edward II – her own husband – along with his supporters, the Dispensers. Their mission was accomplished with the Dispensers killed, Edward III crowned as King, and Isabella appointed as his Regent. A few years later, the young Edward executed her lover, deposed his mother and took back his authority. He remained generous to his mother.

Taking advantage of the goodwill he had built with the king, Eustace de Burneby secured a grant, 'of special grace', of free warren in his demesne lands in Watford and Silsworth. Eustace had won the right to hunt in his demesne, a privilege usually reserved for the king.

The abbot and convent of Sulby sent a petition to the king, saying, 'from time immemorial', the sheriff of Northampton had held the view of frankpledge of the abbot's tenants in Welford and Watford. As commanded, the abbot had taken the fines and paid half a mark yearly to the sheriffs. The king granted the frankpledge to the abbot and convent and said the sheriff shall not meddle anymore, paying to the king one half mark. Frankpledge was a system of law enforcement among the villagers, a privilege of lordship often generating fines which was income the lord of the manor could keep. The abbot's success was short-lived.

A special inquisition *ad quod damnum* took place in 1333. This was another kind of enquiry, held not post mortem, but rather to assess any possible damages to the king following any grant of land held direct from the king. Eustace won his case, and by a charter of 1334 he was granted frankpledge of his tenants in Watford and the hamlets of Silsworth and Murcott. In return, Eustace was instructed to pay 3s annually to the exchequer in addition to the 34s 9d customarily paid to the sheriff.

In defiance, Edmund de Watford saw fit to protest this action by Eustace. He petitioned the king on the basis that granting frankpledge to Eustace was against the king's interests. Edmund said he and all the village of Watford have previously come for view of frankpledge to the king's hundred of Guilsborough. But Burneby had taken advantage of the king's grace to have the view at his court in Watford instead, which was to the king's disinheritance. Whether Edmund succeeded in having the grant to Eustace reversed is doubtful, as there is a note on the file to Chancery: 'the justice is to do what ought to be done'. This sounds suspiciously similar to government-speak of the modern day.

One of Eustace's younger sons was Richard, who was set up with property in his own right. Richard was granted 1 messuage, 4 virgates of land, and 6 acres of meadow in four parishes. The cost was 20 marks of silver, no doubt provided by Eustace. By 1341, Richard was in debt to the tune of two amounts of £40, one due to Roger de Gildesburgh, and the other to two knights of Eyton. Richard does not appear to have made best use of his relatively privileged position in life. A Parles cousin was the sheriff who had to deal with Richard by arresting him more than once – small comfort to Eustace.

11 April 1348. Westminster.[63] Whereas Walter Parles, sheriff of Northampton, by the king's order attached Richard de Burneby of Watford by his body, in Northampton Castle, and afterwards finding the same Richard, whom he had suffered to go at large in the castle for recreation, wandering in the town of Northampton, again attached him and would have brought him to the castle to stay there in custody, and he forcibly resisted the sheriff and did not permit such attachment to take effect but wounded with a dagger Thomas le Yongebonde of Everdon, who came there to help the sheriff; and whereas the said Richard when charged with the contempt and trespass before William de Thorpe and his fellows, then justices of assizes in the county aforesaid, submitted himself to the king's grace; the king, of his special grace and at the request of John Darcy, has pardoned all that pertains to him in the premises, on condition that he stand trial if any one will implead him herein.

The impact of the king's costly wars was inevitably suffered by the populace. King Edward III found it necessary to order his commissioners to collect more taxes. Commissioners were prominent men of each county, and this time included Eustace de Burneby for Northamptonshire. They were to collect the tax assessments of a tenth and fifteenth for the last three years, and now without delay should collect what still remains unpaid, arrest all non-payers and imprison them until further order. Even more, the king is informed that many of the sub-collectors still retain the moneys collected by them and that some persons have refused to pay their portion and others do not permit payment to be made from their goods. All this is to great disgrace and contempt and manifest retarding of important business. Only six months later, the king added: In view of the immense sums of money which he has to pay for the furtherance of the present war and the very urgent business affecting him and the state, he called on the commonalities to pay in advance the tenth and fifteenth taxes. Edward's orders did not state which war – but the Hundred Years' War with France was just beginning.

Eustace de Burneby, though, was charged with more than finding money for such major undertakings as a war. Barely a month after the instructions to collect taxes, Eustace and three companions were given a commission to carry out roadworks on Watling Street – by 1339 already an ancient roadway. They were asked to survey the king's highway called 'Watlyngstrete' which was reported to have many great breaches in the roadway and its bridges as it ran through the counties of Northampton, Leicester, Warwick and Stafford. The commissioners should then find 'men of those counties who should contribute to the repair and maintenance of the ways and bridges and compel them to do so'. The king obviously had his own view as to who and how his citizens should be encouraged to conduct necessary roadworks on the kingdom's highways.

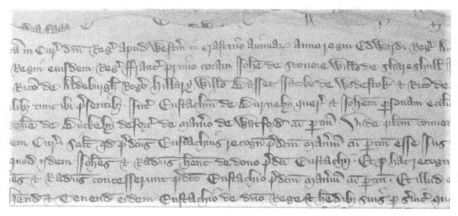

Figure 22: Part of Feet of Fines, Eustace de Burneby, 1340

Only a few years before he died, Eustace de Burneby obtained confirmation that he validly held the manor (see[64] Figure 22). In keeping with the methodology of the time, Eustace gifted two local parsons – of Crick and Long Buckby – with the right to hold the manor of Watford. The two parsons then immediately granted the manor back to Eustace to hold of the king for his lifetime. After his decease, the manor should go to Eustace's son Nicholas de Burneby and his wife Alice, and on to the heirs of Nicholas. The interesting twist in this tale is another protest by Edmund de Watford in the form of a claim against Eustace written onto the back of the scroll (see Figure 45).

Eustace died around Easter in the year 1343, or, in the escheator's complex language, 'He died on Friday next Palm Sunday last'. This was written in a year when Palm Sunday fell four days before the day the report was written. Therefore, Eustace died on the Friday before the last Palm Sunday, i.e. 4th April, 1343. The report recorded Eustace's heir as Nicholas, his son, aged 26 years at last Easter. This meant Nicholas would have turned 27 about a month after the report was written, or born about May 1316.

A summary of Eustace's holdings was assessed in the usual way at the aforementioned inquisition. The escheator reported the basis of Eustace's holdings, i.e., he held three parts of the manor of the king by a fine levied in the king's court in 1340. Successive remainders went to Nicholas and Alice de Burneby and the heirs of Nicholas for ever. The all-important license had been obtained from the king. The escheator then clarified how the three of four parts of the manor were held: Two of the four quarter-fees were held of the king in chief by service of a moiety (half) of a knight's fee. A third part was held of the king in chief at fee-farm, paying the king's Exchequer 16s yearly – should have reported as £20, not 16s. The king then ordered delivery of the three parts of the manor to Nicholas, citing the report of the escheator, and the correct fee-farm rental of £20.

The following[65] ruling by the king many years later completes the story of the unfortunate Richard de Burneby, Eustace's son, and Nicholas's brother:

> Pardon, for good service done in Brittany, to John de Swynford of the king's suit for the death of Richard de Burneby, whereof he is indicted or appealed, and of any consequent outlawry.

In turn the story of John de Swynford might not be done, for John may be the one appearing later in this story in a very different role with Emma de Craunford of the de Watford manor.

Nicholas and Agnes de Burneby: 1343–1406

Like one of his Parles cousins, Nicholas made the mistake of occupying some of his father's lands without first obtaining the king's permission. Luckily for Nicholas, he was pardoned for the misdeed of taking possession of 6 messuages, 6 virgates of land, and 17s 4d of rent in

Watford and Cold Ashby and entering therein without license from the king. The forgiving king also granted him license to keep the lands.

Nicholas de Burneby served enthusiastically as a knight (see[66] Figure 23) in the king's army, irrespective of his obligations from holding most of a knight's fee. While battling the French at Calais, the king issued a pardon to Nicholas 'for good service in the siege of Calais', as attested, in Nicholas's case, by the prince of Wales. The title 'knight' was added after his name, although when Nicholas was knighted is not clear. The siege of Calais became another victory for Edward III against the French, only a year after the

Figure 23: Knight of the mid 14th century

victory at Crécy. And Nicholas's contribution at Calais was undeniably clear to the Black Prince. The city remained an English possession for two centuries.

Archers and their longbows (see[67] Figure 24) were an important weapon of England's armies in the fourteenth century. Nicholas was one of 13 prominent men of Northamptonshire to be given a mandate by the king in 1360. They were to array men at arms and archers in the county. However, Richard de Woodville, one of the 13 mandated, was given a free pass and the remaining dozen men were told to proceed without him. The king explained that Richard was so occupied in the service of the king's daughter Isobel concerning the stewardship of her lands in several counties, he could not attend to the array with them.

Figure 24: Longbowman of the mid 14th century

Nicholas appears to have been a knight before his service at Calais and to have established his reputation as a true knight at arms.

> Inscription[68] of a tablet, on the wall of the Audit House, Southampton, setting forth the Roll of Nicholas de Magdalene, in the company of Lord Thomas de Beauchamp, Earl of Warwick, in the 13th year of King Edward III … who made his stay in Southampton from the 25th day of July, to the 25th day of August 1340, with his retinue, viz: 8 knights, 50 men at arms, and 50 archers.

> One of the Knights is named *Nicholas de Burneby*.
> One of the Archers is named *Thomas de Burneby*.

The second time the de Burneby fee-farm rose to prominence in its own humble way was in 1359 for the consort of Edward III, Queen Philippa (see[69] Figure 25), just after the death of Queen Isabella. Edward and Philippa had married in 1328, less than a year after Edward had commenced his reign. He had initially fixed her dower at that time. Philippa was the daughter of Isabella's cousin from Hainault, France. She was known for her kindness and compassion, thus becoming a popular figure in England. In 1359, Edward saw fit to give 'for life, by the advice and assent of the council, to the king's consort Queen Philippa, beyond the lands already assigned to her in dower which are insufficient for the necessary expenses of her household and chamber ... £2,000 yearly of land &c'. As with previous such orders, included in the long list of lands was: 'the farm of £20 which Eustace de Burnaby renders for the town of Watford'.

Unfortunately for Nicholas, he too became a victim of the second pandemic of the plague in England in 1361. That summer, many of his family and cousins were also taken. Nicholas's inquisition was delayed six years. His holdings in Northamptonshire had increased, possibly due to his marriage to Alice de Clinton, and now included free tenants in four other parishes. His main holdings were the manor of Watford and Silsworth. The manor was held by knight's service, and a third part of the manor was charged with £20 annual rent to the Exchequer and 16s rent to the prior of St Andrews in Northampton for a tenement in Silsworth.

Figure 25: Queen Philippa

Nicholas's next heir was Agnes, who in April of 1367 was aged only 11. She was Nicholas's granddaughter, the daughter of his deceased son and heir, Eustace. After Nicholas died the profits of the manor were paid to the king's daughter, Isobel, because there was no heir of full age. Born 1332 and the eldest daughter of Edward III, Isobel had married Ingelram de Coucy, a wealthy French lord. Ingelram was appointed as the Earl of Bedford in 1366, and the king gave his daughter an income of 1,000 marks per year, which was to come from land rents. The king directed that one of those lands should be the de Burneby fee-farm.

Nicholas's holdings were listed as follows: a manor house of no value, a dovecote worth 3s 4d, a garden with wineries worth 5s, two mills valued at 8s, two carucates of land containing in total 240 acres valued at 6d per acre (£6 total), 19 acres of meadow worth nothing because it lay in the common, 30 acres of wood worth 20s, free and bond tenants in Watford worth £22 6s 8d, and free and bond tenants in the village of Silsworth paying £20 6s 10d per year, barely more than the fixed rent paid of £20. The escheator noted that tenants maintained several 'customs'. One was

72 geese called 'heichges' for rent, and another paid 19 cocks and 67 hens annually. Yet more, tenants were to work the plough for 31 days in winter and at Lent or pay 6d per ploughing, work 31 days mowing the meadows or pay 6d per mowing, also work 'Lovedaies' or pay 3d each work, and finally there were 83 works called 'Metebones' towards food of the lord. The fortunate lord also profited from pleas and perquisites of court, valued at 40s pa.

The jury noted that in 1361, someone had entered and occupied 1 ¼ virgates of land with 1 ½ dwellings in Watford. No one knew why he had done so. The king resolved this a few months later by issuing an order. The aforesaid dwellings and lands should also to be delivered to the king's daughter and son-in-law, the Duke of Bedford, as of the date of Nicholas's death, due to the nonage of Nicholas's heir. The king added that the heir, Agnes, should have the lands when of lawful age, as the king had discovered they were held in Nicholas's demesne as of fee and were a part of the manor of Watford held in chief by knight's service. Lastly, the king required the escheator to get off the premises.

The troubles the de Burnebys faced to keep their manor lands in Watford did not end with Nicholas and his granddaughter Agnes. She was born in May of 1356. With her father and grandfather both dead, she was left as an heiress at the age of five in the wardship of the king. John Estbury of Eastbury in Berkshire was the escheator in the counties of Oxon, Berks and Wilts. He married Agnes de Burneby (see[70] Figure 26) in 1371 when she was aged only 15, which was legal at the time. Her 'proof of age' inquisition was held in May 1371, when several local citizens gave evidence of her birth date and age, thereby supporting the legality of her marriage. One of the witnesses, Richard Alisaundre, aged 50, stated he knew her birth date because Agnes had been 'born at Watford and baptized in the church, and he was present at the baptism and was asked by Eustace her father to be her godfather, which he utterly refused because it was possible for him to survive Eustace and then marry Agnes'.

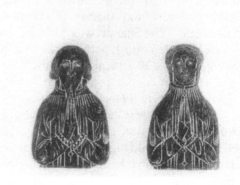

Figure 26: John de Estbury and wife Agnes nee de Burneby

By virtue of his marriage, John Estbury had become 'lord of Watford' for his lifetime. So titled, he was witness to a charter of 1371 by neighbour Sir Richard Mallory, knight, of West Haddon. Sir Richard gave to John de Haddon, sergeant at arms, the manor of West Haddon, with lands, woods, meadows, feedings, pastures, waters, ways, paths, mills, wards, marriages, reliefs, heriots, escheats, rents, and services of free tenants and neifs. Another witness was Ralph de Parles, who held the other quarter knight's fee in Watford.

Agnes died in June 1375, at the age of 19. The inquisition held soon after her death recorded that she held three parts of Watford manor, worth £31 6s after fixed rent outgoings, virtually the same as for her grandfather. Out of the three, two parts were held by service of half of a knight's fee, and the third part was a fee-farm held of the king by service of paying £20 yearly at the Exchequer. Agnes also held lands in Great Creaton of the honor of Chokes and in each of Staverton, West Haddon, Welton, and Cold Ashby, all in Northamptonshire, totalling £5 19s.

Soon after the inquisition, the escheator was ordered to deliver Agnes's lands, including the manor of Watford, to John Estbury, as tenant, for his life. John should hold the manor because he and Agnes had had a child, and the child had died while Agnes was alive. After John died, the manor should go to Thomas de Burneby, Agnes's eldest uncle, who was aged 30 in 1375. However, Thomas died too soon to inherit the estate. So the manor slipped into the hands of the next eldest uncle.

John Estbury died in August 1406. At his inquisition, other than the lands he had of his own right, which descended to his nephew, he was found to hold three parts of the manor of Watford by service of half a knight's fee. He also held 1½ messuages and 1¼ virgates there, by service unknown to the jurors. He held the manor of the king, in chief, by the law or courtesy of England after the death of Agnes his wife, of her inheritance. Remainder was to George, son of Nicholas de Burneby, father of Eustace de Burneby, father of Agnes, as uncle and heir of Agnes. George was the third brother; Eustace the eldest and Thomas the next eldest had predeceased him. The manor was said to be worth 40 marks p.a. beyond the £20 paid annually to the exchequer, again similar to the prior valuation, plus another 25s 8d for 1½ messuages and 1¼ virgates. An order was issued to the escheator of the county of Northampton to take the fealty of George and cause him to have full seisin of the premises.

George and Eustace de Burneby: 1406–1464

Despite the escheator's accurate summary of George's inheritance, reports of his age, possibly rather shyly provided by himself, optimistically suggest he was born about 1365. That cannot be true because his father had died by 1361. More likely he was 50, therefore born about 1355; after all, his elder brother was apparently born in 1345.

George had more meaningful difficulties when he found he could not walk onto the manor land and claim it as his own. Eventually, the king saw fit to order his exchequer to 'no more trouble George de Burneby'. The king explained that upon the death of John Estbury, George inherited from Agnes, John's wife, as her uncle and heir. A fine was paid to the treasury and the king had taken George's homage, so he commanded the ceremony of livery, which delivered George's lands to him.

When the holders of the de Burneby fee-farm were reminded to pay the rent in 1414, the recently enthroned king referred to George's great grandfather. The king's order was given to 'the heirs of Eustace de Burneby and Maud, his wife', the keepers of the farm, to pay £20 rent to the exchequer from their receipts for a messuage, 16 virgates of land, 16 acres of meadow and 19s rent, in Watford. In addition, arrears due since the king's order dated 4 June in 4 Henry IV (1403) had to be paid. Again in 1423, just after the beginning of the reign of a new king, a similar order was issued to the same heirs. This time, like many other payment orders to landholders, the money was part of a dowry of 10,000 marks per year given to Queen Joan for life, with arrears, by the letters patent of 1403.

Married in 1403, Joanna of Navarre (see[71] Figure 27) was the second wife of King Henry IV, and he was her second husband. Regrettably, she was imprisoned in 1419 for witchcraft and her dower revoked. Henry V, her stepson, shortly before he died in 1422, freed her and returned the dower to her, which included the rent from the Watford manor. However, this was complicated by further letters patent issued in 1405. Queen Joan gave 20 marks annually for life out of the £20 received yearly from the Watford farm to two of her servants. They had married by Joan's ordinance and advice, and had little to live on. The charges of witchcraft against Joanna were never pressed and she lived quietly for the remainder of her life.

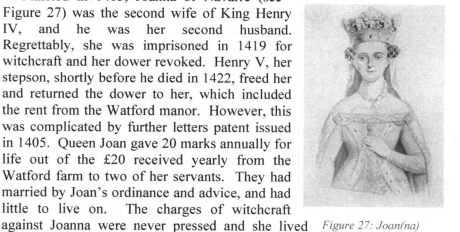

Figure 27: Joan(na) of Navarre

Already an elderly man in 1428, George put his name to a sale of lands without permission, which of course annoyed the king. The buyers were a group of four including John Wythermale, who was George's step-son. For 300 marks of silver, on July 1st George and his wife, Mary, sold 9 messuages, 2 mills, 8 ½ virgates of land 24 acres of pasture, and just short of £4 rent in Cold Ashby, Holwell, Creaton, Staverton, West Haddon, Ashby Leger, Watford, and Silsworth, and a half of the manor of Ullesthorpe. The agreement acknowledged that the moiety of Ullesthorpe was held by Margery Burneby for her life with reversion to George, but did not identify Margery. She was George's sister. Very shortly afterwards, for 40s paid, a pardon was issued to John Wythermale and his companions 'for acquiring to themselves and their heirs from George Burneby, esquire, and Mary, his wife, and entering without license' into the two mills in Watford, held in chief. They were also reminded to grant the same premises back to George and Mary for his life with remainder to Eustace, George's son, and his heirs.

Indeed, John and his trio of friends did give the lands back to George and Mary on September 3rd, 1428, which effectively reversed some of the July 1st sale. There was a 'charter' for this, because it was referred to and 'shown to the jurors' in an inquisition held less than a year later. To sum up, it appears that the first effort on 1st July 1428 should probably have taken the traditional form of an acknowledgement by, and re-grant back to, George and Mary. Or, if the transaction of September was a marriage settlement for George's son, Eustace, then the two transactions should have been dated simultaneously, either in July or September of 1428.

George Burneby died in June 1429 and Mary, his widow, died only two years later in August 1431. An inquisition was held for each of George[72] and Mary,[73] which included descriptions of the manor of Watford and Silsworth, as well as other holdings in Ullesthorpe and Ashby St Ledgers. Both inquisitions reported that the right of George and Mary to hold the manor came from the feoffment to them dated 9 Henry IV, or 1408, which was soon after George's father died. Each inquisition determined George's next heir to be Eustace de Burneby and his wife Philippa, and each was consistent in describing Eustace's age as 30 and 32, respectively. Mary's heir was John Wythemale, who was obviously her son from an earlier marriage. The manor included the manor house and lands held of the king in chief by ½ knight's fee, and a third part of the manor held of the king in chief at fee-farm for rent of £20 per annum:

The Manor House:
> A hall with two chambers, a cook house, two barns, two stables, a watch-tower, and a kiln, all worth nothing in rental value.

The Manor Lands:
> A dovecot, a croft called 'le Orchard', 200 acres demesne land, 20 acres demesne meadow, 40 acres pasture, one enclosed croft, a wood called 'le hay' of 30 acres, 5 stanks (pools), 36 virgates with each virgate containing 24 acres land and 2 acres meadow, frankpledge twice yearly, two crofts with tenants, the rent of pepper and cumin from the abbot of St James Northampton, 6 cottages, 4 tofts. All together, this was worth £17 16s annually.

The Third Part of the Manor:
>Messuage, 16 virgates of land, 16 acres meadow, and 19s rent in Watford and Silsworth. These were worth nothing except the 19s above the 'rent resolute'.

Additional to the Manor, held by George alone:
>A watermill and a windmill, part of Watford manor, worth 20s per year, and a messuage and a virgate of land in Silsworth, worth 20s per year.

In some respects, the manor house roughly 150 years later resembled the house as it had been in 1276 – there was a hall and two chambers with a watchtower (see[74] Figure 28). The structure and its attachments were stated to be worth nothing. This was because the capital mansion house

Figure 28: Medieval manor house

stood on land held by the Abbey of St James, rented back to the Burnebys and therefore did not represent an income. Notable also, that the carefully appraised extent of the manor in virgates and acres of demesne very closely reflected the escheator's summary in 1276 for Sarah and Ellen together.

The third part of the manor of over 16 virgates represented the villeinage and free tenancy lands originally held by Athelina. They were 'rented', rather than held by right of a quarter knight's fee. The quantification of the fee-farm (16 virgates & 16 acres) remained fixed from its original description in the thirteenth century. Also, even though the quantification of a virgate in Watford in 1429 had changed to 24 acres for the manor, the fee-farm remained at the old measure of 20 acres per virgate, fixed at the Exchequer over a century before.

Following the inquisition of 1429, the king ordered that Eustace de Burneby and his wife Philippa be given the estate in Ashby Ledger for their heirs and a messuage and virgate in Silsworth. Two mills in Watford were given to Eustace for his heirs. The king took care to carve out the rent on the fee-farm, which was held by Queen Joanna in the name of her dower.

Yet another order to the escheator followed in 1431, after Mary's death. The manor of Watford was held of the king in chief by service of the moiety of a knight's fee, and Eustace Burneby was of full age and the rightful heir of George. Therefore, the escheator was to cause Eustace to have full seisin of the manor, as the king had taken his oath of faithfulness, and for a fee of one mark he won delay of giving homage until Michaelmas next. King Henry VI also noted that King Henry IV had pardoned George and Mary all manner of gifts, alienations, and purchases of lands held of the king in chief and made by them without licence from the king.

Eustace's bride in September 1428, only shortly before his father died, was Philippa Mallory, sister of Sir Thomas Mallory, author of *Morte D'Arthur*. The re-grant of lands back to his parents in the same month, with reversion to Eustace, must have been his marriage settlement. The Mallory family had been allied with the Burnebys for generations, and had strong associations with the neighbouring parishes of Winwick and Welton.

A fellow named Thomas Burneby appears on the scene, probably a younger brother of Eustace. With no expectations of a substantial inheritance, typical of a younger son, Thomas took up a career in the king's service. He was rewarded in 1443 when the king made a grant for life to the 'king's sergeant Thomas Burneby, esquire', of 20 marks yearly. This was followed in 1450 with another lifetime grant to 'the king's squire, Thomas Burneby, of the office of sergeant of the king's tents and pavilions, with the usual wages and fees.' Between the two crown grants, Henry Beaufort, Cardinal of England and Bishop of Westminster, bequeathed[75] to 'Thomas Burneby, Page to my Lady the Queen, £20, and a cup of silver gilt'. The queen at the time was Margaret of Anjou, whose marriage to Henry VI had been arranged by the Duke of Suffolk.

A commission given to Eustace and four companions required them to follow up on the unexpected turn of events concerning a commitment undertaken by the king. The king had granted to John Gloucester the keeping of all the lands of a deceased heir and tenant-in-chief, John Wichingham, as well as his marriage. But to the king's consternation, certain enemies had abducted the heir. He made Eustace and his companions responsible to find the guilty party and advise into whose hands the heir had been conveyed.

For unspecified reasons, Eustace was granted a general pardon in August 1463. This was near to the end of his life, and may have concerned his excesses as a younger man. Accusations[76] had been levelled against Eustace and his friend Sir Thomas Mallory in the 1440s. Among other things he and Sir Thomas were accused of insulting, wounding and imprisoning Thomas Smith in a nearby parish, and stealing his goods worth £40. The pair were never tried and the charge may have been merely an angry accusation in troubled times.

Eustace's inquisition, held by February 1464, prompted an order a month later from King Edward IV. The King instructed the escheator in Northamptonshire to take the oath of Philippa, widow of Eustace, and assign her dower in the presence of George Burneby, the son and heir. George was 24 years old. Eustace's estate included 'the manor of Watford called Burneby's, held of the king by knight's service', a windmill and a watermill, both in Watford, and in Silsworth a messuage and a virgate, which appears to be the add-on of long ago from the Dumer dispute. In four other parishes, Eustace held 12 cottages and 10 virgates as well as rent of 5 marks in Ashby Leger and 6s 8d in West Haddon. The cottages and virgates in two of the parishes, Cold Ashby and Holwell, seem to be the ancient holdings of the Watford manor originating as far back as three or four centuries.

For the fourth time in a 100 years, part of the Watford Manor claimed a place in the royal politics of England. This time the beneficiary was Jacquetta of Luxembourg (see[77] Figure 29) and her second husband, Richard of Woodville, whom she had married secretly about 1437. With Eustace's estate barely past its inquisition, his beneficiaries had the honour of receiving an order from King Edward IV concerning only the fee-farm rent paid by Eustace Burneby. They were directed to continue paying to Richard and Jacquetta during her lifetime, plus arrears, the annual £20 originally granted to them by Henry VI in June 1440. For particular reasons concerning the royal power, the king added, he had caused the rent on these lands to be seized into his own hands. But, after 'pondering' the estate of the said Jacquetta, the king decided to continue Richard and Jacquetta's grant as made by letters patent of December 1461.

Figure 29: Jacquetta of Luxembourg

The last Lancastrian King, Henry VI, was defeated in battle in March 1461, by the Yorkist King Edward IV. Late the same year he ascended the throne, Edward granted and confirmed to Jacquetta and Richard the dower she had from her first husband, and added confirmation of the small supplement made in June 1440 of the Watford £20 rent. One of the Woodvilles' many children was Elizabeth who married Edward IV, also in secret, sometime in 1464. Perhaps the king's marriage allowed him the charity to renew the grant to Jacquetta only a few months later.

Jacquetta was also accused of witchcraft. But she was granted exoneration on 10 February 1470 after a hearing in the presence of the king, three bishops, five earls, six lords, and three other dignitaries. She complained that Thomas Wake had caused her name to be dragged through a 'common noise and slander of witchcraft throughout a great part of the realm'. Thomas had shown a lead figure to several lords in Warwick saying Jacquetta used it for sorcery. He then asked John Daunger of Stoke Brewerne to say there were two other such images for the king and queen, but John refused to do so.

George and Thomas Burneby: 1464–1535

By fines in 1464 and 1465, George Burneby, son of Eustace, confirmed his inheritance. He acknowledged the right of Philippa, the widow of Eustace Burneby, in the manor and tenements of 'Burnebyes manor' in Watford. Philippa granted the manor, tenements, mills and two minor extras to George and Alice and their heirs, with the remainder to George's right heirs. For this, George and Alice gave Philippa 400 marks of silver.

George's wife was Alice Danvers, the daughter of Sir Robert Danvers of Culworth in Northamptonshire. When Sir Robert died in 1467, he made George Burneby one of his executors and left his estate to Alice and her two sisters. In 1472, George and Alice sold a large portfolio of lands, which probably included most of Alice's inheritance, together with lands in Owneby purchased by George for £20 in 1466, and other lands held by George. The price was £400 and the deal included manors or parts of manors and/or lands in Pykworth, Owneby, Culworth, Netherbury, Crowelton, Byfield, Stareton, Grymmesbury, Aston, Alkryngton, Lee, Adderbury, Magna Boureton, Parva Bourton, Hardwyk, Nethropp, and Bloxham.

Yet another political character was awarded an interest in the Burneby's Watford fee-farm of 16 virgates. In 1476, four years after Jacquetta had died, the same king issued another order with respect to the payment of the Watford rent. This time the order was to pay £10 per year to 'Robert Lord Boyd, a Scotch exile'. Again, the order was issued to the heirs of Eustace de Burneby and Maud his wife, rather than George Burneby who held the lands at the time. Robert Boyd, Lord of Kilmarnock and of Dalry, was a Scottish peer. Around 1467, he obtained possession of the young Scottish King's person and took for himself the offices of chamberlain and justiciary of Scotland, as well as the hand of the king's sister, Mary. His enemies became too strong for him; he was found guilty of treason and sentenced to death. He escaped to England and died in Northumberland about 1480.

About 1482 George Burneby's 'rent gatherer', William Lapworth, brought an action to Chancery vigorously protesting being imprisoned for trespass. George had instructed William to collect the special rent due from the tenant of Wappenbury manor, near Leamington in Warwickshire, who had just died. But another landlord, John Higford, claimed the same special rent, and so threw William in prison out of 'malice and evil will'. George had probably picked up an interest in the manor when he married, but precisely what interest was unclear.

After the short reign of Richard III, Henry VII was crowned king in 1485. One of his first measures in Parliament was to pass an act providing finance for his household by annual payments totalling £14,000 from named persons. At the top of the list were the wealthy duchies of Cornwall and Lancaster, each ordered to pay around £2,500 per year. Well down the list were the heirs of Eustace de Burneby and Maud, his wife, ordered to pay £20 from the farm of a messuage, 16 yardlands, 16 acres of meadow and 19s rent in Watford by the hands of the farmer, receiver, bailiff, or other occupier. Ten years later the King had Parliament pass a similar act, this time for a mere £13,000 annually, which again featured the same Burneby fee-farm and rental.

The years of the reign of Henry VIII in the first half of the sixteenth century appear to have brought great difficulties to the Burneby family and manor estate in Watford. Whether or not this was self-induced by George and/or his children remains an unanswered question. Something seems to have caused George to live for some time – at least in 1470 – at the Hospitaller of Sutton-at-Hone in Kent. The original house and chapel were built by the Knights Hospitallers of the order of St John of Jerusalem during the time of King John. Their early history tells of involvement in the Crusades, and at one point, the Hospitallers were given the property of the Knights Templar. George's reasons for his association are unknown, but from this time, the Watford manor estate was sometimes said to be held of the prior of St John of Jerusalem for a notional rent of two pennies each year.

Burke's peerage, when referring to Alice Danvers, George's wife, states she died without children, and a Danvers family memorial is silent regarding children of George and Alice. She left somewhat of a mystery. Alice is reported to have died in 1467, although was apparently alive in 1472 for a Feet of Fines entry – probably enrolled years after the event. There can be no question that George left children; either Alice and he did have children, or George married for a second time. He had at least three children. His two sons, Thomas, the eldest and heir, and Eustace, the second son, were named after George's elder but deceased brothers. His daughter was named Elizabeth.

In October of 1512, George put together an agreement aimed at taking care of his estate. Whether knowingly or not, he left complexities which in some ways were not unusual at that time. As it turned out, this was only the first of several confusing agreements made over the next few decades by George and his sons. Nonetheless, what nudged George into this action was the impending marriage of his granddaughter, Jane. One of the several purposes of the agreement was to give Jane and her husband an income.

As called for by the agreement, George gave sufficient and lawful title of his estate to eight prominent gentlemen. Secondly, Sir Edward Belknap took possession of George's half of Wappenbury manor in return for providing a rental income to the newly married Jane Burneby, Thomas's daughter and heir at the time. George's estate was to be held by the group of eight for George's use for his life, then for George's eldest son, Thomas, for his life, then for Thomas's heirs, or in default of Thomas's heirs, for his brother Eustace Burneby, and so on with more defaults. The estate included the manor of Watford and Silsworth, valued at £17 13s 4d annually, with 6,240 acres located in six parishes of Northamptonshire. The eight men named were: William Walgrave, Geoffrey Gates, Edward Ferrers, John Spencer, Nicholas Malory, Edward Greville, Gilbert Stoughton, and Eustace Burneby. However, three of the eight men died before or immediately after George. Fortunately, four of the men other than Eustace lived long enough to deal with George's sparring sons after his death. They were Walgrave, Greville, Gates and Ferrers, although the first three of the four did not last too long either, dead by 1530.

George had other reasons pushing him towards such an arrangement. At the time – 1512 – his eldest son and heir, Thomas, had no male heir and 'only' a daughter; the lack of a male heir was seen as less than ideal. At a later date, Thomas said Jane had married several times and most of her husbands were dead, with no heir produced. Furthermore, George did not seem to have full confidence in his heir apparent or of his capabilities. So George chose Eustace as his executor, and named Eustace as one of the eight feoffees for the entire estate, which cannot have made Thomas happy.

Aged over 80 in May 1521, George Burneby died survived by his son and heir, Thomas. The heir was aged 50 and more according to the inquisition of 1526. Therefore, theoretically he was born in 1475, but very likely years earlier, for example, 1470, and might suggest George married again after Alice's death. His inquisition said his estate was the same as listed in the 1512 agreement, specifically a total of 6,240 acres in several parishes. That stated acreage appears wildly exaggerated or plain wrong.

The estate of Eustace, George's father, which carefully specified holdings in the same parishes, was far more reliable. There seems more than a little likelihood the writers of the legal arrangement carelessly mixed the Latin words for thousand with hundred for several of the acreages.

Thomas's first wife was named Alice, although circumstances surrounding her appear shadowy, and she is barely mentioned anywhere. Alice and Thomas's children included three daughters: eldest Jane, who married Richard Cooke among several others, Joanna, who married Thomas Knightley, and Anne, who married Thomas Roberts of Leicester. After her daughters were born, Alice may have been unwell in some way until she died. Thomas's sons were born later, from a second marriage – to Elizabeth Taylor. The eldest son was Richard, his eventual heir, of whom more later.

After his father died, Thomas found himself in financial difficulties. His attempts to extricate himself ended badly. Problems began when the Watford estate was not formally passed over to Thomas in fee. Instead, the survivors of the group of eight men named in the 1512 agreement, including Thomas's younger brother, Eustace, had been enfeoffed with the estate to hold for the benefit of Thomas, his wife Alice, and brother Eustace.

The unsettled circumstances between the siblings may have been exacerbated by the appointment of Eustace as George's executor. Thomas's sister, Elizabeth Hatfield, who by then was a widow, brought a suit against Eustace in his capacity as executor. She complained that Eustace had given her a debt of £50 as her share of their father's estate, of which only £10 was paid. The debtor died, and the meagre proceeds of the debtor's property were seized by the Abbot of Westminster and paid to his original creditors, including Eustace. Eustace retorted with the claim his sister had no legal right to any 'child's part' of the estate. After her initial request, he had been content to give her the debt, but now, due to her unkind and uncourteous behaviour towards him, he reversed the gesture.

Before George died and probably without telling him, Thomas made a deal with the Knightleys that he lived to regret. Thomas desperately needed £30 but before handing over the money Edmund Knightley had insisted Thomas give him a lease of Silsworth fields immediately after George died. On top of that, to ensure Thomas wrote the lease, Edmund obtained a bond from Thomas for £200 secured on the Statute of the Staple.[iv]

[iv] A security for a debt given and recognized by the Mayor of a town (e.g. London), so that if not repaid, the debtor could have his lands seized and income taken by the creditor until the debt was fully repaid.

Sometime around 1523, Thomas's first wife, Alice, died in mysterious circumstances. Alice was the beneficiary to a lifetime pension of 20 marks annually after the death of her father-in-law, George. Eustace noted in one of his challenges to Thomas in the Court of Chancery that Alice's death had triggered the enfeoffment of the four living gentlemen named in 1512.

Thomas committed 'certain felonies and transgressions'. As a result, in February 1524 two justices of the king called Thomas to a court hearing. Four farmers and citizens of Watford stood surety for Thomas, guaranteeing his appearance at the court. The 'transgression' was not specified but was serious enough to be termed a felony, which could only be charged after a grand jury hearing. One can only wonder whether the felony was linked to Alice's circumstances vis-à-vis her relationship with Thomas, or even her death.

At some point, presumably after Alice died, Thomas remarried. Richard, Thomas's son and therefore heir in preference to his daughters, was born late in 1523. Thomas's second wife, Elizabeth, was named in a written appeal to the Courts about 1530. History records that she was Elizabeth Taylor, although little or nothing is known of her origins.

About 1525, Thomas brought suit into Chancery (see[78] Figure 30) against his brother to recover from Eustace the deeds of Watford Manor and other lands which he needed to prove the manor should descend to him. Eustace, on the other hand, brought a counter-suit against his elder brother and Waldegrave, Gates, Greville, and Ferrers for non-payment of the

Figure 30: High Court of Chancery

annual pension of ten marks (£6 13s 4d) owed to him from Watford Manor. Eustace said their father had been dead four years, so Thomas owed him 40 marks. Further to that, he wanted to be set up with the right to collect the pension direct from rents arising from specific tenants, so he wouldn't have to chase Thomas for his money. Eustace went on to refute Thomas's claim about who was holding the deeds, saying that Thomas, not Eustace, held them. Although on another occasion he confessed he had good reason to keep the deeds from Thomas, because they proved Eustace's rights in the lands. By this time, 1526, one of the four gents whom Eustace sued, Geoffrey Gates, had died. The Court heard Eustace's case early in 1527 and to obtain William Waldegrave's story sent a representative to him because he was 'lacking energy, frail and severely ill'. Judgement was given in Eustace's favour in June, only days before William Waldegrave died.

Thomas was forced to borrow money in 1526 and 1527, secured by the Statute of the Staple in London. The sum of £100 came from Thomas Purpointe, another £80 was lent by Michael Dormer. And 100 marks was borrowed from James Danyell, from which Thomas probably paid the 60 marks (£40) he eventually owed for Eustace's pension. All of these lenders lived in London, and all later took action against Thomas in one way or another.

A suit was brought by Edmund Knightley, who claimed £200 from Thomas. Edmund was the brother-in-law of Joanna Knightley, Thomas's daughter. Thomas had the loan of £30 from Knightley a year before George died. After George died, Thomas repaid the £30 from the first year's rent. Nevertheless, Edmund wanted to collect on the £200 Bond and threatened to imprison Thomas, which would leave him absolutely destroyed. Thomas had no receipt for the £30 he had paid and begged the court for relief against Edmund.

Michael Dormer of London saw fit to pursue his £80 in 1529. Dormer had proved the debt and now went to the extent of executing a writ against Thomas. This generated an order from the king to the sheriff of Northampton, Sir John Clerke, knight, to imprison Thomas until the debt was paid and to conduct an inquisition to establish the extent of Thomas's assets. The inquisition of June 1530 reported that Thomas was seised of the Manor of Watford, and 12 messuages, 2 cottages, and a watermill in Watford, all worth £39. Other minor assets in Ashby Leger and Staverton, together produced 61s rent. The sheriff also established that just before the inquisition, Thomas held 300 acres of pasture in Silsworth, which he had leased out to Edmund Knightley at £30 per year for 21 years. He further reported that Knightley had to pay two amounts from the rent: £20 annually to the Crown for rent of the fee-farm at Watford, and £6 13s 8d per year as a pension for Eustace Burneby. That left a balance of 5 marks taken by Thomas, and therefore a total net value for the manor of £45 7s 8d.

Another of Thomas's creditors, James Danyell, a citizen and merchant-tailor of London, confirmed his claim in 1530, possibly acting in conjunction with Dormer. James presented the same inquisition of Thomas's assets as had been established by Michael Dormer. Thomas and his wife, Elizabeth, appealed to the court while Thomas was in prison for non-payment of the debt. Thomas protested Danyell's action of throwing him in prison and attaching his manor of Watford, thus preventing Thomas from discharging his debts to Danyell and many others. The manor was worth about £30 per year, he claimed, but was effectively still in executorship, not yet given to Thomas by his father's trustees. He appealed to the court of Chancery for his 'body' to be 'conveyed' to the court, to conclude and finalise a bargain made through the mediation of friends. The agreement, with an honest merchant of London, would repay all his debts and avoid 'his lands and rents to be sold, wasted and destroyed & he and his heirs disinherited & utterly undone forever'.

The brothers may have sorted out their differences with the encouragement of 'the honest merchant of London', Thomas Purpoynte. In 1532 the brothers signed an agreement with the same Thomas Purpoynte, whereby Purpoynte enfeoffed the manor estate to another group of gents, one of whom was a Commissioner of the Peace. The group were to hold the premises first for the use of Thomas Burneby until he died, then for Thomas Purpoynte until the heir, Richard, reached 21 years of age, when Richard would take use himself. Purpoynte did indeed take possession of the manor and premises and enjoyed the income of the premises until Richard came of age. That certainly would have been good recompense for any loan Purpoynte had made to Thomas.

The year 1533 was important for the Burnebys, the manor, and the country, for this was the birth year of the future Queen Elizabeth, daughter of Anne Boleyn and King Henry VIII. As another outcome of the Purpoynte agreement the year before, the king was able to grant an order addressed to Thomas Burneby, heir and kinsman of the deceased Eustace Burneby, that is, Thomas, son and heir of George Burneby, son and heir of the said Eustace. Others who should take notice were Sir Edward Ferrers, Eustace Burneby, and any other person seized to the use of the lands of Eustace Burneby senior, George and Thomas. The order granted livery for the third part of the manor of Watford, called Burneby's Manor, and all other possessions in England whereof the said Eustace Burneby, senior, and George Burneby were seized. The king's lawyers saw fit to refer back as far as Eustace de Burneby, Thomas's grandfather, as the last Burneby with a reliable summary of the Watford estate on file at Chancery.

Written in the sometimes confusing manner of the time, the order refers to Eustace, deceased, presumably meaning 'Eustace senior'. At long last, for Thomas, the order clarified his rights as heir to the deceased George, and established the place of Eustace Burneby and others 'to the use of' the Burneby manor and lands. Sir Edward Ferrers remained a part of the picture, the last of the seven independent gentlemen named in George's agreement of 1512 remaining alive at the time of the king's order.

Thomas Burneby died in March 1535. Two inquisitions were held in his name, one in Northamptonshire, and the other in Warwickshire. Each advised his date of death and declared Thomas's son and next heir to be Richard Burneby, aged 11 when Thomas died, therefore born about the second half of 1523 and long after 1512 when father George made legal arrangements for his estate.

The Burnebys held rights in half the manor of Wappenbury. Another of George's actions in October 1512 had been to rent out the manor to Edward Belknap for £31 13s 4d annually – apparently this is what Sir Edward meant when he said in his will he 'bought' the manor. Of the rent, £20 went to Jane Cooke, Thomas's daughter, and the remaining £11 13s 4d was to the use of Thomas and his heirs, and failing such heirs, to Thomas's brother Eustace and his heirs. This split of the rent still applied when Thomas died. After Richard Cooke died, Jane married again to John Bartholomew of London.

Thomas held no lands of his own in Northamptonshire, which was an unusual statement by an escheator. Instead, 'for a long time before the death of Thomas', a group of men held the Watford manor and the same (overstated) 6,240 acres in six parishes mentioned in his father's estate together with £10 rent – all for the uses stated in the 1532 agreement. The escheator also clarified that the lands, tenements, mill and other premises in Silsworth, Staverton, Ashby Ledgers, West Haddon, Twyne, and Holowell were held of the prior of St John of Jerusalem in England by fidelity and rent of 2d per year, and was worth £10 per year above outgoings.

Some detail was provided of Thomas's holdings in Watford parish. These included a capital mansion at Watford, closes called Milche, Motte, and Calves, a close called Great Haye, and a watermill with a close called Mille Holme belonging to the manor. Also, eleven more tenements and a house called the Common Bakehouse. All 16 tenements and 200 acres of land, which appears to be the demesne, was worth a clear £10. All premises in Watford were, in profits, worth a clear £20, held of the king in chief for the service of a ½ knight's fee.

About 15 years after Thomas died, his daughter Jane Bartholomew, formerly Cooke, and her husband John took legal action against Ursula Knightley. Ursula was the executor of Edmund Knightley's estate and sister-in-law of Joanna and Thomas Knightley. John said Ursula had not paid rent for the manor of Watford and Silsworth for 13 ½ years. Ursula Knightley replied utterly rejecting the Bartholomew's claim as nonsense. Jane's husband claimed the Knightleys had the lease of the entire manor after the death of Thomas for £20 per year. John seems to have been confused with the £20 annual income granted to Jane from the Wappenbury lease, and was not aware of the 1532 agreement made in the time of 'the late king of famous memory King Henry the eighth'. To decide the dispute, in 1552 the Court sent three well-known men, Sir Richard Catesby, John Spencer, and Thomas Andrews to Watford to take statements from knowledgeable Watford locals. They said the 1532 agreement was applicable. Further, use of the manor after Thomas Burneby died went to Thomas Purpoynte for his life or until Richard Burneby turned 21, then Richard took the benefits of the manor, and still did. One of the witnesses was John Watkyn, who later bought the Catesby manor of Watford.

Richard and Thomas Burneby: 1535–1609

The manor descended to Richard Burneby, who exited his wardship in 1544. Immediately he came of age, Richard took possession of the manor with grant of livery from the king.

About 1720 a local historian described[79] the manor house and grounds. The lord of the manor 'hath here an old seat with good gardens

Figure 31: Watford Manor Hall

and a park of about two hundred acres'. This two hundred acres of parkland is consistent with the 1429 inquisition listing the same 200 acre demesne, part of the Burneby's two quarter-fee holdings.

Shortly after he took possession of his inherited lands, and with the approval of Mr Purpoynte, Richard married Anne Woodhull, who probably brought with her a generous marriage settlement. Richard eventually built the manor house (see[80] Figure 31) that stood in Watford adjacent to the village for the next four centuries. From then, about 1569, Richard kept Court Rolls for the manor, but unfortunately, the Rolls were not well-kept and now are unavailable for examination.

Like his grandfather, Richard executed an agreement to protect the inheritance of the manor. The provisions, dated May 1546, lasted through the next few generations, into the next century. No surprise, landed citizens in those days did not welcome the payment of taxes to the king upon the direct inheritance of property, and many such as Richard wished to see his manor inheritance remain in the family. This kind of agreement took care of both of these intentions.

Richard granted his manor of Watford and

Figure 32: Thomas Vaux, 2nd Baron of Harrowden.

Silsworth to a group of six men, with certain conditions and obligations. The group included prominent representatives of Richard's new in-laws: Thomas Vaux Lord Harrowden (see[81] Figure 32), and William Parr Lord Horton, as well as Christopher Lewis, two Catesbys and one other person. Anne's parents were Nicholas Woodhull and Elizabeth Parr. Elizabeth's father was Sir William Parr, first Baron Horton, a military man knighted by King Henry VIII. One of Elizabeth's first cousins was Kathryn Parr, the last wife of Henry VIII.

In December 1546, Lord Thomas Vaux carried out one of the key obligations of the agreement made earlier the same year. Thomas 'handed over and demised to Richard and Anne his wife the manor of Watford and all messuages etc in Watford and Silsworth'. So Richard and Anne occupied and 'used' their manor on a good legal footing.

Richard was proud of his Burneby name and background. He obtained a certification of Arms of his family in 1554 (see[82] Figure 33). This included quarterings[v] of de Watford (lower left), Burneby (twice), and in the fourth (upper right), Ardern of Watford.

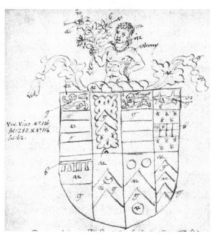

Figure 33: Certification of Arms of Burneby, 1554

In a major tactical move, Richard brought certain lands formerly of St James Abbey to the Burneby manor – the same lands granted to the Abbey centuries before by his ancestors. Back in 1534, before dissolution, the Abbey's major holdings in Watford had been given in two 40 year leases to Henry Wright[vi] of Watford.

One lease included the Rectory of Watford with the capital messuage or mansion place, the granaries, stables, and other houses belonging to the rectory, and all lands, meadows, pastures, tithes and profits going with it, except the tithes of Silsworth. The other lease was for 2 virgates of land with appurtenances in Watford then tenanted by William Sabyn, Thomas Sabyn, John Frauncys and Thomas Haliwell, as well as a granary, four

---

[v] Others: 2nd Revell, 6th Teyes, 7th Besley, 8th Grinden.
[vi] Henry Wright of Watford not to be confused with Henry Wryght of Welton, who appears later. Wright of Watford was married to Audrey and was dead by 1559.

cottages with named tenants, and all related lands, meadows, pastures and profits.

Like all of England's Catholic abbeys and monasteries, St James was subject to King Henry's Dissolution. In 30 Henry VIII, 1538, when St James was dissolved, the total income of the Abbey was surveyed[83] at £274, of which Watford was the largest single contributor after Northampton: *'Watford and Silsworth rents held at the will of the lord king £2 9s 8d; Watford and Silsworth farms £2 18s; Watford rectory £23; Silsworth tithes £2 13s 4d.'* In August 1538, the abbot surrendered the monastery and all its holdings to the king's commissioners. After a while under the King's management, in the 37 Henry VIII, 1545, the site and demesne lands of the Abbey were given to Nicholas Gifford and his descendants.

In December 1559, for £25, Audrey, the widow of Henry Wright senior, late of Watford, conveyed to Richard Burneby the rights to the premises in two leases originally signed in 1538. The premises in one lease were two yardland, one barn, four cottages, and one close called Abbots in Watford. The other lease contained the glebe land, the tithe hay, the tithe of the hayfield, and the tithes and profits of Murcott, and all meads, lands and profits belonging to the parsonage of Watford. On the other hand, Richard granted 1 yardland in the tenure of Edward Watkins, used with a tenement of John Wright, to the use of Henry Wright junior for annual rent of 20s for term of 12 years and 9 months.

Richard wanted full control of the lands on which his manor house was built. So eleven years later, in 1570, by Letters Patent and a fine of 100 marks, Richard Burneby was granted new leases of the same lands. As a condition, Richard surrendered the two leases previously granted by the former abbot to Henry Wright in 1534, which Richard now held due to the assignment in 1559. The new leases were for a duration of 21 years with annual rents set the same as for Henry Wright, that is, £23 for the rectory and capital messuage, and 58s for 2 virgates of land, a granary and four cottages and other premises in Watford. According to the grant, the buildings of the rectory had fallen into decay while in possession of the Monastery of St James, presumably explaining why the rents were not increased. Richard was permitted to take materials from the land to repair the houses and buildings.

In 1577, the lease for 58s (£2 18s) annually of 'our lands' in Watford was one of 20 leases granted by the Queen to George Kirkham. George's lease of 2 virgates, four cottages and a granary was to commence in 1591, at the end of Richard's lease, and last for 40 years. This meant Richard was directed to pay his rents to George, rather than the Queen's Exchequer, from 1591 until 1631. Certain privileges were reserved – the proceeds of court baron, court leet, and view of frankpledge.

The Burnebys had built their manor house on a capital messuage, or manor place (aka scite), held for centuries by St James abbey but rented back to the family by the Rectory. The manor now held the premises of the rectory by right of rent to the crown, fixed at the £23 per year.

There was another of the St James leases that did not find a home with the Burneby Manor. In this case, the lands rented out by the Crown for 49s 8d per year. Their eventual disposition involving the Willes farming family happened decades later. The last of the several lease rentals paid to St James Abbey at Dissolution, the Silsworth tithes of 53s 4d, had been agreed way back in so-called 'time out of mind' and remained with the Crown.

Anne Burneby, nee Woodhull, died at Watford in August 1575, leaving Richard with Thomas, his heir, another son, Benjamin, and a daughter, Mary. Richard married for the second time to Susan Dixwell, by whom he had two more sons, Humphrey and John. Early in December 1590, Richard entered into an agreement with Clement Lewis, Henry Sapcote, and Fulke Woodhull to protect the rights of his heir by his first marriage and of the said heir's children. The second and third of the gentlemen were representatives of Richard's daughter-in-law and his deceased wife, respectively.

The first of the aforementioned three gentlemen was Clement Lewis. One historian, when referring to the Comberford manors, mentions the inquisition of Clement's father, Christopher. The historian correctly noted Lewis's interest in Watford lands, but Lewis never 'held' any of the Burneby lands for his own use or benefit. At best, the Lewis father and son duo played a key role in estate planning for the Burnebys, using the method commonly employed at the time.

Held nine years after his death, Christopher's inquisition summarized his estate, which included minor property interests elsewhere in Northamptonshire. The escheator highlighted the key feature – a long time before 'this' inquisition, Lord Thomas Vaux had partly fulfilled the obligations of the 1546 indenture when he demised the manor estate to Richard senior and his wife. Therefore, first Christopher, as last survivor of the six original feoffees, and then his son Clement Lewis by inheritance, according to this inquisition, was heir to the right and obligation of *reversion* of the manor to the rightful heir at the end of the life interest of Richard senior. With this ruling, the escheator confirmed Clement's legal capacity to fulfil obligations from the 1594 agreement, that is, the enfeoffment to Richard's heir, Thomas.

In the same year as Christopher Lewis's inquisition, the State Papers[84] recorded the following:

> Statement of the case of Rich. Burneby, seized of Watford manor, and a rent of £30, which he enfeoffed to A. B. C. and Chris. Lewis, on condition of its re-assurance to himself and Anne his wife, for life, and of its re-assurance to his son and heir, in tail, within a year after Richard's decease. The surviving feoffee died 24 Eliz [1582]; his heir tendered livery 33 Eliz [1591]. With question whether the pardons of 27 and 29 Eliz discharged him from payment of the mean rates, as there is but a conditional reversion, and nothing due during the life of Rich. Burneby, now tenant for life.

The last living original feoffee, Christopher Lewis, had died in 1582 and Christopher's son, Clement, was heir to his father's interests. The discussion in the Papers about pardons and mean rates may refer to the fee-farm, held by the Burneby family since 1303 for an annual rent of £20. This holding was listed separately in Richard's inquisition with the same description as used since 1303. Also, a lease remained in effect for some of the manor's lands, generating £30 annually, which probably was the Silsworth lands rented out earlier in the same century.

The parties declared the agreement of December 1590 was in consideration of the love and affection Richard Burneby the elder (for Richard the younger was Thomas's son, christened in neighbouring Crick in May of 1577) had for his son and heir, Thomas Burneby. This goodwill extended to the children of Thomas and his wife Elizabeth. Further, the agreement recognized a Jointure to be had for Elizabeth in the Lands and Tenements. Among other things, the agreement said, Clement should make fine before next July for the manor and lands in Watford and Silsworth to the benefit of Richard's family.

When identifying the subject manor and lands, the agreement carefully excluded all those Silsworth closes known by the names of the Highfield alias the Hillfield, and one close now in the tenure of Giles Sharrock, and one other close or pasture called Middlefield. When specifying the subject of any fine or alienation to be made, the premises in two agreements were specifically excepted. One concerned Dixwell, of which more later. The other was dated November 1590, only a few weeks before the December agreement. This agreement was between, first, Richard Burneby, Clement Lewis, and Thomas Burneby, second, John Catesby and William Chibnall (Catesby's lawyer), and third, John Talbott, William Thornbury and Henry Sapcote. By that document the Burnebys sold their manor of Silsworth, which then became one of Catesby's manors of Silsworth.

Among other things, the agreement named 15 of the manor's tenants. The lands attached to the manor included: one close containing the ponds beneath the capital messuage, a close called Milche with two other adjoining closes, all the pastures or closes called the Hayfield, the Birtche close, the Barley close, with the Windmill, the Watermill, and the Bakehouse.

The complex process was brought to a close in the following February of 1591, when the Court of Westminster completed two[85] deeds of 'Final Concord'. On a certain day, Thomas Burneby remised, quitclaimed with warranty by fine and concord, for £400 received, the premises to Henry Sapcote and Fulke Woodhull. On the following day, Richard Burneby senior and Clement Lewis remised, quitclaimed with warranty by fine and accord, also for £400, the same premises to Henry and Fulke. The deeds recited the premises, totalling 1,910 acres:

> re the manor of Watford with appurtenances and 15 messuages, 10 tofts, one watermill, one windmill, two dovecotes, 16 gardens, 1000 acres land, 100 acres meadow, 600 acres pasture, 10 acres woodland, 200 acres furze (gorse) & heath & 100 shillings rent with appurtenances in Watford & Sinelsworth alias Sillsworth.

As called for in the agreement, the fine was levied on the premises in Watford and Silsworth to the separate uses of Richard Burneby senior for life, and after his death to the use of Henry and Fulke with the intention that Richard's son, Thomas, have the rents and profits during his lifetime, and also Elizabeth his wife, during her lifetime for her Jointure. After the deaths of all the aforesaid, the premises should be for the use of Richard junior for his life and after his death for the use of junior's first-born son. And in default of such heir, to a sequential 25 default heirs, all according to the indenture of Elizabeth's Jointure dated December 1590.

Richard Burneby died and was buried in January 1602/3 at Watford, only ten weeks before the death of Queen Elizabeth, whose long reign Richard had witnessed virtually in its entirety. His inquisition named Thomas Burneby as his son and next heir, aged 40 years and more, which was considerably understated; Thomas would have been about 55 years old. Richard left a will[86] dated October 1590. First, he expressed his desire to be buried in Watford church. Richard then gave his brothers, William and Edward, £5 each, and his sons, John and Humphrey, 200 marks and 100 marks, respectively. Through a codicil, he gave another son, Benjamin, £20 and £10 to his daughter, Marie Cure. Richard seems to hint at a connection to Jane Seymour:

> to Thomas Burneby my sonne and heire apparent the hangings of the great chamber of my nowe mansion house in Watford aforesaid and also the bedstead nowe being in the said chamber one featherbed ... one paire of pillows ... and also ...[bedding] ... beinge in the said great chamber aforesaid and the bedstead and ... the hangings of the walles

> being in the chamber called Mistress Seymors chamber next the said
> great chamber … and all the glass beinge in the windows of the said
> mansion house

He left the residue of his personal estate to his (second) wife Susan Burneby, nee Dixwell.

Richard's inquisition provided only a summary of the estate: 'the manor of Watford with appurtenances, a capital messuage, and 16 virgates of land and 16 acres of meadow in Watford and Silsworth and annual rent of 19s', and all messuages, tofts, gardens, yards, orchards, ponds, waters, fisheries, lands, tenements, rents, reversions, services, meadows, pastures, rights of pasturage, commons, woodlands, underwoods, and other hereditaments in Watford and Silsworth. The only obvious additions to the estate were ponds, waters, and fisheries, which Richard probably added when he rebuilt the manor house.

The escheator for Richard senior spelt out his logic for the validity of Thomas's inheritance. At the end, with the demise of the reversion in 1590 by Clement, the escheator concluded that when Richard died, Thomas was duly seized of the premises.

Four months after his father's death, on the 20th of May in the first year of King James (1603), Thomas Burneby came before Cuthbert Pepper Esquire, surveyor of the King, and sought delivery of all the described manors, lands and tenements. The described premises were the manor of Watford and a capital messuage with appurtenances in Watford and Silsworth, worth £10, all held of the king. In addition, there was the fee-farm, although not described as such, rather as 16 virgates of land, 16 acres of meadow, and 19s rent. Thomas declared, therefore, a total annual value of £10 19s for his inheritance.

Nearly two years after his father died, Thomas presented himself once again before Sir Cuthbert Pepper, knight, Surveyor of the Liveries on behalf of the Lord King. This time the key official was Lord Robert Cecil, the Principal Secretary to the king and master of his highness's court of Wards and Liveries. The proceedings recorded the king's agreement to grant Thomas the lordship, manor, lands, tenancies, rents, and other hereditaments with the appurtenances coming into the possession of Thomas by descent from Richard Burneby, his father. That said, the document in several ways and at great length warned Thomas not to undervalue the lands or omit any, and to ensure his grace the king had perfect knowledge of the lands Thomas had inherited.

Stepping back, Thomas had married Elizabeth Sapcote about 1575, and Richard, their eldest son, was baptised at the neighbouring Crick parish church in May of 1577. However, there was one other Burneby baptism recorded before that date, which was in 1566 at Watford, for 'Anna

Burnabye'. While the record does not state 'filia of' anyone, the 1590 marriage Jointure tells us that Thomas's eldest daughter was Anne. The Watford register records the baptism of the other eight children of Thomas, also listed in the 1590 indenture. Four other baptisms took place after 1590, therefore not named in the 1590 indenture. All but one of the latter four died. A total of 14 children were born to Thomas and Elizabeth Burneby over a span of 20 years. Small wonder – Elizabeth Burneby, wife of Thomas Burneby, died and was buried at Watford church in June 1598.

Thomas spent most of his adulthood following his own pursuits. His father lived a long life, and Thomas did not become lord of Watford Manor until an advanced age. He took an interest in other domains, for example, the arts. His name appears in support of the performing arts in London. He became friends with Robert Greene (1558–1592), who was an English author popular in his day. Three of Greene's works of prose written later in his life were dedicated to Thomas Burneby, Esq.

One of Thomas's brothers, John, died and was buried at Watford in December 1608 and his will was proved at PCC in January of 1608/9. John held the manor of Rugby which he left in a complex arrangement involving a bailiff, whereby two parts of the rent of £24 were to be paid to his heirs during the life of Mrs Duncombe. While there is no other information regarding Mrs Duncombe, Mr Duncombe held the 'Oad Ground' in Silsworth. One of John Burneby's bequests was to his uncle Erasmus Dixwell, to whom he gave his lease of a messuage and farm in Watford, which then was in John's own occupation.

Thomas Burneby himself died on 11 March 1608/9, a few months after his brother, and was buried one day later at the church in Watford. Thomas's inquisition reported that his son and next heir was Richard, aged 25 years or more as of October 1609. Given the christening record for Richard, dating his birth in May 1577, he was actually about 32 years of age. There followed a lengthy recitation of events already described earlier leading towards the validity of Richard's inheritance, from the 1546 agreement, the demise later in the same year by Lord Vaux, and the Recoveries of 1591. The inquisition for Thomas provided the same summary of the Watford Manor estate as was given in February 1591 with the two fines and Final Accord.

According to Thomas's escheator, Richard senior had become seized of the manor by a fine 'by force of' the *Statute of Uses* of 4 February, 27 Henry VIII, 1536. This was a statute pushed through Parliament by Henry VIII to stop a practice becoming too common among landholders. They avoided taxes, called fines, by passing an estate to a third party 'for the use of' a person chosen by the initial title holder, often himself or his heir. Both Richard senior and his grandfather George had indulged in the practice. By this Act, Henry VIII awarded title automatically to the person designated 'for the use of'. Therefore, said the escheator, a fine paid according to this Act meant Richard senior was seized when he died and Thomas was permitted to enter and enjoy the manor and premises. As Thomas was in possession when he died, title validly fell to Richard junior. Nonetheless, Richard's title was subject to the restrictions of the intail.

Sir Richard Burneby: 1609–1626

At the age of 31, Richard became Sir Richard, knight bachelor, in February 1608/9, only a month before his father died. Following his father's burial at Watford in March, Richard inherited the manor of Watford and Silsworth. His wife was Elizabeth Reade to whom he was married about 1603. Elizabeth was one of the seven daughters of John Reade of Cottesbrooke and brought with her a marriage settlement – part of her father's substantial estate. Elizabeth's father died in 1604 and in the same year, Richard sold for £300 Elizabeth's inheritance of lands and rights in several parishes including Cottesbrooke.

A few years later, by which time he was accustomed to the mantle of lord of Watford's Burneby manor, Sir Richard signed a number of farm leases for some of his manor lands. They were all dated September of 1612 and all but one carried a particular covenant. The lands leased were certified 'anciently demisable lands of the manor of Watford' and the rents payable were 'the true ancient and accustomed rents … usually payable' for the premises. That ancient rent was set at the rate of 20s per yardland, low enough to contribute to Sir Richard's mounting financial difficulties. Part of each farmer's consideration for a lease was the surrender of his interest in 'diverse years yet to come' in the lands and tenements already in his occupation. Sir Richard must have had some rationale to rewrite his leases – something he gained in the new leases in order to give up the old leases.

Richard Gilbert represented a very long-standing farming family of the parish. Sir Richard Burneby leased to him for 21 years a messuage or tenement and 2 yardland at an annual rental of 33s 4d, which was less than the ancient 'standard' rate. However, Richard Gilbert agreed to provide other services in addition to the rent. Every year he was to carry and bring to the Burneby manor house two buttresses of pitt coal from any pit within 20 miles of Watford. Generously, Sir Richard felt obliged to pay for the coal and provide 'meate and drinke' for the workers and hay for the horses. Gilbert should also provide a team and 'two sufficient servants' with the team to carry hay for Sir Richard for one day at the time of the hay harvest, another day for the 'corne harvest', a third day for the 'pease harvest', and yet another man for a day to mow grass and make hay in the hay harvest. And each year Gilbert shall grind at the mill and bake at Sir Richard's bakehouse, while using those facilities for others as much as possible, or pay one penny for each shricke of corne not baked there. Not done yet, every year Gilbert was to plant and maintain four trees (of Oak, Ash or Elm) somewhere on the premises. Finally, Richard was to deliver two capons at Whitsuntide, four hens in February, and 12 chickens between Easter and August, and deliver a true terrar to Sir Richard every seven years. Nothing was found in the lease to suggest the precise location of the Gilbert farm within the town of Watford. There seems some likelihood his were two virgates of farmlands situated within the Manor Park itself. If so, it is not surprising that Richard Gilbert provided such additional services to the Lord of the manor and his mansion. The family dwelling lay on what became lot (n), the last in a row of messuages adjoining lot 31 with its nearly 40 acres, both owned by William Gilbert in 1771, and located where the village road opens to the church and the manor lands. Several closes in Watford bear the name Gilbert.

One of the three farmers with a lease at the 'ancient' rate took on a messuage and 1 ¾ yardland at 40s annually for 21 years. Another farmer in Watford leased a messuage and 1 ¼ yardland for an annual rent of 25s. At the same time, he leased another messuage, 1 yardland, and the Old Mill Close, paying Sir Richard 20s per year. By 1623, he leased only 2 yardlands, the difference possibly accounted for by a quarterne sold in 1641. And lastly, one more husbandman of the parish signed up for a messuage and 1 ¼ yardland, paying 25s 4d annually. One wonders what the common factor might be that tied these tenants to 'ancient' rates?

In 1615, a few years after Sir Richard sorted out some of his own farm leases, a certain John Lambe took on the lease of another Silsworth manor from the Catesbys. Sir Richard Burneby immediately entered a plea to demand payment for tithes from John Lambe on those Silsworth lands. Richard claimed £600, being triple value of the tithes of Silsworth belonging to the Rectory of Watford, which the Burnebys had leased since 1570. He said his claim was according to the Statute of King Edward VI, requiring the payment of threefold the value for tithes not paid in kind. Not surprisingly, within a few months, John Lambe entered a Bill to Chancery refuting Sir Richard's claim for tithes. Not content with that, Sir Richard entered an answer contradicting John's claim that Richard's claim for tithes was invalid. The dispute lay undetermined for an extended period of time.

Ten years after the dispute over tithes first appeared the case resurfaced, but with the parties in opposite seats. In October of 1624, John Lambe, a knight by that time, filed a new Bill in Chancery claiming tithes payable by all owners or occupiers of Silsworth lands, including Sir Richard Burneby and Robert Catesby jnr. Sir John claimed he had bought the rights to tithes in Silsworth in or after 1615. Two of the many from whom Sir John claimed tithes were Sir Richard Burneby and Edward Shugborough. The two owned the Rectory of Watford, Sir John said, but not the tithes of Silsworth. Following Sir John's claim, the Audience Court heard a Statement of Proceedings. About three months later, Sir Richard Burneby and Edward Shugborough filed answers to the bill of Sir John Lambe, vehemently denying they owed anything to Sir John. In November of 1626, a writ restraining proceedings between Lambe and Shugborough was filed in the Court of Audience. Sir Richard had removed himself from the controversy – his holdings in Silsworth were sold. After Sir Richard completed his manor sale, Edward Shuckburgh leased about 210 acres in Silsworth from the new owner. For his own financial security, he added a covenant protecting himself from any legal suit brought by Sir John Lambe for tithes on any lands in Silsworth he then or previously held.

By 1620, Sir Richard realised he had much greater financial problems to deal with than he could surmount with his annual income. He had eight children, his eldest son about to enter Oxford University, his daughters all expecting a marriage settlement, various family members looking for help, let alone existing debts. To provide some immediate ready cash, and remove himself from the day-to-day management of a part of his manor estate, Sir Richard signed a six-year lease. William Halford took on the core of Sir Richard's Watford manor for an up-front payment of £200 plus ongoing rentals. Three parcels of lands each bearing a different rental were leased: First: the Manor House, its orchards, gardens, brewery, the stables attached and four adjoining closes; second, the Hay Field; and third, Cumberford's farm. For the manor house with brewery and closes adjoining called the Warren, the Barley close or Bowling Leyes, the Holme close, and the Milche close the annual rent was £60. For the Hay Field, the annual rental of 12 increasing to 22 shillings per acre was payable. The four yardlands of the inheritance of Robert Lord Spencer, known as Cumberford's farm, yielded £32 per year.

The Cumberfords' four yardlands had been obtained by the Burnebys centuries before to make farming in the immediate area much more practical. This acreage appears to be the four virgates enfeoffed in 1330 by the Parles family to the Burnebys. The enfeoffment meant the Burnebys held the lands effectively as an everlasting lease, provided they continued to pay the rent. The four farmers on Cumberford's farm were named, while Sir Richard himself occupied the Hay and the manor closes. The lease allowed for ingress and egress of various tenants to and from their tenancies.

Sir Richard Burneby decided[87] to sell his manor of Watford and Silsworth, officially giving the reason – 'for Payment of Debts, and raising of Portions for younger Children'. However, to put together an effective sale of the manor to a third party, Sir Richard had to break the intail specifically preventing such an action. One way of accomplishing this was to seek an Act of Parliament, rather than obtain a license as might have sufficed in medieval times.

Richard found a buyer for the manor in George Clerke, supported by George's father-in-law, Robert Palmer. They signed an agreement[88] dated 20th November, 21 James, or 1623, for the sale and purchase of the manor. The price was to be £9,400, with £500 paid upon signing, two other amounts due within a year, and the last and largest amount due the March 25th following Sir Richard's son and heir, Eustace, attaining the age of 21 years. The deal was conditioned on Richard's wife, Elizabeth, and Eustace validly added their 'assurance' to the conveyance. Eustace had to agree to the sale because as the eldest son and heir, he was caught by the intail. The parties also agreed to delay payment of the last £1,000 by George Clerke.

Prior to signing up for the sale of the manor, Sir Richard took care of another family obligation. He wanted to officially remove certain parcels of land from the manor so they would not be sold as part of the whole manor. So he signed a series of agreements to sell one of the manor's farms to his sister, Susanna, and her husband, Thomas Eyton, for £550. The premises were a dwelling, two closes and two yardlands in the occupation of Humphrey Dixwell.

Just after the Manor sale concluded, Susanna's premises were the subject of a second sale agreement. This time Richard's legal heir, Eustace, was included as a seller, while the purchasers were Richard Lane and Robert Greene of Northampton, and the occupants of the premises were the Eytons, Mr Dixwell having departed or been evicted. The first sale was to remove the lands from the manor premises so George Clerke could not get his hands on them. The second 'sale' set up the false process of Common Recovery, which was required to break the intail, as necessary for this small parcel as for the manor itself.

A bill was presented to Parliament on the 23rd April 1624 for the sale of Burneby's manor. After a discussion on 7th of May 1624, Parliament was divided on the question, and the final vote was 'Noe, 104 and Yea, 99'. The bill was rejected. Nonetheless, the sale process continued, but with a different angle of attack.

Only a week after parliament vetoed the proposed sale, George and Richard signed a modification to the agreement written on the back of the original document. Part of the premises turned out to be of lesser value than expected, so the sum of £200 would be deducted from the last payment. With modifications in November and December 1624, the parties made several changes to delay the final close of the deal to allow for the alternate plan. Price adjustments were made deducting £400 for lesser value so the total price would be £9,000. The Burnebys then agreed they would 'forbear' George Clerke delaying payment of the last £1,000 until the 2nd February 1626, and the account and payment due on 25th March 1625 would not be due at that time. Finally, they recorded that Eustace Burneby was now signed up as a joint seller.

Sir Richard acknowledged he had received £2,300 of the price, which was probably a payment directed towards his debts, now necessary due to the delay in close and to clear an encumbrance. Separately, on 22nd May 1624, Sir Richard (see[89] Figure 34) bonded himself to the extent of £2,000 guaranteeing adherence to all agreements made and delivery to George Clerke of all deeds, evidences, court rolls, surveys, indentures, leases, or any writing concerning the manor and premises intended to be sold.

Figure 34: Signature of Richard Burnebie

The agreement of sale documented the manor of Watford, with all rights and members, the Manor house and all demesne lands in the occupation of Sir Richard Burneby or his assignees, farmers or tenants. Specifically:

> All those twoe pasture grounds called Cookesfield and Viccars fields with the meadows thereto belonging

> All other the lands tenements and hereditaments of the said Sir Richard in Sillesworth … with the rights members and appurtenances thereof parcel of the Mannor of Sillesworth with all rights profits and comodities … in Sillesworth … now being in the tenure or occupation of Sir Richard … his assignees, fermoes or penden tennants

> All manner of houses, edifices, byldings, barnes, stables, outhouses, gardens, closes and inclosed grounds, lands tenements, meadows, pastures, feedings … whatsoever of Sir Richard to the manner of Watford and Silsworth

> All that the Rectorie or parsonage Impropriate of Watford … and all manner of tenths, tythes of corne graine and hay

> All that messuage ('MS') or tenement ('T') and 2 yardlands ('YL') in lands ('L') meadow ('M') commons ('C') and pasture ('P') with their appurtenances ('App') to the same belonging in Watford ('W') aforesaid

in the tenure or occupation ('Occ') of one William Hollys or his assigns ('A') [abbreviations added by the author]

All that MS or T and 1 ¼ YL in L, M, C, and P with App in W in the Occ of John Murcott or his A

All that MS and 2 ¼ YL in L M C and P with App in W in the Occ of William Sabyne or his A

One other MS or T and 1 ¾ YL in L, M, C and P with App in W in the Occ of William Cornish or his A

All that MS or T 1 ¼ YL in L, M, C and P with App in W in the Occ of Robert Cattell or his A

One other MS or T and ¾ YL in L, M, C and P with App in W in the Occ of Edward Justine or his A

One other MS or T and 1 ¼ YL in L, M, C and P with App in W in the Occ of Joan Paybodye or her A

One other MS or T and 2 YL in L, M, C, and P with App in W in the Occ of John Marrytt or his A

One other MS or T and 1 ½ YL in L, M, C and P with App in W in the Occ of Richard Cattell or his A

One other MS or T and 1 ½ YL in L, M, C and P with App in the Occ of Robert Lucas or his A

One other MS or T and 2 YL in L, M, C and P with App in W in the Occ of [space] Gilbert widow or her A

One other MS or T and 2 YL in L, M, C and P with App in W in the Occ of John Eares the younger or his A

All that one cottage or T with App and one peece of M called Ashby Hooke and the comonninge ... pasturinge and feedinge for three lease [plural of lea or ley] and twentie sheepe at all comonable tymes in all places comonable in W in the Occ of Rafe Pyke or his A

One other cottage or T and one close with the App and the comonninge ... pasturinge and feeding for three beastes and twentie sheepe at all times in all places comonable in W in the Occ of William Roberts or his A

One other cottage or T and one cowe comons with the App in W in the Occ of William Baylie or his A

One other cottage and one close and one cowe comons with the App in W in the Occ of William Hankin or his A

All that one Water Mill and all the Meadows and Mill Hylmes thereunto belonging with the App in W in the Occ of Sir Richard or his A

All that one Windemill and the ground and soyle whereupon the same standeth with the App in W in the Occ of Sir Richard or his A

And also Courte Leete and Court Baron and ... fines and forfeytures and all other profits ... belongeth

All manner of Cheete tentants quittrate rents royalties and privelidges duetyes customs and services whatsoever

Also one Comon Backhouse with the App and all manner of duties rights customs and privelidges belonging

Alsoe all those severall pastures inclosures and inclosed grounds with their severall rights members and appurtenances in Watford and Sillesworth ... called by the severall names of the Bowlinge leayes Hay field Nasborowe Cookesfield Viccarsfield Chermick Closes or by any other name ... nowe in the severall tenures ... or occupation of the said Sir Richard Burneby Simon Norton, Robert Cattell, Edward Shuckbrugh Esq and William Halford Esq or some of them ... or some of their severall assigns farmors or undertennants

Alsoe all other the messuages lands tenaments meadows comons and comon of pasture fouldel and foulde courses closes emoluments and hereditaments whatsoever ... in Watford and Sillesworth

All the rent and rents, revercon and revercons, remainder and remainders, and services of all and singular the aforesaid premises ...

And also all the estate right title interest clayame and demannd whatsoever of the said Sir Richard ... to the foresaid manor messuages lands tenements hereditaments premises or any of them

And all deeds and indentures wills charters writings ... and minuments whatsoever ... and all copies ...

Excepte and reserved out of such bargaine and sale ... one messuage or tenement and two yardlands with appurtenances ... in the occupation of Humphrey Dixwell or his assigns And also the glebe lands lying in Watford and Martoll [Murcott?] And the tyeth of Martoll [Murcott?] ... formerly souled to Edward Shukbrough Esq by the said Sir Richard Burneby

And the foresaid Manner house in Watford aforesaid with all lockes dores keyes benches settles wainscot portals windows glasses shuttings for wondows ovens coppers leads casks coopers and all manner of burninge vessels or vessel not defull for own and all barrows houshees and other caske thrulls or seats whatsoever and all other things usually kept in such like cases together with all kacks mangers planckes cowe slabs shaiders honells pales postes and kayles in and about the foresaid premises

The conclusion of the conveyance process occurred in late 1625 and early 1626. At Westminster, in December 1625, for £12 paid to the Exchequer, King Charles granted Letters Patent to Sir Burneby, Knight, Elizabeth his wife, and Eustace Burneby Esquire, son and heir apparent of Richard. They were given permission to grant, alienate or acknowledge by fine or recovery the manor of Watford with appurtenances situated in Watford and Silsworth. The beneficiary was named as George Clarke, to have and to hold to George, his heirs and assigns, forever.

Armed with the king's permission the transaction could be finalised. On the 12th February 1626, in the first year of the reign of King Charles I, Sir Richard Burneby, his wife, Dame Elizabeth and his son and heir, Eustace, appeared before a Justice of the Court of Common Pleas at Westminster. By fine and common recovery, they demised, released and quitclaimed all amounts due from George Clerke for the mentioned premises, except for the sum of £1,000 unpaid by George. So the Justice of the Common Pleas conducted a 'Common Recovery'. This was a collusive action by all parties – a fake legal procedure performed by the court, commonly used to break an intail. The descendants of Richard senior, his son Thomas and Thomas's son, (Sir) Richard the younger, were restricted by intail from passing title in the manor lands to someone else – in this case, George Clerke. Hence the need to break the intail, which this process accomplished.

The premises were described as: the manor of Watford with all its rights, 12 (or 16)[vii] homesteads, four cottages, one watermill, one windmill, 16 gardens, 16 orchards, 380 acres of land, 150 acres of meadow, 700 acres of pasture, 4 acres of wood, 50 acres of heath and gorse, £4 of rent, and common of pasture for all manner of cattle, view of frankpledge with rights in Watford and Silsworth, and the Rectory of Watford, with rights and all manner of tithes belonging.

Duplicating the main Manor transaction, in December 1625 Sir Richard Burneby and his son, Eustace, obtained a license to sell certain premises to Lane and Greene for Richard's sister. By exemplification of Common

---

[vii] The document listed premises in two places, one noted 16 homesteads and the other 12 homesteads; the correct number appears to be 12. The count of 4 cottages was also correct, with each cottage also declared as a tenement or close (which was also a tenancy). The two together make 16 tenements.

Recovery on 13th February 1626, the premises were said to contain a house, a dovecot, a garden, and a total of 128 acres.

The Burneby manor of Watford was sold to George Clerke, almost to the day, 350 years after its creation. That had been brought about in February 1276 when the escheator created the four daughter's manors by splitting the single manor of Eustace de Watford IV. Going back further to when Agnes de Ardern was given the entire manor, the Burneby manor in Watford lasted, all told, nearly 500 years through her direct descendants, ending finally with Sir Richard Burneby.

As sold, the manor included 19 ½ yardlands, which accounts for the declared 380 acres of arable land. The manor's remaining 904 acres of pasture, meadow, and unusable land is another reminder of the generous extent of appurtenances in Watford parish. Although the declarations of extent in official documents such as a Common Recovery are not necessarily 100% accurate, some exploration of the information is possible. Despite that reservation, the recitation in the Recovery was precisely accurate regarding the number of messuages or homesteads, cottages and tenures, which can be counted in the agreement of sale as listed above.

Some pasture and meadow in Watford was naturally attached to yardlands. Watford town had a good number of large enclosed fields that were pasture, such Naseborough in the east as well as Middleton, Cringles and Overende in the west, which total over 300 acres. The Burnebys included in the sale what was called the Manor of Silsworth, which may total 390 acres or may be an understated 300 acres in Silsworth identified a century before by the Sheriff. And Sir Richard specifically named his pastures in Silsworth, Cooksfield and Viccarsfield, which amount to 150 acres.

The Fee-farm must have been part of the manor lands handed over by Sir Richard. Documents kept at the Northamptonshire Record Office indicate the Burnebys continued to pay rent for the fee-farm until 1638, although obviously George Clerke must have paid the rentals in the name of the Burnebys from 1626. George Clerke himself continued to pay the same fee in his own name from 1639 until 1642. In the last year, the fee-farm carried virtually the same description as more than 300 years before: 'one messuage & 16 virgates of land & 16 acres of meadow & 29 shillings rent in Watford & Silsworth'.

The declared areas in 1590 and 1626 differ to the tune of about 500 acres of land, allowing for what was peeled off for Susanna Eyton. This difference ties in with the approximate size of the de Watford manor, later known as the Catesby manor. While technically, this manor owed homage to the Burneby manor, times had moved on since the medieval period, and George Clerke planned to separately acquire that manor in due course.

Knowing he would eventually pay a fine for the Catesby manor, George had every reason to exclude that acreage from his declaration in 1626 to avoid paying tax twice.

Sir Richard and most of his family seem to fade from the public eye. In fact, few records of his family exist. Other than the record of (Sir) Richard Burneby's christening, to date no record of his marriage to Elizabeth Reade or the birth of his eldest son, Eustace, has been found. Oxford Alumni reports Eustace Burneby, the son of a knight, matriculated 16 November 1621, aged 16, suggesting he was born about December 1604 – therefore aged 21 in December 1625. In error, *Visitations of Northamptonshire made in 1564 and 1618*, on page 172, reports Sir Richard's eldest son to be a Richard, and no mention of any Eustace is made among the seven children listed. Furthermore, no record has yet been found of the death of Sir Richard, or of any related will. It might be tempting to consider a 'True Bill' – a report of the murder by the thrust of a sword to the chest of a Richard Burneby on Holborne in London. However, this occurs on 14th February 1625, in the last days of King James and therefore must be ignored, because Richard's signature exists on a document dated a year later, February 1626, in the first year of King Charles. Perhaps this unfortunate Richard Burneby was the servant at the *King's Arms*, buried at St Clement Danes, Middx on the 18th February, 1625.

Sir Richard died about 1629 or 1630. Lady Elizabeth Burneby died in or before June 1633, at Stoke next Coventry in Warwickshire. The date she wrote in her will was January 1631, by then already describing herself as the widow of Sir Richard Burneby. Her personal goods, mostly clothing, were inventoried at a value of just over £13 and given to one of her daughters, Susanna or Theodosius. In the will, she mentioned a bond of £200, the interest then being paid to herself, which after her decease was for her son, Eustace Burneby. He lived in Coventry for many years, appearing in at least eight legal actions, often with Alice Knightley, concerning a bond and tenement in that city. Eustace Burneby of Coventry, whose will was proved in May 1684, is likely the same Eustace of Watford, son of Sir Richard.

PART 3: The Parles and Cumberford Manor

Joan de Watford and William de Parles: 1276–1309

From 1276, Joan, the third daughter of Sir Eustace de Watford, held the fourth quarter of the Watford manor direct of the king. William de Parles was her husband and so her manor became known as '*The Parles manor of Watford*'. The Parles name (see Arms[90] Figure 35) was well-known in medieval times, but not always for the best of reasons. Joan and her husband were the first of ten generations[viii] to hold this quarter of the Watford manor and associated knight's fee, initially as Parles and in later generations, as Cumberford.

Figure 35: Arms of de Parles

The de Parles family's primary seat was Honesworth (Handsworth) in Staffordshire. William's father was John and his grandfather, another William de Parles. Records featuring the elder William in Sandwell exist back to the outset of the thirteenth century. He set a tone for the family when he supported the Barons against the king in the First Baron's War of 1215 – 1217, and as a result was one of many who had his lands taken away by the king.

> [91]The Sheriff of Staffordshire is ordered to cause Robert de Teuray Knight of the County of Chester to have land which was of William de Parles, who is with the enemies of the lord King, in Huneswro' with all its appurtenances, for as long as it pleases the lord King.

Like many others, William senior got his lands back when he returned to loyalty and once again gave homage to the king.

Two generations later, Joan's marriage to the younger William de Parles was another marital alliance that increased Eustace de Watford's influence and reputation in Northamptonshire. William was a man with a mixed reputation, whether deserved or not.

> [92]From the early years of the 13th century the priory of Sandwell was involved in disputes with three generations of the Parles family over lands

---

viii see Appendix 2.

in Sandwell, Handsworth and the advowson of the priory. The climax of the priory's relations with the Parles family was reached in 1260 when William de Parles led an armed band of assailants against the prior, who was fortunate to escape.

This apple hadn't fallen far from the apple tree. William featured in the assizes (courts) a number of times in the thirteenth century, before and after his marriage. The aforementioned case in 1260 was only one example. Another enquiry held by the sheriff of Stafford found Nicholas de Swinefen had entered the park of William de Parles in Honesworth and took and carried away one buck and two pigs. In January 1266, William le Brune (Parles' brother-in-law) and Eustace de Watford (his father-in-law), among other notables, acted as pledge for William de Parles. He had taken the side of the rebels in the second Baron's War and faced the consequences. He was imprisoned at Gloucester for crimes against King Henry III and the king's son, eventually King Edward I, as well as the Constable of the king's castle at Gloucester.

On one of two other occasions, William entered a plea against 38 men for 'cutting down and carrying away his trees at Hunesworth to the value of £60'. On the other occasion, 18 tenants claimed the right to pasture on William's lands in Honesworthe. In November 1275, William de Parles was one of several who stood guarantor for a friend thrown in prison for 'diverse trespasses'.

In yet another case, the king issued a mandate for his representative with a jury to hear the case brought by William de Parles against eight men, particularly Geoffrey de Lucy, for the abduction of William's underage ward named Hamon, the son of Hamon. The malefactors had removed the youngster at the very instant an arraignment was being taken by William against the same parties who had snatched one of his tenements from him. Their act was against the peace and in manifest contempt of Court. Geoffrey and his cohorts had come armed and captured the boy to prevent the assize being taken. When William raised a 'hue and cry' with a horn, the local bailiff prevented William from pursuing the scoundrels by taking away his horn. The defendants were ordered to be arrested.

Sometime in 1275 William gave his son, John, the manor of Honesworth, or so John claimed at a later date. Afterwards, William travelled with his family to Northamptonshire leaving his servants at Honesworth. They attended to the estate of Eustace de Watford early in 1276 when Joan inherited her share of the Watford manor. After staying three weeks, the family returned to Staffordshire where William continued to act as any other lord.

William was not shy of annoying his mother-in-law. Not long after Lord Eustace was gone, his widow Margery de Watford brought a suit against William de Parles 'concerning a trespass committed upon her'. She 'put in her place' William Petri or Thomas de Bray to conduct the suit before the king on her behalf.

William de Parles was one of many summoned in December 1276 by the writ of King Edward, *Longshanks*, to meet at Worcester in July of 1277. There he acknowledged the service he owed on account of holding one-fourth of a knight's fee in Watford, the inheritance of his wife. That summer he performed his service as a knight in the successful war against the Welsh, and then returned home.

The end of William de Parles was as dramatic as his life. He was hanged for murder. The felony was committed in the summer of 1278, after which William was arrested, imprisoned, tried, and hanged in November of that year. As a consequence of William's crime, his lands were taken by the king in whose possession they remained until December 1279.

Following William's encounter with the gallows, several inquisitions were held between May 1279 and March 1281 to sort out who should have his estates. One inquisition dealt with William's chattels and three addressed disputes over entitlement to William's lands in Honesworth and Great Rollendrich. An escheator said William held two carucates in Great Rollendrich of John de Parles, his son. The escheator elaborated: Eustace de Parles, William's other son, 'had no seisin of the said land' and indeed, no other person other than William himself had been enfeoffed with those lands. Another escheator said the lands had been granted to Roger le Burd by William for 10 marks yearly. This escheator was even more emphatic in his comments about Eustace de Parles: 'William never enfeoffed Eustace de Parles, but Eustace falsely, to the prejudice to the right of the king and the said John, pretended to be enfeoffed, and not by collusion between him and the said Roger.'

Fortunately for Joan de Parles, her rights were clarified promptly. In December 1278, the king directed a rather testy order to the sheriff of Northampton. 'Order to deliver to Joan, late the wife of William de Parles, daughter and co-heiress of Eustace de Watford, the lands that fall to her purparty of the lands of Eustace de Watford, which were taken into the king's hands by reason of William's death, together with the corn sown in the lands … [and] … the other goods and chattels that belonged to William upon her finding security to answer for the price thereof … and to restore to Joan any of the goods that the sheriff may have alienated, the king having previously ordered him to deliver the lands but he has done nothing in the matter, to the king's surprise.'

An inquisition followed, which indicated Joan had been delivered of the goods and chattels from the king's hands at a valuation by the king's order. In contrast to his action with Joan's lands and chattels in Watford, the king ordered William's goods and chattels on Honesworth be given to his consort, Queen Eleanor.

While Joan's right to certain lands may have been clear – given she was a direct heiress of her father – her family faced great struggle with William's lands. A year after the order in favour of Joan, William's son John also obtained an order, to at least some effect. The sheriff of Oxford should pay John Parles the annual 10 mark rent due on William's lands in Great Rollendrich until the following Easter, when the king would see justice done for persons claiming rights to the lands. Two enquiries, four years apart, were needed to establish whether William was seized of the manor of Honesworth on the day he committed the felony.

William and Joan de Parles had at least five children: sons John and Eustace, obviously named after the father of each parent, another son Walter, and daughters Sarrah and Alice. Eustace, apparently the younger of the sons, may have taken on some of the aggressive characteristics of his father. In 1282, John put his brother Eustace in his place to stand for him in a suit before the king, presumably because Eustace was better able to present a defence. The suit was between Queen Eleanor, the king's consort, and John concerning a trespass committed by him. This probably concerned the lands of Honesworth. Only a few years later, the backing of six men, including Eustace de Burneby, was required to stand guarantor for Eustace de Parles. The king then ordered the sheriff of York to deliver Eustace de Parles from prison to appear before the king to answer for his trespasses.

The Parles family did not easily give up the fight for their right to William's lands. In the Easter session of 1290, 'the children of William de Parles' petitioned the lord King Edward at parliament for the restitution of their father's lands. They claimed William had been unjustly hanged which had become clear through the confession of others. They requested the king show them grace in the matter of their father's lands. Their petition,[93] which spells out the whole sad story, was appended with the notation – 'Nothing is to be done for them'.

The children of William Parles pray our lord the king and his council that pity be taken of them and of the wrong that was done to their father in contempt of the commandment of our lord the king and to their disinheritance, that is to say, that when their father was arrested by a false accusation against him of the killing of Philip son of Robert and they heard said that sir Ellis de Hauville was procured by the enemies of their father to be the justice in this case to ensure the condemnation of their father, Eustace their brother approached the court of our lord the king and prayed a remedy for this and that too hasty judgment be not given until the country could be better informed of the aforesaid death. So he was granted a writ of *de odio et athia* and a writ to the aforesaid sir Ellis that, whatever the inquest found, he should have it returned to the court of our lord the king. The aforesaid Ellis, when he understood the tenor of the aforesaid writ that was of a later date than his warrant and defeated his power in respect of the giving of judgment, he took and had taken the aforesaid Eustace, the bearer of the aforesaid commandment of the king, to the contempt of our lord the king and of his commandment and in the presence of the whole country and imprisoned him until he had done his will on their father and then released him. So the aforesaid children pray for God's sake and for the sake of the souls of the ancestors of our lord the king and of his children that since those who killed the aforesaid sir Philip have been arrested and admitted the said deed, some in the same area and some at Newgate and Warwick, so the country is now better informed on this killing than it was before and that their father was not guilty, that they be not disinherited by this falsehood and that they may put those who plotted this to answer in the council of our lord the king, if it please.

Years after proving her right to hold all of her own lands, Joan de Parles again had to prove her right to a small property. One of Joan's tenants, John de Dumer, died in 1306 and his inquisition was instructed to ascertain what lands he held and by what right. The escheator concluded John de Dumer held in Watford three homesteads and 51 acres given to him in 1279 by Joan, who held the lands in chief, and another 12 acres by the gift of Ellen de Watford. But that was not the end of the story.

Even for this small plot of land the king's governmental machinery ground into action. The escheator for Northamptonshire was ordered to take back the lands which John de Dumer had obtained from Joan de Parles without the king's license. The lands should not be returned to Dumer's son until the next parliament, and Joan should be warned to attend a hearing to defend herself, otherwise the lands would be restored to Richard de Dumer. After a delay, in March 1311 another order told the escheator not to molest Richard de Dumer for the profits of the lands in Watford his father had held without royal license. The resolution of the dispute favoured the Burnebys, the chief lords of the manor. As a result, two parcels of land, closely resembling the two acreages listed by the escheator in 1306 and 1307, were granted to the de Burnebys.

In yet another related inquisition of November 1308, the escheator was asked to find out only one thing about Richard de Dumer – his age – to ensure he was old enough to inherit. The common process for this kind of enquiry was to ask local residents how they knew the subject's age. One witness in Richard's case stated Richard was born at the feast of St Luke, 14 Edward I (18 October 1286). His reasoning provides a unique insight into an important part of the history of the church at Watford: 'Oliver, sometime bishop of Lincoln, dedicated the church of Watford in the same year'. Each witness gave his name and age. The witnesses and their birthdates included residents such as Richard Golafre 1268, Roger Capel 1248, Simon de Taillour 1248, and William Freman 1245. Many of these names are familiar from the list of villeins and free tenants in the Watford of 1276.

John de Parles and Walter de Parles: 1309–1361

John, the son of Joan and William de Parles, inherited the Parles estates of Watford in 1309, but he tripped himself up with the process. Without license from the king, John acquired in fee from his mother a dwelling, 11 ½ virgates of land and 5 acres of meadow in Watford parish, all held in chief. The king took back the lands because John had not obtained a license. So a special inquisition *ad quod damnum* was held to decide whether the king would be disadvantaged if John de Parles was allowed to have the lands. The answer was no damage, because John was the son and rightful heir of Joan de Parles. The inquisition took care to value the quarter-manor at £9 1s 8d annually, including: 1 mark p.a. for the dwelling, 1 mark p.a. for each virgate, and 3s p.a. for each acre of meadow. To redress his trespass, John paid a fine and obtained a pardon, and the king granted the Watford lands back to him.

Both the king and John were happy. The king had collected money for agreeing to overlook John's ignorance of the rules. John had the king's formal ruling which could be produced any time in the future should he need to prove he held these lands.

Not long after, Joan gave her daughters a home and income. She granted Sarrah a dwelling and 10s rent in Watford, and Alice, another dwelling and half a virgate, also in Watford. The gifts to both daughters were 'in chief'.

Six years later, with a 10 mark fine, John was granted another license. This time all was done correctly. He granted lands to John Squier with re-grant by Squier back to himself and Eleanor, his wife, and their heirs. Even better, he made sure another inquisition *ad quod damnum* agreed in advance that the king would not be damaged by the grants. On the other hand, the lands seem to be worth nearly a third less, or £6 7s 6d p.a., a plan probably orchestrated by John to reduce his fine for the grants. The dwelling was now worth 5s, the 11 ½ virgates of land 115s (10s per virgate), and 5 acres of meadow earnt 7s 6d. The grant[94] (see[95] Figure 36) itself summarised his lands and included reference to the two houses given to his siblings. He gave:

> all my manor in the town of Watford ... with appurtenances with houses, building, gardens, curtilages, vineyards, fisheries, apiaries, meadows, pastures & pasturings, and all homages, services, rents, customs &c. And also with all my right & claim to all my lands & tenements with appurtenances &c within & without the towns of Watford, Morkotes, Wykenhul, Senelesworth. Saving to Walter my brother & Sarah my sister rents of the messuages which the said Walter & Sarah had for term of their lives as appears by a certain deed made

John wanted to be sure other landholders understood what he was doing and would be able to bear witness to the extent of his landholdings if called upon. His witnesses included the Lords of four local parishes – Daventre, Watford, Ashby Legers, and Crick.

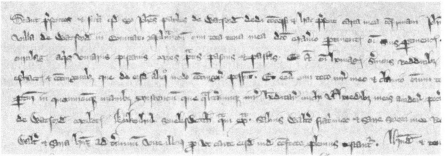

Figure 36: Extract from Grant by John de Parles of Watford, 1315

No record of the demise of John de Parles is available. However, he must have died in or by 1327, by which time his widow, Eleanor, held rights to the land. She gave to her son, Walter, and Alice his wife a house in Watford, for as long as Eleanor lived. Walter reconfirmed Eleanor should have for her life the lands John Squier had given to his parents paying any required service fees to the chief lord of the fee of Watford. After her decease, the lands should revert to Walter and his heirs, except for the crops on the land. Once more, witnesses included the nearby lords of Daventry, Crick, and two from Watford.

In the same year, Walter de Parles acknowledged he owed £100 to Eustace de Burneby. If Walter ended up in default of payment, Eustace could take Walter's lands and chattels in Northamptonshire. Within the next three years Eustace must have pressured Walter to settle the debt, which Walter did by giving land to Eustace. For this, Walter Parles needed a licence. So the path had to be cleared through a yet another special inquisition *ad quod damnum* held in Walter's name.

First, the inquisition acknowledged Walter Parles held 8 virgates of land in Watford and Murcott by right of a quarter knight's fee. He was licensed to grant rent and the eighth part of a knight's fee in Watford and Murcott to Eustace de Burneby, held in chief, but retain the reversion of a dwelling and land in Watford.

Second, Walter held another 9 dwellings and 7 virgates of land in Silsworth and Watford, which he kept. He was licensed to grant those lands in fee simple to Roger de Waldeshef after the lifetime of Eleanor, to be immediately granted back to Walter, his wife Alice and heirs in tail. If Walter had no heirs then the lands should go to Eustace de Burneby in fee simple.

The special inquisition approved the grant of land to Eustace de Burneby because switching lands from one holder-in-chief to another holder-in-chief, within the same knight's fee, did not disadvantage the king. Walter granted Eustace a half of his quarter knight's fee *to have to him and his heirs by service owed and of right accustomed for ever.* This did not transfer title in fee, but rather the right to use the land – probably for a nominal rent – forever. In summary, the inquisition recognised Walter held 15 virgates of land, allowed him to give 4 to Eustace, leaving him with 11 virgates, and all the dwellings. Another half-virgate given in 1310 to a daughter, 'in chief' may have come back into the picture in later years. Reports of land holdings in different inquisitions were not always arithmetically precise or exactly consistent.

Years later, Walter obtained an 'exemplification[ix] under the seal now in use' of the second license. This was the normal response to prove his right to hold lands or finalise the gift of lands to another person.

Walter, as Sheriff of Northamptonshire, was occasionally asked to perform public duties. Along with three others, he was appointed to arrest William Cransley. William had falsely claimed title to the church of Foston, which was held by the king due to the 'temporalities' of its owner, the priory, on account of the war with France. William had acted in 'derogation' of the king's right to present the pastor of the church, and had 'often entered and still enters the [church] with armed force, holding the tithes and profits thereof, and so threatens the men and servants of the king's [pastor], that they have not dared to do what is incumbent on them,

---

[ix] A copy or transcript attested to be correct by the seal of an officer having custody of the original.

in contempt of the king'. William was to be imprisoned in Newgate goal until further order.

In another case in the same year, but somewhat contrary in nature, Walter was appointed along with Eustace de Burneby and another to arrest Adam de Kaylmersh, a chaplain. This time the king had presented another pastor to the church of Temesford because the gift of the presentment was held by the king due to the temporalities of another priory. Adam had presented his pastor 'by a pretended provision from the court of Rome' and 'has intruded himself into the church, and holds the tithes and profits thereof, and dilapidates it in many ways, in contempt of the king'. Being in 'contempt' of the king was obviously a bad place to be.

Walter sued to regain the manor of Honesworth, which he claimed his grandfather, William de Parles, had given to John de Parles, his father. After the death of his father, he argued, the manor should descend to him as son and heir. The respondent denied the allegation. A few weeks later, a hearing decided William de Parles had not given the manor to John. Therefore, the unsuccessful Walter was fined for making a false claim.

Figure 37: Battle of Crécy, 1346

Like his second cousin, Eustace de Burneby, Walter was occasionally required to provide for the king's wars. He paid 40s at the Exchequer for an archer, and the arrayers of Northamptonshire were ordered not to molest Walter for the expense of an archer to go with the king at his next crossing beyond the seas. The king was unwilling that this, done in urgent necessity, be drawn into a precedent. As events turned out, the next crossing of the English Channel only a few months later in 1346 led to an important victory by King Edward III against the French at the Battle of Crécy (see[96] Figure 37) in northern France during the 100 Years' War.

Walter had a brother, Thomas Parles. With the consent of his mother, Walter gave to Thomas for his lifetime an adjacent house in which (aunt) Sarrah used to live. The nominal annual rent was one rose. Two known children of Walter Parles were Nicholas and Ralph. While Ralph inherited Watford and other lands, Nicholas held Upton, west of Northampton.

Eleanor Parles, John's widow, died on the 6th December 1345 and an inquisition followed within two weeks. Walter, aged 36 years, was named heir to Eleanor and John. Theoretically, he was born in 1309, but likely earlier. The Parles manor was deemed properly held by fine levied in the king's court, with the king's charter of license.

The manor consisted of typical components. First, a capital messuage with a dovecot, worth 5s p.a. Second, 11 ½ virgates of land, which included 100 acres arable land at 4d p.a. per acre, total 22s 4d, while three parts of that land lay fallow each year with no value because they lay in the common field, plus the service of 6 villeins, each with one virgate of land for rent of 6s p.a. and no work. Lastly, 5 acres of meadow worth 10s p.a.

The Northamptonshire escheator was ordered to deliver the manor to Walter Parles. Another license was issued allowing Walter to enfeoff a cleric with lands and for the cleric to re-grant them back to Walter and Alice his wife, with remainder to Walter's heirs. This applied to a carucate of land (4 virgates), 5 acres of meadow and 2 acres of wood in Watford, held in chief.

Walter seems to have specialized in taking action for the king with reference to churches and the parsons appointed to them. He, as Sheriff, along with another individual of authority, was ordered 'to arrest all those who had intruded themselves armed into the church of Grafton and collected, carried away and consumed the tithes, profits and faculties thereof'. Their action was contrary to the king's right of presentation against the prior of Wylmyngton. The king's two appointees should bring those accused away from Grafton and into council with all such things they found prejudicial to the king's rights.

The day before the aforementioned order, another order was issued to sheriff Walter Parles to remove Walter Parles (himself) from the office of sheriff of Northamptonshire because 'he cannot exercise the duties of the office'. A coroner should be elected in his place. Nonetheless, orders to Walter as sheriff continued; he did not appoint his own replacement for some time. One such later order (April 1348) to Walter involved a distant relative, Richard de Burneby, which put Walter in the difficult situation of having to arrest and restrain Richard.

Another special inquisition *ad quod damnum* took place in 1347 in Walter's name, which was two years after his mother's death, and clearly respected the orders of 17 years ago. He settled a messuage, a carucate of land, 5 acres of meadow, and 2 acres of wood in Watford, all part of the ¼ manor of Watford and worth 4 marks annually, on himself, Alice his wife, and the heirs of their bodies, with remainder to his own right heirs. He retained 9 messuages, 7 virgates of land in Watford and Silsworth, the residual of the ¼ manor of Watford, worth 12 marks. He also held lands and rents in Byfield, Shitelhanger, and Aldrington, worth another 9 marks, which was an estate that likely came to him via his marriage to Alice.

There were occasions when the king was moved to show special favour[97] when confronted with unusual events encountered by one of his citizens. In one case a thief was convicted, hanged until dead but miraculously came back to life, whereupon King Edward III generously decided not to hang him again:

> Whereas William Prest of Somercotes was lately convicted before William de Leyghburn and Hervey Riband, then bailiffs of the late bishop of Lincoln of his liberty of Louth, of having broken the house of Richard de Cateby and carried away goods of the said Richard and of Walter de la Dale and for that cause was adjudged to death and hanged, and afterwards as a dead body was cut down from the gallows and carried to the church of St Erifrida, Louth, to be there handed over for burial by the church, and whereas after lying for a long time in the churchyard of that church before burial he miraculously came to life again. The king, because it has been testified before him that the same William was not guilty of what was laid to his charge, willing to shew special favour to him in respect of the incomplete execution of the said judgement against him, had pardoned him the execution of the judgement, the felony and all that pertains to the king in this behalf, as well as any outlawry published against him herein.

Walter died in the summer of 1361, like two of his distant cousins, during the second great outbreak of the Black Death. The writ for his inquisition was one of many ordered that summer and the hearing was held in Northampton in August. Walter's heir was his son Ralph Parles, 26 years old. Walter's holdings in Watford parish comprised the familiar messuage, 11 virgates of land, 5 acres of meadow, 2 acres of wood, a dovecot, all worth a net 10 marks, plus another 10 marks rent from customary free tenants. As before, these were held of the king in chief by a quarter knight's fee. In this case, the obligation of knight's fee was conveniently clarified as finding at the holder's own costs a fourth part of a man-at-arms for forty days when the white banner is raised for the king's war against Scotland. An order followed, instructing the sheriff to deliver to Ralph his father's lands. He also held 10 marks rent in Byfield probably of the manor, shared with his son Ralph Parles, but nothing outside Northamptonshire.

A few days later, the escheator reported that each virgate held by Walter in 1361 contained 16 acres – this quantification of one virgate in Watford has been quoted[98] in research. It is unusual for any parish to see different values utilised at separate times – in this case, 20 acres in 1276, and 24 acres in 1431.

In the same year Walter died, an inquisition was held for Roesia (Rose), late the wife of Nicholas de Parles, Walter's other son. In 1347, 'Nicholas, son of Walter Parles', aged 21 and more had been named the heir of Roesia's father, Nicholas Cancellis of Upton. Nicholas de Cancellis had granted the manor of Upton to Nicholas, son of Walter Parles, and his wife Roesia and their heirs in 1344. Nicholas Parles was apparently the elder[x] of Walter's two sons, but had died before 1361 without children.

Ralph de Parles and the wardship: 1361–1440

Ralph lived a long life, during which he married three times. Three years after his father's death, Ralph Parles and his first wife Katherine Talbot acquired an estate from John de Harewedon of Chiselhampton for the sum of 200 silver marks. The estate was similar in extent to his manor of Watford, comprising 9 messuages, 2 mills, 11 virgates of land, 18 acres of meadow, 10 acres of pasture, 100 acres of wood, and 40 shillings of rent, but spread through four parishes – Stoke Brewere, Shitelhangre, Shawe and Aldryngton.

Nearly 100 years after the death of his great grandfather, Ralph made his own bid to regain the lands lost when William de Parles was hanged. In 1365, Ralph sued for the manor of Hunesworth. He was unsuccessful. The court remembered the manor had been given back to a superior barony, whose descendants still held the lands today.

In Watford parish, the Daventry family had been free tenants of 11 virgates of land in Murcott since the 12th century. The lands were part of the Parles manor, held by the Daventrys by service of a ¼ knights fee. In 1381, Simon de Daventry remised and quitclaimed himself from the free

---

[x] Nicholas's age of 21 suggests birth in about 1325, possibly earlier if he was 21 in 1344. This calls to doubt the birth year of 1309 for his father, Walter, determined at his father's death. Walter's birth could be closer to 1300.

tenancy his family had occupied for about two centuries. Along with the 11 virgates of land, there were 11 dwellings and 1 toft. For that, Ralph Parles and Elizabeth Lewknor, his second wife, paid Daventry 200 marks of silver. From that time, Murcott became a direct holding of Ralph Parles and his successors, without an intervening free tenant.

In 1403, the king noted to the treasurer and barons of the exchequer that four prominent men of Northamptonshire, including Ralph Parles and John Catesby, had never received a writ of commission sent by the late king. So he repeated the writ. The commissioners were to make inquisition as to why public passage of ships and boats on the king's rivers was hindered, and why the meadows, pastures and nearby sown lands were flooded and wasted owing to the excessive raising and straightening of weirs, mills, stanks, pales and kiddles there.

Shutlanger, a parish south of Northampton, is recorded[99] as the home of the Parles family with a fourteenth century house (see[100] Figure 38). Land between[101] the church and Shutlanger was sold to become an independent estate called 'Parles Park' ultimately centred on 'The Monastery'. By the early fifteenth century, the property seems to be held[102] by Ralph Parles. He was granted a three-year license in 1410–11 by the Bishop of Lincoln to celebrate divine services in his manor of Shutlanger, thus inspiring the name, 'The Monastery'.

Ralph supported the king. He was one of eight, including the sheriff of Northamptonshire, who were given a commission of array 'for defence against the king's enemies, who have lately invaded the realm'. In the first ten years of his reign after deposing Richard II in 1399, King Henry IV spent much time fighting rebellions.

Figure 38: Shutlanger 'Monastery' from the south

Chief among these was led by Owain Glyndŵr of Wales and Henry Percy of Northumberland. Just before this commission of array, King Henry had successfully fought the Battle of Shrewsbury, after which some of the rebel leaders were publicly hanged, drawn, and quartered.

Ralph Parles lived a long life for those times. By 1413 he had become blind and was too aged to execute the office of verderer for Whitilwode forest. This was a medieval hunting forest in the south of Northamptonshire, near Shutlanger and Silverstone. From Westminster, the king ordered the sheriff of Northampton to elect a new verderer in Ralph's place.

At the age of 80, and with an eye on his estate, Ralph 'adjusted' his holdings of the tenancies originally acquired in 1364, at the cost of another 100 marks of silver. Nicholas and Maud Wilby remised and quitclaimed themselves from the tenements, acknowledging them to be the right of Ralph and his (third) wife, Alice de Harewedon, and six clerics. Ralph's son had died and to ensure his estate was handled as he preferred, he directed the lands should be given to the heirs of one of the clerics. In turn, the cleric would ensure Ralph's estate would descend to his right heir. The lands were somewhat fewer than when acquired some 50 years before, now comprising 8 messuages, 2 mills, 7 ½ virgates of land, 17 acres of meadow, 6 ½ acres of pasture, 44 acres of wood, the moiety of 1 acre, and rents of 5s 7¾d and a grain of corn, situated in Stokebruere, Shutlanger, Alderton and Shawe.

Ralph Parles died on the 27th of August 1420, aged 85. Another Ralph Parles was named as his kinsman (grandson) and next heir. Ralph jnr was the son of Walter who in turn was the son of the recently deceased Ralph Parles snr. Walter had predeceased his father, but left Ralph senior a grandson. The Parles family had paid a fee of £10 in gold to Queen Katherine for the marriage of Walter. Grandson Ralph was a minor aged only 11. When he died, Ralph senior was seized in his demesne of Watford manor in fee of the king by knight service. The annual value of the manor was 100s (£5). He was also seized of lands in Shittlehanger (Shutlanger) including a ruinous mill, Stoke Bruern, Alderton, Wappenham, Helmdon, Yelvertoft, and in Byfield, 'Parles Maner'.

For the next 20 years the Parles estates remained in the wardship of William Tresham and two others. Tresham and company were given[103] 'the keeping of all manors, lands, rents and services late of Ralph Parles, esquire, tenant in chief by knight service, during the minority of Ralph, son of Walter Parles ... with the marriage of the latter ... paying £100 to the king ... [and] finding a competent maintenance for the heir, maintaining the houses, enclosures and buildings and supporting all charges.' At the same time, the Tresham threesome signed an indenture with Alicia, Ralph's widow, by which Alicia signed over all the rents of the manor. In return, Alicia would receive from them an annual income of 18 marks (£12).

Reports by the Collector for the Parles Manor in the 1430s show that rents received for lands in Watford, Silsworth and Murcott were around £25 per year. A heche goose was also payable to the Lord as rent in kind. Additional small amounts were received for Manor Court fines and use of pasture. The Collector paid out about £4 for carpenters and materials for repairs to a tenant's house. He also paid various fines or rents often accumulating to about £14, and a fee for himself of less than £1. In some years the Collector was pardoned for Murcott rents, and in others, he paid a fixed rent of £4 for pasture. The remaining net of receipts and payments owed to the Lord was carried forward to the next year.

By 1441, Tresham's two companions had died, and not only had Ralph junior died but also Ralph's next younger brother, William. The inquisition held for the young William Parles in November 1440 was instructed to establish what lands and tenements came to King Henry V by the deaths of Ralph Parles senior and grandsons Ralph and William.

John Parles: 1440–1460

The escheator in November 1440 recorded the death of young William Parles in May 1430, which left his brother, John, as the next heir. John was reported to be aged 21 on the 1st October last. The extent of the Parles holdings in Watford was described in no more detail than for Grandfather Ralph in 1420: the Parles' manor in the hamlets of Watford, Murcott and Silsworth, worth 100s annually. He also held in Stoke Bruerne, Alderton, and

Figure 39: Church of St Peter & St Paul, Watford

Shutlanger, unfortunately with the same ruinous mill.

A special inquisition for John Parles in February 1441 was not 'post mortem', but rather had been convened by '*writ de etate probanda*', a 'proof of age' for John. In this case, each of the jurors stated John Parles was born on 1st October 1419 at Watford and was baptised in the church of St Peter (see[104] Figure 39) there. The jurors' reasoning, which seems to focus on a fire at William Wright's house, follows herewith:[105]

> John Cranesley, 60 and more, carried a waxen candle before John Parles at his baptism. Richard Holwell, 56 and more, carried a towel around his neck. Thomas Burgeys, 49 and more, carried a silver basin. William Wright, 62 and more, knows because his house caught fire immediately after the baptism. John Hykman, 46 and more, carried water to extinguish the said fire after the baptism. Thomas Smyth, 55 and more, saw his wife carry John Parles to the church. Henry Bray, 46 and more, rode for the godfathers of John Parles on the same day. Richard Hyde, 48 and more,

rang the bells discordantly (*pulsavit campanas contrarie*) in the church belfry because of the fire at William Wright's house. Henry Humme, 60 and more, rode on the same day, for the vicar of the church to baptise John. John Wright, 50 and more, knows because his wife gave birth to his first-born son on the same day. Thomas Bramcote, 44 and more, saw his wife carrying John Wright's son to the church to be baptised on the same day after the baptism of John Parles. John Modery, 48 and more, was asked in the church by John Wright, during the baptism of John Parles, to be godfather to his son.

The king followed the inquisition with an order given in the customary jargon: the sheriff should 'give John Parles brother and heir of William Parles brother and heir of Ralph son of Walter Parles of Watford son of Ralph Parles esquire, seisin of the lands of Ralph Parles esquire, the said Ralph the son and William having died within age in ward of the king, as he has proved his age before the escheator, and the king has taken his homage and fealty'.

John Parles died in May 1452, aged only 32. John had been married to Margaret Walwyn and their daughter, Joan, was aged only five.

The king had to send two writs to the escheator instructing an inquisition after the first one was lost. The inquisition found John held Watford manor by knight's fee worth 100s per annum including 20s rent from free tenants. This time, the report showed John was seized of another 6 messuages and 10 virgates of land, worth 6s 8d per virgate, in Murcott. Like his grandfather, John's other holdings included a mill called Twyfordsmyll, lands in Shutlanger, which included a ruinous watermill worth nothing, Stoke, Alderton, Yelvertoft, Wappenham, Weldon Parva, and Parles manor in Byfeld. The family holdings in Murcott seem to have mysteriously shrunk by 1 virgate.

The king issued his order to the escheator of Northamptonshire – he was 'to remove the king's hand and meddle no further with the manor, rent, messuages, and land hereinafter mentioned, delivering to Margaret wife of John Parles' the lands and issue from them. The order continued by specifying the lands so inherited and by what service. Long before his death, John had been seized of the lands by the demise of Ralph Parles, John's grandfather.

By Letters Patent issued in the year John died, the king granted custody of the manors and lands of John Parles to Messrs Ingleton and Tanfield, until his daughter Joan reached full age. The two gentlemen were also given the right to determine who Joan could marry. She was born in 1446. That was about a year before John's charter of April 1447, which recorded the basis of John's holding of Murcott lands. John would have written the Charter to guard the inheritance of his new-born daughter.

Margaret Parles married again to Robert Catesby, whose brother, Sir William Catesby, already held land in Watford parish. Robert and Margaret had a son, William Catesby. When Margaret died in July 1459 the ensuing inquisition stated her previous husband, John Parles, had died seized of Parles manor in Byfield, Watford and Silsworth, so Margaret was allowed to remain in the manor by right of marriage. However, the heir of Margaret's Parles estate was Joan Parles, aged 12 when Margaret died. Her heir was not William Catesby because Joan was the child of John and Margaret Parles, whereas William was not. Margaret's inquisition attested Letters Patent, dated the year John Parles died, which granted the Parles lands to two custodians.

John Cumberford and Joan Cumberford, nee Parles: 1460–1508

In turn, Joan's custodians granted her custody and marriage to William Cumberford (aka 'Comberford'), a prominent citizen of Staffordshire. Joan was committed as a ward to William until she came of age. The wardship included holding all the lands which Margaret Catesby, formerly Parles, held on the day of her death due to Joan's inheritance from John Parles. The wardship would last as long as the lands remained in the king's hands by reason of Joan's minority. For this, William paid the Exchequer a yearly farm rent of £10.

The wardship did not last long for in August 1461, the escheator of Northamptonshire was ordered to take the fealty of Joan Parles, heir of John Parles, and give her the Parles lands. Joan had proved her age before an escheator. She was now 15 years old and 'of age'. For half a mark, the king delayed her homage until the following July 7.

In an obvious strategic move, William Comberford arranged the marriage of his ward, Joan Parles, to his son, John, and consequently the Parles lands of Watford manor became known in Watford as the 'Comberford manor'. In 1482, the Cumberfords saw fit to secure Joan's inheritance of lands to the Cumberford descendants, possibly on the occasion of their eldest son turning a key age. John and Joan gave the manor of Byfield to three men, including Christopher Cumberford, who promptly gave the estate back to John and Joan and their heirs forever, and in default, to the right heirs of Joan. The Byfield manor consisted of 14 messuages, 839 acres in Watford, Murcott, Shutlanger, Stokebruern, Shawe, Alderton, Wappenham, Byfeld, Yelvertoft, and the fourth part of the manor of Watford. A large part of the manor area appears to have been associated with the Watford manor lands in Watford, Murcott, and Silsworth.

In 1504 John Comberford, together with his son Thomas and daughter-in-law Dorothy, sold for £100 a total of 364 acres of the former Parles estates in Stoke Bruerne, Shutlanger, Alderton and Wappenham, but not Watford, to Richard Empson of Easton Neston. The sale included eight messuages, six tofts, one mill, 200 acres of land, 24 acres of meadow, 100 acres of pasture, 40 acres of wood and 14 shillings rent.

The Comberfords did not rest after selling the Parles lands. On the same day, Thomas Comberford enfeoffed his father John Comberford of 1 messuage, 10 tofts and 340 acres of land, meadow, and pasture in Silsworth, with reversion upon John's decease to Thomas and his heirs forever. That number of acres seems to comprise approximately 315 acres of the Parles/Comberford manor in Silsworth, plus another parcel of perhaps 25 acres purchased by the Comberfords in 1493.

At about this time, Sir Richard Empson wrote about a 'young' Comberford, presumably Thomas, who tried to make a case to Richard for increasing the £3 semi-annual rent by a noble (half a mark) for the Comberford lands in Silsworth, occupied and rented by George Catesby. The young landlord had also indicated a desire to occupy the land himself. The result – Sir Richard talked his way into short-paying Thomas Comberford by the same noble (6s 8d), out of the rent amount agreed years before.

Back in September 1487, John Comberford leased to Sir John Halyghewell, knight, for 20 years, all his lands, meadows, pasture and crofts in Silsworth for rent of 10 marks or £6 13s 4d per year (£3 6s 8d per half-year). This was around the time Sir John Halyghewell occupied all of the Catesbys' Silsworth lands consequent to William Catesby's execution. Comberford's lease and the 1504 enfeoffment demonstrate the Parles manor included lands in Silsworth, which, therefore, could not have been held in fee by the Catesbys in the late fifteenth century.

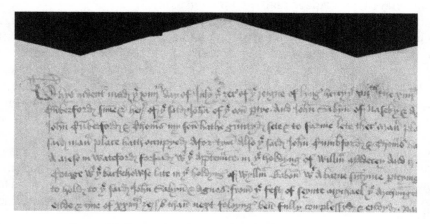

Figure 40: Extract from lease by Cumberford to Sabyn, 1499

Again acting together, John Cumberford of Cumberford and Thomas Cumberford, his son and heir, wrote a lease (see[106] Figure 40). Remarkably, given the year, 1499, the indenture, or agreement, was written in Old English rather than Latin and the transcriptions below retain the form, structure and spelling of that period. The 'indent' or wavy cut across the top that gave such documents their name is plain to see. The lease, granted to John Sabyn of Naseby and his wife Agnes, was to last for 24 years, from September of the year 1500 ...

> *paying yerly ... vii £ & x s sterling at too tymes of the yer'. [The Cumberfords] 'grauntyd & sete to farme lete ther manor place of Watford with all the appurtenance as the farmers of the said manor place hath occupyed afor tym*

This referred to the historic central place of the Parles then Cumberford manor in Watford town with its attached lands lying in and around Burneby's premises. Also granted

> *to farme lette ... a mese in Watford aforesaid with appurtenance in the holdyng of William Moderey and ii [two] cotags oen late in the holdyng of Herry Boteler and anoyther cotage with the backehowse late in the holdyng of Wyiliam Sabon with a barne sumtyme perteyning to the said manor late in the holding of Roger Horne'.*

There had indeed been a manor held by Roger Horne, which was the de Watford manor of the Catesbys. Tenants John & Agnes Sabyn had specific obligations to work the Hay fields, they

> *shall dyche & rukesete the haye at any tym that yt be departyd bytwyx the said John Comberford or hys heryes*

The chief lord of the Watford fee also had commitments to the Cumberford manor and its lessee, John Sabyn, to supply loads of wood for stakes to mend fences

> *And George Burneby at the pur coste & charge of the said John Sabyn & Agnes and the said John Cumberford & Thomas hys sonne shall fynde to the said John Sabyn and Agnes ii [two] lode wode to make stakys of for monndyng of the said parte of the haye And the said John and Agnes shall carye & clene yt to make stakys of at ther pur cost and charge*

After her husband died in 1508, Joan Cumberford obtained a license of entry for her son and heir, Thomas Cumberford. This allowed her son to take possession of his Cumberford inheritance.

Thomas, Humphrey, and Thomas Comberford: 1508–1563

Thomas Comberford, son and heir of John and Joan Comberford, inherited several manors and lands from his parents including the former Parles lands of Watford manor. The eldest son and successor of Thomas and his second wife was Humphrey. Just to be different, Humphrey Comberford's elder two sons were named Thomas and another Humphrey.

The elder Humphrey died in 1555 possessed of many estates, including a quarter of the Watford manor. Other than leaving most of his manors to his son, Thomas, he specified in his will that his Watford manor lands were to be held by his second son, Humphrey, for 60 years. In the event, Humphrey the younger died unmarried in 1545, ten years before his father, and so the lands designated for him were inherited by Thomas, the elder son.

At about this time a certain Henry Wryght[xi] of Welton enters the picture. And his lands later became another transaction with the Spencers.

In September 1540 'Henry Wryght of Welton, yeoman', was married. As part of the marriage settlement, Henry granted five men annual rents of 17s issuing from his lands in Watford, lately purchased from Thomas Osborne, to the use of his wife, Etheldreda. In September of 1542, the same Henry Wryght of Welton purchased Watford lands from the Catesbys. Valued at an annual 47s 7d, these were two parcels each of a yardland and a croft, one tenanted by Richard Coleman and the other by Alice Fraunces, as well as two crofts, two roods of land, and certain other land valued at 8s per year.

Four years later, Henry Wryght of Welton granted lands to William Welche of Watford to hold forever of the chief lord of the fee by customary services owed. William's lease brought him 1 virgate in Watford, two homesteads near one of Richard Burneby's, a ½ acre next to the Abbot of St James' land, and another ½ acre within Overend Meadow.

About 1550 Humphrey Cumberford found himself the subject of a suit reaching across manors to one of his tenants. John Watkyn, as the tenant,

---

[xi] Henry Wryght of Welton not to be confused with Henry Wright of Watford. Mr Wryght of Welton was married to Etheldreda and was alive in 1561.

not owner, of the de Watford manor, laid claim on a bond for rent payable in malt by William Sabyn for a house and land in Watford.

After Humphrey died in December 1555, an inquisition for his Northamptonshire estate was held a year later. He held the manor of Watford, worth £10 per year. The tenant, William Gifford, had 280 acres of land, meadow, pasture, and waste land 'in Watford' paying £9 10s annually. A further 10s rent arose from two cottages. Another 260 acres of land, meadow, and pasture with two messuages and cottages also said to be 'in Watford', was worth £4 2s. And not least, in 'Morecote', were four messuages and 340 acres[xii] of land, meadow, and pasture, all worth £8. All in all, the 885 acres in Watford parish was worth £22 2s annually. Lastly, the jurors said Humphrey was seized of 6d 'capital rent' in Watford. This may be the notional rent received for 1 ½ virgates originally held of the Parles manor by the abbey of St James near Northampton.

The Cumberford's tenant, William Gifford, held other lands also formerly of St James abbey, which were held by the Burnebys. Nicholas Gifford was 'of St James abbey' and had been given St James' lands at Dissolution, indicating not only how Gifford got his lands, but also that part of the Parles Manor was held of St James abbey.

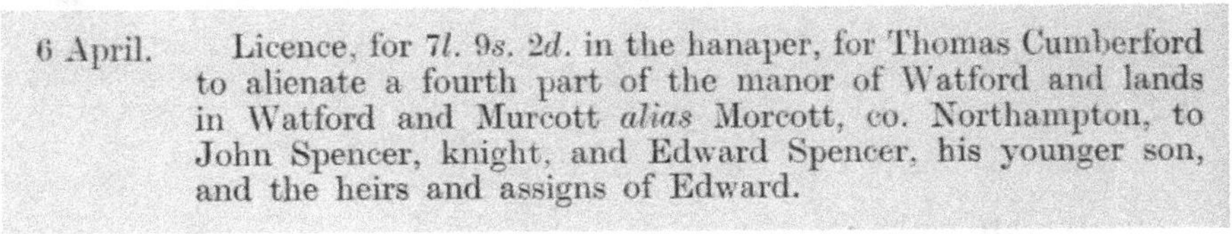

| 6 April. | Licence, for 7l. 9s. 2d. in the hanaper, for Thomas Cumberford to alienate a fourth part of the manor of Watford and lands in Watford and Murcott *alias* Morcott, co. Northampton, to John Spencer, knight, and Edward Spencer, his younger son, and the heirs and assigns of Edward. |

Figure 41: Sale of Cumberford lands, Patent Rolls, 1563

By 1563, without young Humphrey to inherit, the eldest son, Thomas Cumberford, held the Watford manor lands. He sold (see[107] Figure 41) his Watford manor to Sir John Spencer. Sir John intended the manor lands for his son, Edward, but Edward died in 1584, aged only 23. When sold, according to the fine, the manor included 840 acres of land, meadow and pasture, plus 46 acres of wood, heath and furze. The former Parles and Comberford lands descended from their buyer, Sir John Spencer, to his son John Spencer, himself knighted in 1586, and in turn to Sir John's son, Robert Spencer.

[xii] The IPM reported another 500 acres of gorse and heath in Murcott, which is impossible because all Murcott amounted to only 680 acres. The '500 acres' taken to mean 5 acres, i.e. a total of 345 acres in Murcott.

The Earls Spencer, from 1563

With possession of the Comberford lands, the Spencer family began a permanent presence in Watford parish, holding lands in all three 'towns' – Watford, Murcott, and Silsworth.

Back to the story of John Wryght, son and heir of Henry Wryght, late of Welton. John wrote two similar leases, both dated 15 October 1567. One was for George Cosford, husbandman, his wife Margaret and son Henry, for their three lives. The lease was for one yardland of arable and one close of pasture in Watford, already leased to George since April 1561 by Henry Wryght, for the annual rent of 25s. The other lease was to William Rogers (see[108] Figure 42), husbandman, his future wife and child if he 'shall fortune to have', for their three lives, of a homestead, ½ yardland arable and 2 closes of pasture for the annual rent of 26s 8d. William Rogers and George Cosford were father and father-in-law of Thomas Rogers, one of the first Pilgrims to America in 1620 on the *Mayflower*. John Watkyn was a witness to both leases.

Figure 42: Extract of lease by Wryght to Rogers, 1567

John Wryght had a third tenant named Richard Smithe, who occupied a virgate of John's land. Richard's lease may have descended to him from another Richard Smythe and his daughter Elizabeth Hill. Generations before, the father and daughter leased a homestead, a croft, 1 virgate, and also a ¼ virgate of 'odd lands' in Watford town.

Six years after acquiring the Comberford's Watford manor, for £120 Sir John Spencer purchased[109] from John Wright of Watford:

> all that his messuage or tenement with a haulf yarde lande with the appurtenances scitnate lyinge and beinge in Wattford aforesaid in the saide Countie of Northt and nowe or late in the severall tenure holdinge or occupacon of one William Rogers And all that his tenament and ohne yarde lande with appurtenance sett lyinge and beinge within the territorie of the towneshipp or hamlett of Wattford aforesaid and nowe being in the tenure or occupacon of one Richard Smithe And all that his one yarde lande with appurtenance and one Close skitnate and being within the parishe hamlette and fyldes of Wattford aforesaide and nowe in the severall tenure holdinge or occupacon of one George Cosford husbandman And all that yerelie rente of eighteen pence issuinge and

goinge out of a tenement in Wattford aforesaid appurteyning to one
Nicholas Marston of Wattford

The agreement included John Wright's warranty confirming he was
solely and lawfully seized of the premises with power to convey the lands.
Furthermore, the lands were warranted free of all encumbrances except
rent to the chief lord of the fee. Eighteen months later another agreement
was signed for the purposes of common recovery before the Justice of the
Common Pleas, allowing Thomas Spencer, Sir John's son, to gain good
title. This was one of the methods utilised at the time to transfer (or
'recover') title. The document usefully provided another view of the lands
'sold' by John Wright:

All those his four messuages in Watford with the appurtenances ... and
all lands tenements and hereditaments reputed as parcel or to the same
messuages belonging with all and singular their appurtenances in County
Northampton, By the name or names of four messuages four gardens four
orchards threescore acres of land ten acres of meadow twenty acres of
pasture and eighteen pence of rent

The documents indicate the premises sold included at least one or as
many as four homesteads, three closes of pasture and two and a half
yardlands, all of which encompassed 90 acres. A fourth tenement of some
kind, producing 18 pence annual rent, could be a cottage used with a
separate farm then in the hands of the Marston family in Silsworth.
Wright's sale included lands bought from the de Watford and Catesby
manor, explaining the origin of Lord Spencer's holding of de
Watford/Catesby lands.

An interrogatory survives featuring Robert Spencer, before he was Lord
Spencer, as complainant, and Richard Burneby, defendant, dated 1595.
Eleven questions were posed and answered by three Watford residents:
William Richardson aged 40, a shepherd, John Sabin aged 53, and John
Ravesby aged 62, both farmers. An ancestor of this John Sabin likely
includes the John Sabyn signed up as Cumberford's tenant in 1499.

The answers clarified the boundaries of the Comberford lands lying
within the 'Hayfield'. Robert Spencer appears to believe his rights were
being trampled on by Richard Burneby and Richard's tenants. The
Hayfield was a large inclosed ground divided into many parts, somehow
shared among chief tenants, Richard Burneby and Robert Spencer. The
name 'Hay' is mentioned as far back as 1276 and survived in several
derivations until modern times.

Two of the witnesses stated that the Comberford manor within the Hayfield included 22 'peeces' of arable lands and leys. They continued with descriptions of 24 locations, citing boundaries, totalling 174 lands and leys.

One farmer in particular seems to have been a concern, William Sabyn, who, according to one of the witnesses (not John Sabyn), had been a tenant farmer on the 'Comberford peece in the Hayfield' for about 50 years. For the most part, Sabyn kept there 30 or 40 great beast and cattle, and of sheep, 80 in summer and 120 in winter.

The boundaries of the area under contention, the Hayfield (Great Hay, Barne Hay, Haysith, Hayway), were prescribed by fieldnames as follows, working clockwise: Silsworth Field in the north and northeast; in the east, Navesborowe and Heygate; in the south, both Barley Pieces, then Freeman's Croft; and in the west, Middleton, Blackwells and Bretts. All this ground stretches from Richard Burneby's capital messuage northwards to the Silsworth and Crick boundaries. Another field mentioned with a name unknown in later times was Crabtree, which is very likely the close fitting nicely between Blackwells and Freemans Croft.

Presumably the parties respected the manor boundaries explained from the local knowledge of the three witnesses. If not, then the matter was resolved decades later by changes in land ownership.

Lord Robert Spencer addressed another irritant concerning his holding in Murcott. Other than lands in Watford town, Robert Lord Spencer held 'a meadow called Sandford, alias Twinney Meadow', purchased from Edward Griffin. 'Sanford Meadow' had originally been purchased by the Sheriff of Northamptonshire, Robert Braybroc, in return for a rent of 2 shillings p.a. and given to Daventry Priory. Successive inquisitions of Braybroc descendants indicates the meadow provided a rental income of £4 per annum, often delivered by the hands of the prior of Daventry. Finally, Thomas Griffin then Edward Griffin, in 1565 and 1569, possess the lands, which they sold to Spencer.

Daventry Priory, dissolved in 1526, was an early victim of the Dissolution. The lands were given to the Pope and granted to Cardinal Wolseley. When the Cardinal fell from power, King Henry VIII took the lands for his new college at Oxford. After Dissolution, a grant of a large package of lands was made including a meadow called 'Sandford meade' alias 'Watford meade' in Watford. The meadow was 'formerly belonging to the late royal college commonly called King Henry the Eighth's College in the university of Oxford and once parcel of the lands of the late monastery of Daventry'. Later, these were the Twinney meadows in Murcott town of Watford parish. Like George Clerke, Spencer found some of the grounds he had acquired were occupied, and so he bought the lease. Lord Robert's inquisition links the name Sandford Meadow to Twinney Meadow.

Included in his discussion of Watford, when describing the descent of the so-called Comberford manor lands, a noted historian stated the following:[110]

> In the twenty-fourth year of Queen *Elizabeth* died *Christopher Lewys* Gent possessed of a Manor in *Watford*, probably the same which belonged to the family of *Comberford*, in which he was succeeded by *Clement Lewys* his son and heir. [Reference given: Esc anno 33 Eliz n 60 p 1]

> *Robert* Lord *Spencer* was seized of it at his death in the fourth year of *Charles* I and left it with certain lands and tenements in *Watford* and *Silsworth* formerly purchased of *Thomas Comberford* to *William* Lord *Spencer* his successor and son. [Reference given: Esc anno 4 Car I n 8 p 2.]

This correctly recorded that the *Comberford* lands became part of the *Spencer* family holdings, but incorrectly implied any *Lewys* family participation. The *Lewys* family merely played a legal role with the *de Burneby* lands in Watford (as explained under the *Burneby manor*), but never 'held' those or any other lands in Watford parish for their own use. The same inquisition, referred to above, 4 Charles I (March 1629), also reported that Lord Robert Spencer held 2 messuages, certain other lands, and rent of 18s, all purchased from John Wright.

The heirs of Robert Lord Spencer were persuaded that a swap involving their lands in Watford was a good idea. But before agreeing to any exchange, Sir William, Lord Spencer, leased a farm of 2 ½ yardlands in the town and fields of Watford for 21 years to William Sabyn. Rent was set at £15 per year … which compares to £7 10s twice yearly payable by John Sabyn for his lease in 1499. Sabyn took on the responsibility for maintaining the house and land, not unlike John Sabyn's obligations many years before. William Sabyn took on more – including providing a carriage service at Muscott (another Spencer holding) with his cart, teams and workers, and each year taking 15 hundredweight of coal to Althorpe, and planting and looking after 80 trees on the land he leased.

In June of 1631, George Clerke, merchant of London, and Sir William, Baron Spencer of Wormeleighton, agreed[111] to an exchange of lands. On the one side, the agreement acknowledged George Clerke had procured a parcel of lands from Thomas Wilbraham and caused them to be conveyed to William Lord Spencer and his heirs. The parcel comprised the 'moiety of the manor of Radborne … and several inclosed meadow and pasture grounds in Radborne …containing by estimation 604 acres'. George had paid Wilbraham £200 of 'his own proper money' and Baron Spencer the other £140, of the full price of £340, to Thomas for the Radborne lands. Radborne had been part of the Catesby empire for many years.

On the other side of the deal, Baron Spencer would convey to George Clerke his 'Manor of Cumberford in Watford only and not in Murcott ... being a hamlet of Watford ... of the yearly value of £126'. Baron Spencer or his heirs would not conclude the conveyance until the Baron's eldest son and heir reached the full age of 21 years. William Spencer did not convey the lands before he died in 1636, but his eldest son Henry did complete the intent of the 1631 agreement.

Eight years after agreeing to make the exchange, Henry Lord Spencer, son of William Spencer, together with his uncle Richard Spencer, made another agreement[112] dated 26 June 1639, which gave their lands in Watford town to George Clerke. In 1631 George had taken back a lease of the Radborne lands for 500 years, as assurance William Spencer would carry out the conveyance of the Watford lands to George. In accordance with the 1639 agreement, George gave up the lease. Henry, Lord Spencer, fought and died in 1643 in the English Civil War on the side of the Cavaliers, aged only 23.

The 1639 agreement included the following list of lands given up to George Clerke [with additional detail from the 1631 agreement]:

The Scite[xiii] of the Mannor of Cumberford in Watford with the appurtenances adjoyneinge to the Court yard and lyeing neere to the Capitall Messuage or mannor howse of George Clerke

Two yard land of arable meadow and pasture with the appurtenances lying and being dispersedly in the common fields of Watford heretofore used with the said Scite

One messuage or farm house in Watford known by the name of Kites house with the appurtenances

Two yard land of arable meadow and pasture with the appurtenances in the common fields of Watford used with the said farm house

Diverse and sundry several pieces or parcels of pasture ground containing by estimation 100 acres being dispersedly and intermixed in certain inclosed grounds of the said George Clerke in Watford called the Hayfield and Barley Piece

Five severall closes in Watford called Blackwell Close the Crabbtree Close the Bryer Close Cocks [Coxe] Close and Guilberts Close

---

[xiii] 'Scite' = The ground on which (in this case) a capital messuage stands, irrespective of who holds the ground.

Three other closes in Watford to and with the said Scite of the Manor and farm house called Kites house used or enjoyed

One farm house in Watford with the appurtenances and two closes and half a close and two yard land and a half in Watford with the appurtenances in the tenure of William Sabin [rent: £15]

And one other farm house two closes and a half yard land with the appurtenances in Watford in the tenure of William Rogers [rent: 26s 8d]

One yard land and one close with their appurtenances in Watford also in the tenure of the said William Rogers [rent £7]

One cottage and one close with the appurtenances in Watford in the tenure of John Butlin [rent: 10s]

Another cottage [with appurtenances] in Watford in the tenure of William Braunson [rent: 6s]

One cottage and close with the appurtenances in Watford in the tenure of Nicholas Eaton [rent: 14s]

One cottage with the appurtenances in Watford in the tenure of John Harvey [rent:10s]

Diverse other houses buildings common rights members and appurtenances to the said several messuages cottages closes yardlands and premises generally belonging or therewith used as severally belonging

All that the Manor or reputed Manor of Cumberford in Watford aforesaid only and not in Murcot in the said county of Northampton with all and every the appurtenances in Watford aforesaid only And in several quitrents thereunto belonging

All of which said Manor and premises are of the clean yearly value of £126 or near thereabouts

In July 1639, George Clerke and Henry Spencer appeared in Court to finalize the sale of the manor of Cumberford. They agreed the manor and all its belongings included 8 dwellings, 100 acres of arable land, 25 acres of meadow, 200 acres of pasture, 5 acres of heath and furze, for a total of 330 acres. Apparently, the scite of the manor counted as one dwelling, Kites a second, with six more identified in the second parcel of lands, totalling the eight homesteads.

The Cumberford manor in Watford town, reported as 330 acres, fell into two parts:

The first seven items in the agreement describe the premises originally leased by George Clerke in 1626, paying £100 annually: 2 homesteads, 4 yardlands 'in the common fields of Watford', 100 acres of pasture, 5 named closes, and 3 unnamed closes.

The second seven items summarise leases of six tenants for annual total rentals of £25 6s 8d issuing from 6 cottages or houses, 4 yardlands 'in Watford', and 7 ½ closes.

Fitting those 330 Watford acres within the 885 (give or take) total acres in the parish held by the Comberfords in the mid sixteenth century is not straightforward. Best guess, sticking to other available references as far as possible: 260 acres situated in Watford, 280 acres in Silsworth, and 345 acres in Murcott. The Spencer's Murcott holding probably condensed to about 285 acres after the impact of enclosure in the eighteenth century. The Silsworth lands may represent the sum of Silsworth Field of 170 acres, 150 acres of the Oad ground and the Hill Meadow, less 40 acres of wood, heath and furze. The lands in Watford may have comprised the 330 acres as sold, less about 70 acres of de Watford/Catesby lands included in the lands sold to Lord Spencer in 1569.

Doubtless, George Clerke found he was obliged to untangle what had evolved into a complex land ownership structure in Watford town. He vented his frustration when buying the Cumberford manor by speaking of some lands 'lying very much intermixed with the lands of the said George Clerke both in his inclosures and elsewhere inconvenient to either party'. The parcel of 100 acres is described as lying dispersedly and intermixed in George's incloses called the Hay and Barley Piece.

Reaching back to 1276, the demesne share of each daughter was allocated as a quarter each of 27 different fields. Therefore, each daughter's demesne was a checkerboard of quarter-fields strewn across the entire demesne of almost 400 acres. That methodology for sharing, enshrined in the Close Rolls, rather than dividing the 27 fields as six or seven fields for each daughter, added plenty of colour to George's frustration with the 100 acre demesne.

The premises included in the first part of the deal – the Manor of Cumberford, the Scite and Kites house with four yardlands in the common fields of Watford, and three unnamed closes used with the Scite and Kites house – resemble the description of a demesne. George had leased these premises in 1626 when he bought the Burneby manor. Presumably he did so because access to those lands was essential to effective use of the Burneby manor premises. This is consistent with there being no named third party occupant of the four virgates. These four yardlands seem to be the demesne enfeoffed to the Burnebys in 1330 by Walter Parles, and one and the same as the 100 scattered acres.

Hardly clarifying the matter, a parcel of 100 'indifferently' measured acres had been one side of the deal[113] done in 1615 between Sir Richard Burneby and Robert Lord Spencer, whereby the two exchanged parcels of 100 acres of land. Unfortunately, a somewhat indifferent lawyer wrote into the agreement the ambiguous phrase:

'Spencer should have one hundred acres of land in exchange for other land of his lyeinge in the Hey feilde in Watford aforesaid',

which with punctuation could be read as either: –

'Spencer should have one hundred acres of land, in exchange for other land of his, lyeinge in the Hey feilde in Watford aforesaid' or,

'Spencer should have one hundred acres of land, in exchange for other land of his lyeinge in the Hey feilde, in Watford aforesaid'.

Depending on where the second comma is placed, the 100 scattered acres, later included as part of Spencer's Comberford manor, could have been located either in the Hay or elsewhere in Watford. One might hope the inclusion of the same acreage with the Comberford manor meant the 100 scattered acres had been given up by Burneby to Spencer. Alas, the good gentlemen landowners further confused the issue with Spencer's agreement to lease back Spencer's 100 acres to Burneby for £100 p.a. Therefore, the Comberford manor's 100 intermixed acres could have been either held or leased. Spencer never did produce a lease document. But when George Clerke bought the Burneby manor, the unwritten lease of Spencer's 100 acres was assigned from Burneby to Clerke. Regrettably, the assignment does not clarify the nature or location of the 100 acres of land on the other side of the deal. Presumably they had been included in Clerke's acquisition of the Burneby manor in 1623-26.

According to historian John Bridges, who described the area in about 1720, Cumberford was 'a depopulated village in an inclosed manor, now reduced to one house ... the Crown ale house'. The alehouse is unknown in modern times. However, 'Kites house', as named by George Clerke, could be both the 'one house' and the 'manor house' of Cumberford described by Bridges almost a century later.

The Parles / Comberford manor lands in Watford parish were located in the central, northern and southeast quarters of the parish. That is to say, the furlongs north of the manor house and northwest towards Crick, the scattered acres north towards Crick and Silsworth in the Hay and Barley

Piece, plus large parcels in Silsworth and Murcott. Thus, a view sometimes expounded on modern maps locating the Parles / Comberford manor west of the Watling Street in the western corner of Watford, is incorrect. As discussed in the section following, the western lands of Watford were originally part of the de Watford manor, subsequently and for some time, the 'Catesby manor of Watford'.

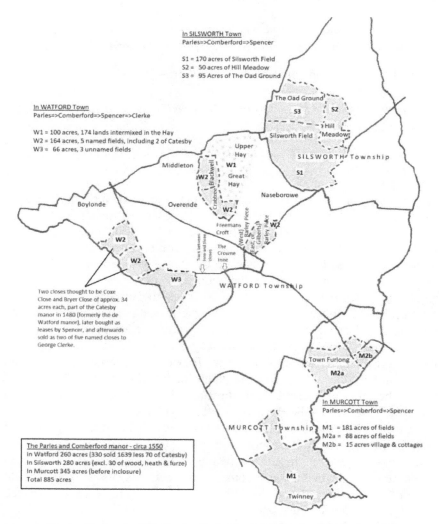

In SILSWORTH Town
Parles=>Comberford=>Spencer

S1 = 170 acres of Silsworth Field
S2 = 50 acres of Hill Meadow
S3 = 95 Acres of The Oad Ground

In WATFORD Town
Parles=>Comberford=>Spencer=>Clerke

W1 = 100 acres, 174 lands intermixed in the Hay
W2 = 164 acres, 5 named fields, including 2 of Catesby
W3 = 66 acres, 3 unnamed fields

Two closes thought to be Coxe Close and Bryer Close of approx. 34 acres each, part of the Catesby manor in 1480 (formerly the de Watford manor), later bought as leases by Spencer, and afterwards sold as two of five named closes to George Clerke.

In MURCOTT Town
Parles=>Comberford=>Spencer

M1 = 181 acres of fields
M2a = 88 acres of fields
M2b = 15 acres village & cottages

The Parles and Comberford manor - circa 1550
In Watford 260 acres (330 sold 1639 less 70 of Catesby)
In Silsworth 280 acres (excl. 30 of wood, heath & furze)
In Murcott 345 acres (before inclosure)
Total 885 acres

Figure 43: Lands of the Parles & Comberford Manor in Watford, c 1550

PART 4: The de Watford and Catesby Manors

Before the Catesbys gave their name to a manor of Watford in the 14th century, the lands were known as the de Watford Manor. Like the Catesbys, the de Watfords also demonstrated moments of rebellion. Some of the five Edmunds de Watford grasped at independence whenever they could.

The Edmunds came from one of the two families continuing the *de Watford* name. Both families held lands in Watford at the time of Sir Eustace's death in 1276, and both holdings were part of the nearly 31 virgates allocated to Sarah de Burneby, nee de Watford. Both were free tenants of the Burneby manor and therefore owed allegiance to the de Burnabys whether they liked it or not. Of the two, Edmund de Watford held the larger of two holdings – 14 virgates.

Those two holdings of de Watford lands eventually became the Catesby Manor of Watford, one by marriage and the other, by purchase. However, this manor lasted only until 1485. Afterwards, the Catesby manors in the parish held lands only in Silsworth. In all, the manors of Watford and Silsworth descended through 14 generations, or 12 if counting after Eustace de Watford IV.[xiv]

The Watford Manor of Edmund de Watford

Edmund de Watford (the first and second): 1276–1291

The first Edmund de Watford and his brother John de Ardern were grandsons of the first Eustace de Watford (see[114] Figure 44). While Edmund remained in Watford becoming part of the establishment of the parish and its surrounding area, John left Watford to live in Cheshire.

Edmund I may or may not have taken part in the First Baron's War. But his son did join the rebels of the East Midlands and took part in the Second Baron's War. Edmund II is listed

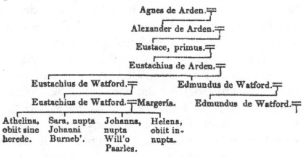

Figure 44: Nichol's Reproduction of Vincent's Chart

---

as 'Edmund de Arderne' alongside Eustace de Watford and Philip de Daventre. They were taken captive after the fight to defend Northampton castle in April 1264. Henry III of England had mounted a siege of Northampton Castle and succeeded in defeating Simon de Montfort's supporters, who defended the Castle.

Edmund II inherited Watford lands from his father, likely a parcel put together when John de Ardern gave his 7 virgates to Eustace III, the chief lord of the manor, to make a healthy holding of 14 virgates. No doubt Edmund II made very sure his lands were recognised as a manor when Eustace IV died.

With the death of his cousin Eustace, Edmund found himself owing homage to the de Burneby family rather than to Eustace, the lord of the whole parish. Even so, Edmund was one of three executors of Sir Eustace's will. The second executor was Henry de Bray, the escheator for the territory, and the third was John de Burneby, Sir Eustace's elder surviving son-in-law. All three executors had to defend themselves in litigation brought against them by Sir Geoffrey de Leukenore, knight, before the commissary of the archdeacon of Northampton. It seems Sir Geoffrey was unhappy with the trio's actions as executors of Sir Eustace's will.

On the same day as the executors were defending themselves, Edmund II and William de Parles witnessed a document relating to their duties as executors. Sir Eustace's widow Margaret (aka Margery) gave the wardship and marriage of her niece and nephew to Robert de Chokes of Great Creaton. This was an important duty because the right to give in marriage represented a source of income. Someone with a suitable marriage partner for the niece or nephew would pay good money to marry a son or daughter to an heir.

Six years after the death of Sir Eustace de Watford, Edmund de Watford witnessed a deed by which Ellen de Watford granted a cottage and its land called 'le Cotes' to Sarah de Burneby. Edmund was a well-known and fully informed resident of Watford, so adding his name as a witness increased certainty the document would be respected.

Edmund II died in 1291, leaving a will proved in February 1292 at Long Buckby, before the court of the Archdeacon of Northampton. Edmund said his body should be buried in the church of St Peter in Watford in front of the rood and asked that his horse, named 'le morel', be with him in his tomb. He left numerous donations to the church, various citizens, several clerics, and friars of various priories. Edmund asked his neighbour, Nicholas de Cranford, to pay 10s per year to his widow, Emma, to support his first wife's elder daughter. The remaining parts of his estate were left to Emma and his sons and daughters for their support. The name 'Emma' was a favourite carried forward to later generations.

Edmund took care of Emma, one of his daughters by his second wife of the same name, before he died. Roger Roys of Sprotton gave a house and land valued at 4s 6d rent to Edmund de Watford for Emma his daughter in marriage. Assuming Emma was young but of the legal age to marry, say between 16 and 18, she was born around 1270–1275.

Edmund de Watford (the third): 1291–1317

The Edmunds were no stranger to controversy, and when needed fought for the independence of their manor. They were not afraid to object to any perceived threat to their autonomy.

Richard Golafre, born 1268, was probably the son of Eustace de Golafre, a free tenant of Athelina in 1276. In an undated deed, Richard Golafre gave a half-acre of arable land to Emma, widow of Edmund de Watford, in exchange for another half-acre. The exchange would not become permanent until ratified by Edmund's heirs when they reached full age. Early in 1303, Edmund, son & heir of Edmund, confirmed the earlier qualified deed. This indicates Edmund III, the son of Edmund II, came of age in 1303 and was therefore born about 1282.

The exchange between Richard and Emma is a good demonstration of how complex such transactions were in the thirteenth and fourteenth centuries, even for a mere half-acre. Presumably, someone realised that better use of the lands would be achieved by swapping the disparate patches to make contiguous pieces. Initially, as noted above, Richard Golafre swapped the half-acre conditionally with Emma de Watford, mother of the young Edmund. In the later confirming transactions, the abbot of St James near Northampton gave land in Watford lying in *Wylfurlong* to Emma and her son Edmund de Watford in exchange for other land in Watford on *Grotenecroft*. On the same day, Ellen de Watford and Eustace de Burneby swapped a half-acre with Edmund son of the late Edmund de Watford. Ellen and Eustace gave a half-acre arable in the south field of Watford on *Wylifurlong* between land of the abbot and Edmund's land. The half-acre given by Edmund was also in the south field of Watford, but lay between land of William the clerk and Edmund's own land. Obviously, the abbot of St James held land in the south field of Watford, next to lands of Edmund de Watford.

In contrast to some of his cousins, Edmund seemed able to lend money, rather than find himself in debt. John de Haldenby acknowledged he owed £20 to John de Boudon and Edmund de Watford. If he defaulted payment, the money could be taken from his lands and chattels in Leicestershire.

Relationships between Edmund de Watford, free tenant, and his 'Lord', de Burneby, were not always friendly. What might have been a longstanding dispute about the rights of either party to use certain Watford lands, such as the common grazing lands in the open fields of the parish, was resolved with an agreement:[115]

> reciting that whereas controversy and discord had arisen between Eustace (*Enstachium*) de Borneby, lord of Watford on 'le Heth' of the one part and Edmund son of Edmund de Watford on the other, at length by the intervention of friends it was agreed between them that the said Edmund and his men and his heirs should freely and without hindrance have their hedge (*hechium*) in all their lands in fallow in the fields of Watford for ever because that was lawful to them by ancient use, and Eustace and his men to have the like. Watford, Sunday before the Translation of St. Edward, 9 Edward II. Witnesses: — William Wardedieu and others (named).

That ruling may be the genesis of what centuries later became known as many 'odd lands', scattered across the parish. Typically, these were hads, leyes, balkes, and other pieces of land, all of an acre or less, carved out of the edge of various host fields. Even after resolving the dispute over land use, Edmund had other issues to bring against Eustace de Burneby. When Eustace officially confirmed his holding of the Watford manor, Edmund protested by recording his 'claim' (see[116] Figure 45) against Eustace on the reverse of Eustace's document.

Figure 45: 'Edmund de Watford puts in his claim'

There is no known record of Edmund III's demise. An estimate puts the date at about 1317, given the large number of deeds from that time of one kind or another, such as made when an heir newly assumes the role of lord upon the death of his father.

Edmund de Watford (the fourth): 1317–1353

Edmund was a thoughtful man, who lived at Watford in parallel with the long and successful reign of King Edward III. He made sure his manor was properly accredited and his family well taken care of. Eventually, to strengthen his family through a strategic alliance, Edmund reached out to a well-established neighbour.

Edmund de Watford IV himself was married to a Margaret by 1316. As many as eight deeds through the next 21 years refer to 'Edmund and Margaret his wife' – so the authorities knew his wife had good standing. Other deeds name a messuage *Emma "en le Mor"*, which may be a salute to Edmund's grandmother and to his aunt, Emma Roys, nee de Watford. Yet another deed conveniently names Edmund's mother, the wife of Edmund III, as Cecily.

Figure 46: Medieval watermill, c 1330

By another deed, Edmund took advantage of his mill. He demised to William de la Vale, for life, his watermill in Watford, a homestead with its land, ten rods[xv] length of his court with the water-course of the millpond, and the yearly suit at the mill of all his bondmen and cottars. In return, William should grind Edmund's malt without cost and find a competent man to cock his hay for one day and reap or bind his corn for one day in the autumn, i.e., on his boon day called 'Mecelene'. The de Watford's watermill was an important part of farming life in Edmund's community. His tenants were obliged to grind their corn at the lord's mill (see[117] Figure 46).

Edmund de Watford secured official confirmation of his tenements by fine in 1321. First, the tenements were acknowledged to be the right of two court officials, which they had because Edmund had given the lands to them. Then, the same holdings were granted back to Edmund and Margaret and the heirs of Edmund to be held forever, owing service to the chief lord of the fee. The tenements comprised 10 messuages and 10 virgates of land in Watford.

When Edward III began one of England's longer reigns in January 1327, Edmund de Watford attended the new king's court. This time he

---

[xv] One rod, also known as a perch or a pole, equals a quarter of a chain or 5 ½ yards.

gave his 'manor of Watford with all its rights and possessions, except 10 messuages and 10 virgates of land', to the king's recently appointed Exchequer – William de Boudon. The excepted lands clearly referred to the 1321 fine and grant. Two days later, William de Boudon granted the same lands back to Edmund and Margaret de Watford and his heirs. The manor itself, without the 10 virgates of tenancies, presumably added several more virgates of demesne to the overall holding.

Edmund IV and Margaret had at least six children: Emma, Edmund, Roger, Lucy, Nicholas and Margaret. While two children, Edmund and Margaret, had their inheritances provided for separately, the other four were given 4 messuages and 4 virgates of land to provide them with some income. In addition, for the marriage of his daughter, Edmund paid 30 pennies to Eustace de Burneby, to whom he owed any service fees for his manor. Although the name of the daughter concerned was not specified, she may have been Lucy, who married into the Clopton family.

Nicholas de Watford was given land in Overend Meadow lying in Watford beside a meadow of the abbot of St James. Overend was a large meadow lying in the west of Watford, straddling what is now the Union Canal, north of the road from Kilsby to Watford village.

Robert de Craunford, the spouse found for Margaret de Watford by her parents Edmund and Margaret,[xvi] represented an alliance with a well-established neighbouring family. An agreement[118] drawn up in 1348 recorded the settlements made on the marriage. Edmund 'granted Robert 35 marks so that Robert shall marry his daughter Margaret'. Accordingly, Edmund granted to the bride and groom 'in frank marriage ... rent from a messuage and virgate of land in Dyngole ... in discharge of

Figure 47: Arms of Craunford

13 of the said 35 marks, also the rents issuing from land ... and cottages held in Ashby Leger, in discharge of 10 marks ... [and] of the residue, he will pay Robert 8 marks on the day of marriage, 2 marks on Lammas day [1st August], and 2 marks on St Luke's day [18th October] following'. In return, 'Robert shall grant ... Margaret for her life a messuage in Ashby Leger, worth 6s yearly, and 32 acres land there which [his father] Nicholas de Craunford gave the said Robert to him and his heirs for ever'.

[xvi] Birthyear estimated 1330, therefore married in 1348 or 1349 at age of about 19, daughter Emma born 1350.

Robert was a son of the prominent de Craunford family of neighbouring Ashby St Ledgers, whose arms (see[119] Figure 47) can be blazoned: *Gules, a fret or, a chief argent*. His parents, Nicholas and Catherine de Craunford, held Ashby Legers for which Catherine, as a widow, paid fine for one knight's fee in 1346. The Craunfords had been lords of Ashby Legers since the time of King John, and long before the advent of the Catesbys.

According to the marriage contract, Edmund also agreed Margaret could live with him until the end of the following September, indicating the marriage was expected by September 1349. But the marriage must have taken place within six months. In May of 1349, Roger de Watford granted land in Ashby St Leger, formerly belonging to Nicholas de Craunford, to 'Robert de Craunford and Margaret his wife'. Not to be forgotten, later in the same year, Roger and Nicholas were granted for their lives a messuage and virgate of land in Watford by their father, Edmund. Another 1 virgate may have been given to Edmund's daughter, Lucy, when she married a 'Clopton', although no record has been found of such a gift. At around this time, Edmund's original legacy of 14 virgates seems to shrink slightly to 13.

Edmund de Watford IV died early 1353. The faithful administration of his goods was certified by an official of the archdeacon of Northampton, discharging the executors from providing any further account.

Edmund (the fifth), Roger and Margaret de Watford: 1353–1405

Edmund IV had lived a long life but compared to him, Edmund V was not destined for a long stretch as manor lord – the plague took its toll. Nor did he seem to readily pick up the mantle of manor lord.

After their father's death, Roger and Nicholas de Watford took care of manor operations. In one case, they gave a house and land in Watford to a new tenant, which had been formerly held in villeinage by John Golafre of Edmund, their father. In the medieval world, a villein held a rank higher than a serf because he paid rent to the lord for his tenancy, often a virgate of land, and worked it himself. On the same day, the brothers leased out what they had been given in 1349, a messuage and virgate of land in Watford, which Thomas Watts formerly held of their father in villeinage. The rent was 24s payable quarterly at the manor belonging to Edmund. Clearly, the many Edmunds de Watford maintained a manor house in the tradition of a lord, even though they were subservient to the chief lords of the fee, the de Burnebys.

Roger and Nicholas acted in tandem once again a year or so after their father's death. They leased to William Saunsum of Watford, a messuage and land in Watford. Evidently, Nicholas de Watford decided to extend his home. Seven years later, William gave back to Nicholas a place to the west of his house in Watford, measuring 18ft by 16ft, to build a chamber thereon.

The brother-in-law of the de Watford brothers, Robert de Craunford, had died by 1356. Walter Wright of Watford acknowledged receiving from Margaret, 'late the wife of Robert de Craunford', various items of farm equipment. They agreed values for the items: 9s for two horses, 17s for two cart-horses, 40d for two coalters and plough shares, 40d for two iron harrows, and of greatest value, 12s for each of eight oxen. All the farm implements, or their agreed value if lost, were to be returned to Margaret by September 29 next coming.

Edmund de Watford, the fifth and last of the name, appears to have acted only rarely to manage his lands. Apparently only a few days before he died, Edmund demised a half-acre of arable land and two acres of meadow in the fields of Watford, formerly held by Nicholas his brother. Edmund must have become aware he was seriously ill, Nicholas had already died, and therefore he had to act on behalf of his deceased brother.

These were the times of the second major outbreak of bubonic plague in England. Edmund himself, like two of his distant cousins, fell victim to the Black Death in the summer of 1361. Presumably, a pardon granted to Ralph Swon in 1364 for not appearing before the justices to answer for a debt of 40s to Edmund de Watford was the result of efforts by Edmund's executors to collect an old debt.

Following the issue of a writ dated 16th September 1361, Edmund's inquisition was held in Northampton ten days later. The escheator noted Edmund had died on 4th September and his heir was Roger de Watford, his brother, aged 24 years and more as of September 29 last, nearly a year ago. Roger was within days of his 25th birthday, and theoretically[xvii] therefore was born September 29, 1336.

On the day he died, Edmund did not hold anything of the king in chief, but he held lands in Watford, Creaton, Newbottle, and Ashby Leger. The holding in Great Creaton generated 18s rent of free tenants, held of the heirs of Roger Roys by service of a rose each year. These were very likely the lands originally given to Emma de Watford's husband about 1290.

[xvii] Appears very unlikely, as Roger demised property in 1349 for his sister's marriage, which he cannot have done aged only 13; accordingly estimate Roger was born about 1322 (and e.g. Emma 1318, Edmund 1320, Lucy 1325, Nicholas 1327, Margaret 1330). Alternatively, the Roger and his brother Nicholas who demised, and were demised to, in 1349 and 1340 were *uncles* of Edmund V, i.e. *brothers* of Edmund IV.

Further, they may be the lands demised by Edmund IV and Margaret, his wife, in 1337 to Adam and John le Vyneter of Middleton, both chaplains, and Alice, their sister – a toft and virgate in Great Creaton, for their lives, at 18s rent. Although the property rented was in Great Creaton, the Vyneter family lived in Middleton, which could either be a parish some distance to the northeast of Watford parish, or a field in the west of Watford town abutting Crick, where the Vyneter family were lords. In Newbottle, Edmund had 24s annual rent by service of 2d, and in Ashby Leger, he had 7s rent by knight's service.

In Watford itself, Edmund V held:

> 6 messuages, a water mill with 2 crofts, 9 virgates of land, 4 pieces of meadow called 'Bradmede', 'Boylond', 'Fletlond' and 'Rodemore', and 30s rent of customary tenants in Watford. In the principal messuage were certain buildings not valued, but there was a dovecote valued at 2s pa and 5s rent issuing from the five other messuages. All premises were held of the heir of Nicholas de Burneby, a minor in the king's wardship, as of the manor of Watford, by service of rendering a pair of gilt spurs or 6d yearly. Two parts of the nine virgates were valued at 40s pa, each acre 6d, and the four pieces of meadow with two crofts were valued at 26s 8d, and the water mill, nothing because it was ruined. And:

> Roger de Watford, Nicholas de Watford, Emma de Watford and Lucy de Clopton held jointly for their lives, 4 messuages and 4 virgates of land of Edmund de Watford, by gift of Edmund de Watford, their father, by service of rendering a rose at Midsummer.

Four meadows are named. At least two, Boylond and Rodemore, can be traced forward hundreds of years to early modern times. Boylond lay in the western corner of Watford town. Rodemore, sometimes Radmore, on the other hand, was in the opposite corner of Watford town in the northeast. Another meadow in Watford was Overend. Often Watford's meadows were large fields in their own right. The escheator summarises 13 of the de Watford's original holding of 14 virgates, so 1 virgate must have been given away at some point.

A few years after Edmund's death, his brother Roger was already describing himself as a 'chaplain' (see[120] Figure 48). But Roger himself did not live in the Watford manor house – his life lay elsewhere. So he leased to Walter Wright of Watford, for life and a year over, the heart of his manor. The manor house and demesne lands were described as

'Morezeue Halle' with the old grange, watermill, 'and land his father used to plough with his own ploughs in the field of Watford'.

Roger's work was not restricted to Northamptonshire. In 1356, King Edward III granted Master Roger de Watford 10 marks yearly for good service to the king and his eldest daughter, Isobel. The pension should last for life or until the king ordered otherwise for Roger's estate.

Given his chosen occupation as a chaplain worthy of the king's attention, small wonder Roger de Watford decided his estate should provide income to the church. By a deed dated 1374, Roger gave all his lands and tenements in Great Creaton to William Haddon and Thomas Haddon, for their lives. Roger did the same thing with his lands in Watford and Newbottle. For Watford, the beneficiary

Figure 48: Medieval cleric

was William de Southo, vicar of the parish between 1372 and 1382.

Sometimes inconsistencies between various official documents became apparent. The date of Roger's grant of Creaton, 1374, conflicts with an entry in the Close Rolls dated 1368. In the Rolls entry, a John Duke, who evidently was another who performed good service to the king, was sent to the abbot and convent of Thorney, Cambs, 8 miles east of Peterborough. At the king's request, John was to live in the abbey to the same standard as the deceased Roger Watford had done. Furthermore, the pension of 100s yearly which the king had been giving to John must end immediately. To clean up the documentation, John had to give back the king's letters of direction for the pension so they could be cancelled. John could not have both!

The date in the Close Rolls must be correct. The evidence for this is a special inquisition after Roger's death in 42 Edward III, 1368, required by the king due to Roger's excellent service to his daughter. The sheriff reported – 'Roger de Watford, yeoman of the king's daughter Isobel, died at Watford on the Sunday after the Nativity of St Mary [8 September] in the manner of plague'. Roger's deed granting lands was probably entered into the Roll years after his death.

Decades after Roger had died, William de Southo, former vicar of Watford, and in 1398 the Master of Aynho Hospital, gave up the de Watford lands. He wrote a release in 1404 with quitclaim and warranty: 'from me William de Southo, vicar of Watford, to Margaret de Craunford, sister and heiress of Roger de Watford, chaplain, deceased, of all my right in all the lands & tenements, rents, services, both freehold and copyhold, which I had by grant of the said Roger in the towns of Watford, Newbottle & Creaton'.

The de Watford lands now passed to Margaret de Watford under her first married name, de Craunford. Margaret had three daughters – the eldest was Emma by her first husband, Robert de Craunford. The next two were Margaret and Joan, daughters by Simon Cresholm (see[121] Figure 49), her second husband. By the end of the fourteenth century, Emma's two sisters were married to Edward de Mettele and Robert Burdet, respectively.

Figure 49: Arms of Cresholm impaling arms of Watford

Emma de Craunford and John de Catesby: 1365–1418

Emma de Craunford, niece of the last Edmund, was the last of his de Watford family line. With a strategic marriage, she merged her manor lands into the Catesby estates. Although before the Catesbys came into the picture, Emma took another direction.

John de Swynford became Emma's husband around 1366. Her mother Margaret made sure certain obligations concerning the Craunford lands would be respected. John de Swynford signed a bond for £200, which would be cancelled on two conditions. First, if Margaret died during Simon Cresholm's and Emma's lifetimes, and the former Craunford lands in Ashby Legers descended to Emma, then John should pay an annual sum of 100s to Simon for his life. Second, when Emma came of age, John should give security of all the said lands to Simon and Margaret for however long Margaret lived. To sum up, Margaret had the benefit of Emma's inheritance during Margaret's lifetime and if she, Margaret, predeceased Simon, then he would have an annuity for the rest of his life.

By a separate deed, Emma's uncle, Roger de Watford, had granted the manor of Ashby Legers and 10 marks rent in Ashby to Margaret de Craunford. That might have been a marriage settlement. The grant was for Margaret's life with reversion to Emma, her husband John and her heirs. So Emma was designated to possess the manor of Ashby Legers, which became an important part of her future life.

Rather cleverly, Roger made the grant of Ashby six years after he died. However, Roger's sister was remarried in his lifetime and his niece did the same at about the same time. Therefore, Emma may have been only 15 years old when she married John de Swynford. Not the case today, but at the time this was the legal marriageable age for young women. So her 21st birthday in 1374 may have been the trigger to formally enrol the settlement of lands previously sealed by Roger when Emma married. John de Swynford died in January 1381, leaving Emma with his Newbold lands.

Only three months later Emma married again, this time to John de Catesby. That brought[122] her former husband's lands in Newbold with her Watford lands and manor of Ashby Legers to the Catesbys. And the influential Catesby family to Northamptonshire. From this time onwards, the de Watford manor became known as the 'Catesby Manor of Watford', and was only one part of the broader chronicle spanning the next century of the growing Catesby empire. The story becomes more about the Catesbys, their descendants and landed estates, somewhat burying the identity of the manor of Watford. The many Catesby arms displayed in the church at Lodbroke include the arms of families who married various members of the Catesby family. In the 10th and last (see[123] Figure 50), John's quartered arms impale the fret of Craunford.

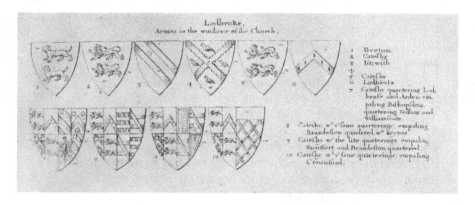

Figure 50: Arms of Catesby and others at Lodbroke

The heiress Emma had married a man with substantial land resources of his own, making an alliance of landed families – a common purpose at the time. The newly created Catesby family preferred Ashby Legers as their home and never lived in Watford.

John de Catesby and his father, William, held lands in Coventry, Warwickshire, among other places. There are many deeds, initially bearing the name of his father, William de Catesby, and later, John's name, stretching through the fourteenth century. William de Catesby came from Radborne in Warwickshire, next to Ladbroke, another of the key Catesby holdings. These two parishes were closely aligned and both were held by Turchil de Ardern at the time of Domesday. One of Turchil's descendants, Joanna de Arderne, daughter of the third William de Arderne of Rodborne, married William Catesby, and this couple were John's parents.

The first William de Ardern of Rodburne was the brother of Letitia, both children of Henry de Ardern, the elder grandson of Turchil. The arms[124] of Ardern de Rodburne, featuring ermine with the gold and blue checkerboard design across the centre of the shield (see[125] Figure 51), were the basis for the arms of Ardern of Watford (see Figure 7).

Figure 51: Arms of de Ardern of Rodburne

Rodbourn included several different parcels of lands. The abbot of Combe created one of these, known as Radburne Grange. Radborne manor was granted by William de Arderne de Radburne to his son, William, who in 1369 delivered the manor to John Catesby, son of William Catesby. The different lordships within Radburne were not easily distinguishable, but the Grange played a key role in the seventeenth century with regard to George Clerke's acquisition of Watford lands.

The Catesbys had held lands in Coventry for many years. Even as far back as 1381 landlord John Catesby saw fit to protect his interests by giving careful instructions in a lease to his future tenant. He made sure the tenant's house would not overlook the Catesby's house when granting the lease:

> for twelve years, of a messuage in Coventry, paying yearly a rose, for the first four years, 6s. 8d. the fifth year, and 20s. yearly, for the remaining seven years; the said [tenant] is to build a new house in the first year, within the said messuage, of six posts not making any windows towards William de Catesby's tenement there, except at such a height that no one can see out.

Emma and John de Catesby (see[126] Figure 52) lived in Ashby Leger. John died there about 1404. He signed a letter of attorney the year before and is referred to as the 'late' John Catesby in a deed of grant a year after.

About the same time, and with the demise of Margaret de Craunford, a dispute arose between Emma and her two half-sisters concerning the lands and tenements lately belonging to Roger de Watford, their uncle. The three daughters called for arbitration in

Figure 52: John de Catesby & Emma de Craunford

December 1406 to settle the dispute. Margaret de Cranford, sole heir of Edmund de Watford, had given to her daughter Margaret and her husband Edward de Metteley a messuage and land in Watford that came to her by right of inheritance after the death of Roger de Watford. Witnesses included two neighbouring lords, John Estbury and Ralph Parles. Thus the pie to be sliced up between the sisters was reduced by 2½ virgates of land.

The arbitrator decided: first, Margaret de Craunford shall have all the profits from all the lands and tenements during her lifetime. Second, Emma de Catesby and William, her son, shall release to her two half-sisters and their husbands their rights in all the lands and tenements formerly belonging to Roger in Watford, Newbottle, Great Creaton, and Ashby Leger. Third, Emma's two half-sisters, Margaret and Joan and their husbands, should grant Emma de Catesby and her heirs forever the capital messuage with all the lands, demesne, crofts, meadows, pastures, and all other appurtenances lately held in Watford by the demise of Margaret de Craunford. Further, they should confirm all of that by fine with warranty. And all deeds for the lands and tenements were to be placed in one chest with three keys for the use of all parties.

As instructed, Emma de Catesby released to her sisters all her right in the premises that the sisters had been given by Margaret, formerly wife of Robert de Cranford. In return, sisters Margaret and Joan and their husbands delivered to Emma the specified premises in Watford. Emma would hold the lands of the chief lords of the fee for customary services, forever. Both deeds were witnessed by George Burneby, Ralph Parles, and others. To legalise Emma's title, the two sisters made the official fine for 1 messuage, 1 carucate of land, 16 acres of meadow, 2½ acres of pasture and half a mill, with all attached rights, in Watford. Finally, they acknowledged all tenements to be the right of Emma and quit themselves from any future claim.

One might wonder why the estate given to Emma was only 1 carucate, which is 4 virgates, when the Edmunds de Watford originally had 14 virgates. The capital messuage and demesne – possibly Boylonde only – were often not described in virgates. The 'lands' and 'tenements' likely included some or all of the former de Watford manor's tenancies.

The arbitrator had decided Emma would have the Watford lands, while her two sisters received all the lands outside Watford, in Newbottle, Great Creaton, and Ashby Ledger, formerly held by Roger and the several Edmunds. Although Emma gave up any Ashby Ledger lands inherited from her de Watford mother, there was no doubt she held the Ashby Ledger lands inherited from her natural father, Robert de Craunford.

Two years later, Emma leased to the vicar of Watford for 20 years at 40s and six capons yearly the manor (see[127] Figure 53) described as 'her capital messuage in Watford', specifically 'one hall with two chambers at the end of the hall, one long house situated lengthwise by the royal highway [Watling Streete], one dovecot & the whole orchard & garden' next to the messuage, 'one croft called Goscroft together with le mulnedam', and 82 selions, butts and other lands in Rodemore 'in the north field', Lortyngore, Sondylond, and Brodemore furlongs, representing 20 ¾

Figure 53: 13th Century Manor House

acres. Emma and John Catesby sealed the lease at their residence of Ashby Leger, one of the holdings assuredly hers as a result of her mother's intervention at the time of her marriage.

Following the death about 1407 of her eldest son, William de Catesby, Emma took steps to clarify rights in her demesne lands for her next heir. In 1412 she obtained the right of free warren on her lands, which could be granted only by the sovereign. This gave the grantee the right to hunt game free from prosecution by the *Forest* court. In this case, Emma's grant extended to her demesne lands, and carried the advantage of no less than the king's authority formally naming her lands.

> Grant[128] to Emma, late the wife of John Catesby, deceased, and John her son, and their heirs, of free warren in all their demesne lands in the towns of Rodbourne, Loddebroke, and Shukkeburgh, co. Warwick, and in Assheby Leger, Welton and Watford, co. Northampton.

The 'Rodbourne' lands in Emma's grant was 'Rodborne Grange', previously mentioned.

In the manner typical of the time, four documents were required for Lady Emma de Catesby and one of her sons to complete a settlement of the family lands. Emma granted, with warranty, her Watford lands and tenements to her third son, Robert, and he granted the same lands back to Emma for her lifetime. There are many deeds after this time signed by her now eldest surviving son, John, together with his mother, Emma.

For example, in 1414, Emma and John bought a messuage, 20 acres of land, 4 acres of meadow and nearly 56 shillings of rent in Welton and Ashby Leger for 20 marks of silver. A feoffment a year later by Emma and John of a messuage and half a virgate in Welton carried witnesses of influential men in the region: John Mallory, lord of Welton, George

Burneby, lord of Watford, Robert de Catesby, Emma's son, and one other. The Mallory family of Welton had been associated with the lords of Watford for more than a century.

Emma Catesby's last appearance was about 1418. Her name is on documents mid 1417 but not afterwards. From late 1418, her son John Catesby alone attaches his seal to deeds.

John Catesby and Sir William Catesby: 1418–1478

John, and eventually his son William, continued to build the Catesby collection of manors. Some of them took an important place in future events involving the Catesbys. Both John and William seemed to make a point of adding yet more Williams and Johns into the Catesby family.

For £100, half the manor of Lapworth was added to the family holdings in 1418 by John Catesby of Ashby Leger. These were the lands of John's wife, Margaret de Montfort, daughter of Lady Rose de Montfort. The lands were immediately leased back to Lady Rose for her lifetime. Nine years later, after Lady Rose died, this moiety (half) of the manor of Lapworth was granted back to John and his wife Margaret.

John Catesby and Margaret bought the manor of Olthorpe for 100 marks of silver in 1429. This was another major addition to the Catesby holdings, which remained in the family until 1508.

John Catesby died in July 1436, leaving seven children of whom William, later, Sir William, inherited the Watford and Ashby Leger lands. Another son, John, held the manor of Olthorpe and became a Sergeant at Law in 1469. In 1435 a third son, Robert Catesby, made a grant to Nicholas West of Daventry and John Freman, vicar of Haddon, for rents of 13s 4d (one mark) receivable from lands and tenements in Bobenhull, Warwickshire.

William Catesby was knighted in 1449, and over the next few decades, many land or manor deeds were completed by William Catesby, knight. Until 1454 many also named William's mother, Lady Margaret. In another case in the 1460s, Sir William fought and eventually won a dispute concerning the manor of Lapworth.

Naturally, the Catesbys did not ignore their holdings in Coventry. Following the example set by John Catesby in 1381, Sir William in 1464 demised[129] a messuage in Coventry for 60 years, conditioned on the lessee rebuilding a house on the premises – three bays long on Catesby Lane – according to the careful instruction provided:

> a house and chamber occupying the whole space of the said messuage
> before Midsummer next, viz. of oak timber with posts (*postibus*) 15 feet

high on stones 1½ feet high, fit for plaster of 'Parys' on all the walls except the walls (*muribus*) called 'les helowe wowes'; the chamber with its 'flore' to be, &c.; the chamber to be 'giteyed' for two feet toward the lane; doors and windows to be made with good 'gryse'

John Catesby was a Sergeant-at-Law, meaning he was an officer of the court. His son, Robert Catesby received the commitment of the Treasury for keeping the manor of Little Weldon for 30 years. The manor had fallen into the king's hands after the death of the widow of the previous lord. In about

Figure 54: Manor House of Ashby St Ledgers

1454 this Robert Catesby married Margaret Parles, the former wife of John Parles, lord of Parles Manor in Watford. Unfortunately for Robert, his marriage did not allow him to keep the Parles estates for himself, because John Parles had left an heir. Robert Catesby is believed to have died at Weldon Magna in 1465 or 1466.

The Catesbys continued to regard the manor house at Ashby Legers (see[130] Figure 54) as their primary home. They went to the extent of obtaining a license[131] to found 'Catesby chantry' in the church at Ashby Legers. Sir William Catesby, knight, wished to celebrate the ...

Holy Trinity, the Salutation of St Mary the Virgin and St Leger, at the altar ... within the church of St Leger, Ashby Leger

This was intended for:

the souls of John Catesby, esquire, and Margaret his wife, father and mother of the said William the father, and Philippa, sometime wife of the latter, and their ancestors

Sir William wanted and was given more:

Grant also to William the father that he may impark 300 acres of wood, land and pasture and a way between his land in Ashby Leger, now enclosed with a dyke and hay, so that he cause another way to be made on his land, and 1,000 acres of wood, land and pasture in Lapworth, co

Warwick, now likewise enclosed; so that none enter the said parks to chase or take anything thence without his license under pain of £10

One could be led to believe Sir William had ulterior motives for his gesture in giving the chantry ... to gain license to develop two of his primary manors.

A short report of receipts and payments for the year 1462–63 covered Sir William Catesby's estate in three parishes – Welton, Watford and Hinton. The Watford account was written by 'Henry Cokkes clerk, collector of rents there' – he was vicar of Watford parish from 1464 to 1484. Henry recorded fixed rents received of £7 3s 9d and 12 hens. Payments totalled £4 4s 5d, including fixed rents of 3d to Eustace Burneby, and 6d to the abbot of St James for a croft called Newecrofte. Other payments covered: four doors for tenants, 5s; the vicar of Ashby Leger for a hospital, 40s; to John the abbot under a bond, 12s; and to a 'servant' probably a lawyer or other professional, 26s 8d. Of the net 59s 4d, the 'accountant' deducted 20s he paid over to the lord and was allowed to carry forward 30s 5d for the Welton accounting and another 8s 11d for the next Watford accounting.

In a flashback to the past, a Thomas Meteley turns up – he was a grandson of Edward de Mettele, the husband of one of Emma Catesby's half-sisters, who shared in their mother's estate some 50 years before. For the short period of 3 ½ years from March 1464, Thomas Meteley had demised his 2 ½ messuages and 2 ½ virgates of land in Watford to Nicholas Cowley. In December 1467, the Catesbys and their associates acquired all the lands and tenements held by Thomas Meteley in Watford. Witnesses included George Burneby, Richard Knightley and Richard Hill. The land was a useful addition to the Catesby manor in Watford.

Only two years later, Elizabeth Hill, widow, the daughter and heir of Richard Smyth of Watford, brought yet another parcel to the Catesbys. She gave up lands in Ashby Ledger to the Catesbys but in exchange was enfeoffed with a messuage, a croft, 1 virgate, and also a ¼ virgate of 'odd lands', all in Watford town. Nonetheless, the Catesbys retained use of the Watford lands in a lease, for which they paid rent, and so re-leased the lands for rent received.

The Watford Lands of Thomas de Watford

The Catesbys had established a good foothold in Watford by a strategic marriage during the 1300s. Several additions had been made to the manor lands in the 1460s and by the 1470s another advantageous parcel held appeal. They set their sights on lands held by John Watford and his son, Thomas. These were lands originally held by Thomas de Watford, younger brother of Eustace de Watford IV. Since 1276, this carefully guarded family landholding had descended through six generations of de Watfords. So we look back 200 years ...

Thomas and Robert de Watford: 1276–1316

Originally, Thomas de Watford's land lay within the manor of Sir Eustace de Watford. Thomas was alive around 1270 to witness deeds made by Sir Robert Mallory of Welton, a longstanding associate and neighbour of the de Watfords. The deeds are undated, but were witnessed by Sir Eustace de Watford, Thomas and William de Watford both cited as 'brothers of Sir Eustace', as well as four other local landlords. Thomas also witnessed a deed by which Sir Eustace gave land to his three married children (see Figure 16).

Thomas's homestead and its land was situated north of Eustace's capital messuage. He died before 1276, leaving his two children, Robert and Agnes, as wards of his elder brother, Eustace. At the time Eustace died the escheator said Robert held 2 virgates of land in Watford, for which he paid a notional annual rent of 6d.

By an agreement dated about seven months after Eustace died, Dame Margaret, his widow, appointed Robert de Chokes as the ward of Robert and Agnes. She also gave him the right to allow or refuse either child in marriage. Robert de Chokes held the Honor of Chokes in Great Creaton, a parish not far to the east of Watford. Along with the children, the widow Margaret gave Chokes 40s in annual income until the children reached majority. And just to make sure Margaret was happy, Robert de Chokes paid 50s to Margaret. The document was witnessed by relatives William de Parles and Edmund de Watford, among others.

As was common at the time, Robert de Chokes took advantage of the rights he had been given and arranged the marriage of Robert de Watford to one of his own daughters. The young Robert and his lands would have been a worthwhile target for local prospective brides.

Robert de Watford willingly took on the responsibilities of a local landholder. Along with others of good reputation he made an appearance as a juror in the special inquisition held in 1309 for his cousin, John de Parles. Robert himself passed away in December 1316 and his inquisition named his heir as William de Watford. Robert had become Lord of Creaton after Robert de Chokes. The inquisition recorded the lordship there included 4 virgates and 100 acres of arable land. He held the land by service of a ¼ knight's fee and paying homage every three weeks at the Chokes' manor of Gayton. In October of the same year, William and his wife, Joan, made fine with the king to secure their holdings in Great Creaton.

After Robert's elevation in Creaton to lord of the manor, his Watford lands became part of the manor of Creaton. In his former home parish, he held a messuage valued at 4s per annum, 2 virgates containing 48 acres of arable land worth 24s per annum, and 1 acre of meadow, valued at 20d, all held of Eustace de Burneby, by service of a tenth of a knight's fee and 6d rent.

William, William and Thomas de Watford: 1316–1456

At the time of his father's inquisition, William de Watford was a young man of 21, but he took his responsibilities seriously. His father had died during the Great Famine, one of its great many victims. The famine started with bad weather in the spring of 1315, continued with crop failures through 1316 and lasted beyond the summer harvest in 1317. William took over his manor at a difficult time after many deaths, with famine, disease and crime extending across vast areas of the country. Nonetheless, he chose to live in the manor house at Great Creaton and not in Watford.

Years later, William leased his capital messuage with its manor house and land in Watford for six years to Roger Waldeshof, vicar of Watford, at an annual rent of £4. Clarifying his status, William was described as the son of Robert, lord of Great Creaton. The same William de Watford of Creaton won a court order in 1341 for £4 15s 9d for 32 stones of wool taken from him by Warin le Latymer. For commercial purposes in medieval times, wool was graded by weight, with a stone equal to 14 pounds weight. Wool was a significant product of the English countryside, exported as high-quality product to cloth weavers in Flanders among other places.

While no record of William's death is found, very likely he died in 1348 at the time of the first great outbreak of the bubonic plague. The Black Death swept Europe and Britain, taking about a third of the entire population. With little defence against the disease, serfs and landlords equally fell victim, including many people driving the nation's legal infrastructure. Fortunately, later records enable the de Watford trail to be found once again.

In 1370, William de Watford, lord of Great Creaton, leased to William Haddon a meadow and arable land until he had received seven crops of hay and corn. Two years later, another transaction spoke of William's heritage and fondly mentioned the lands in Creaton. William, the son and heir of William Watford of Creaton, issued a rent receipt for the next six years to William Haddon for half a virgate of land, which his father, William de Watford, had rented to him for the term of his life at 8s annual rent.

Continuing the family line, in 1398 William de Watford of Great Creaton gave all his lands there to his son, Thomas. William took this step while he was able to do so, ensuring a clear line of succession. Later deeds confirm William did the same for his Watford lands.

Years after he had taken over from his father, a court summoned Thomas for not appearing before Justices of the Bench to answer for a debt of 100s, as well as a plea for 104s by a fishmonger of London. Similarly, John Freman, the vicar of West Haddon, and William Tresham of Northampton brought suit against Thomas Watford of Great Creaton for debts of 10 marks and 5 marks, respectively. Other than making a nuisance of himself over debt, Thomas had a generous streak. In 1442, he was one of the many licensed to grant property to the abbot and convent of St James by Northampton – in his case, a garden in Northampton.

Thomas also took care to preserve his holding[132] within the family in the usual way. His father had left his lands to Thomas 'in tail', which meant Thomas could not choose anyone other than his male heirs to inherit his lands. Evidently, Thomas's chief lord, to whom he owed homage, had either persuaded or forced Thomas to increase his annual rent from the nominal 6d to 8s and 8d.

> Thomas Watford of Northampton made his homage to Eustace de Burneby, lord of Watford, & acknowledged that he & his male heirs, hold of the said Eustace & his heirs all lands & tenements which are in the town & fields of Watford, by homage & fealty & suit of court twice a year, paying for relief annually one gold ring price 8s 8d.

John and Thomas Watford: 1456–1481

John Watford was the last in the line of his family after 1276 to hold these Watford lands. First, however, he established his own title when in 1456 five men fulfilled their legal obligation to pass the lands to the designated heir, John. His father, Thomas, had given the lands to his representatives with directions of what to do after he died. Accordingly, the five gave John Watford, named as son of Thomas Watford, and John's wife Elizabeth, and their heirs all the land in Watford they had been given by Thomas prior to his death. If John had no heirs then Thomas's daughter, Alice Prestwych, should have the lands. And if Alice had no children, the beneficiary should be William Watford, younger brother of Thomas. If even that failed, then the lands would be given to whoever the law designated as the rightful heir of Thomas Watford.

This kind of process was standard procedure at the time. The original deed naming the five men was likely written many years before by Thomas de Watford. The grant was designed to come into force if the heir was already of age following Thomas's death, or when the heir came of age years after Thomas's death.

The five men has been tasked to complete a significant action – arranging title to lands. They wanted to make sure their actions could not be questioned at a later date, so they arranged important men of the area to be witnesses to the deed: Sir William Catesby, knight, John Catesby, Eustace Burneby, and two others, each of whom added his seal.

All that concerned only the Watford lands. More deeds were required specifically concerning the manor of Great Creaton and other lands. With a similar methodology as for Watford, John Watford, now of Northampton, was given formal title to the manor of Great Creaton, anciently called 'Chokes'. Along with the manor, he also inherited at least eight different tenements, cottages and gardens on various streets in Northampton. Elizabeth, John's wife, had likely brought the Northampton lands into the marriage. She and John proceeded to sell surplus properties. They were paid £20 for a goodly package of a house, 1 ½ virgates and rent of 16 shillings and 4 capons in Waldegrave, and gave Elizabeth's warranty of good title. They also sold two of their Northampton tenements. John Watford, now of Weekley, sold another house and virgate in Great Creaton. In this case, John had to sign a bond of 100 marks to guarantee the buyer would not be troubled by anyone claiming title or in any way being a nuisance, spoiling the new owner's happiness with his purchase.

Back to Watford. Although the Watfords couldn't foresee the future and be aware they would eventually sell their lands, their actions from this point set up the complex sale process that took place some 20 years later. One way or another, three parties were given rights in the family's Watford lands.

By deed dated 1458, John Watford leased his Watford lands to William Chamberlain and William Walsh of Watford. The 'lands' were two crofts of pasture, with all of John's other land in Watford. The rent was fixed at a rose for the first six years, and thereafter 26s 8d (two marks) yearly for the term of 33 years. Members of the Walsh (or Welche) family were associated with various Watford lands for centuries. But halfway through the lease, William Walsh seems to have forgotten his lease was time limited.

After Chamberlain died, by deed poll, Walsh recited that the charter of 1458 had granted the two crofts of pasture with all John's lands in Watford to William and himself 'forever'. Regardless, William Walsh then leased the same lands to Nicholas Walsh (probably his son) for a period of three years from the end of September. As a side note, Nicholas Walsh's lands eventually appear in a financial report prepared by a Catesby steward.

The second interest in the Watford lands was set up in 1462. John Watford esquire leased John Umfrehay of Barton Hanred and Eleanor, his wife, the same two crofts of pasture and all John's other lands and tenements in Watford, formerly belonging to his father, Thomas. Sir William Catesby was one of the witnesses to the deed.

John's sister, Alice Prestwych of Northampton, steps into the picture in 1473 with the third interested party. She leased to Nicholas Walsh, William Willis of Watford, and Thomas Hanwell, son of Richard Hanwell, all her father's lands in the town and fields of Watford. This time, a witness was Henry Cokkes, the vicar of Watford. The document has an additional note in Latin, undated, but added some time later, reading: *'This a daughter of Thomas Watford sister of John Watford whose heir he is and is a warranty of corlis distended on the aforesaid John because Alice is dead without heir of her body'*. So John was stuck with Alice's warranty. While still alive, Alice issued a letter of attorney addressed to Robert Fenne and another instructing the lands be delivered to the same three men. And as instructed by Alice, William Grymbold released his right in the lands to Walsh, Willis, and Hanwell.

In January 1477, a group of men led by the Catesbys launched the complex process of buying the de Watford lands held by John Watford. No doubt, the sophisticated Catesbys were used to such convoluted proceedings. They had to address each of the three groups holding interests in the targeted lands.

First, William Walsch granted to Sir William Hastynges, lord of Hastynges, Sir William Catesby, John Catesby, sergeant-at-law, another John Catesby of Olthorp, and three others, the same two Watford crofts of pasture with all the various lands belonging. John Watford had granted the lands to Walsch and Chamberlain in 1458, although Chamberlain was since deceased. Second, William Walsch, Nicholas Walsch, William Willis of Watford, and Thomas Hanwell, son of Richard Hanwell, released to the same group, Sirs Hastynges and Catesby and friends, all their rights in John's two crofts etc in Watford. Third, Robert Fenne and his wife Eleanor, formerly wife of John Umfrehay, delivered Umfrehay's rights to Sirs Hastynges and Catesby et al with the two crofts of pasture in Watford. This third transaction was witnessed by George Burneby and Nicholas Catesby, among others. John Sabyn had been appointed to deliver title to the lands – he was reeve (steward of a manor) in Watford and was the chief tenant of the Catesby's Watford manor at the time.

Little did they know, but there was another document lurking in the background. Six months after completing the three agreements, the Catesby group found another legal matter requiring their attention. As far back as 1412, Thomas Watford had written a charter giving the manor of Great Creaton with its Watford lands to another group of men including William Reeve, vicar of Ravensthorpe. None of the original group remained alive except William's heir, John Reeve. John signed a deed poll releasing to Sirs Hastynges and Catesby and friends all his right in all those lands in Watford that were originally Thomas Watford's. About the time Thomas's son John was born, he had charged the vicar of

Ravensthorpe with the responsibility of getting valid title to John. So to ensure the purchase was legally effective, the Catesbys had to take care of the vicar's rights and responsibilities.

The deal with the Watfords was finalized a full year after the arrangement was initiated. John Watford and his son, Thomas, granted all their lands, tenements, rents, services and any other rights they had in the town and fields of Watford to the Catesby trio and companions, with warranty and quitclaim.

But the Watfords were not done with their lands in Great Creaton. A few months before, John Watford and his son, Thomas, had granted to Dame Anne Osbern for six years the annual rentals of 26s 8d from all the lands the Watfords held in Great Creaton. The grant came with a bond of £20, guaranteeing Dame Anne would be paid the rent without any deductions or missed payments. If she did encounter such problems, the bond would become payable. Dame Anne, a widow of Northampton, may have been a relative. In any case, her name might be the source of 'Osbornes', the name given to the lands of this de Watford family.

In other news ... 'John Watford of Weekley, gentleman' was sued for not appearing before the justices of the Bench to answer the prior of Launde for a debt of 10 marks. Perhaps the Watfords also owed money to the Catesbys, providing additional rationale to sell the manor.

Yet three more documents were needed to finally seal the purchase of the Great Creaton manor and its Watford lands. A Memorandum acknowledged the Watfords owed William Catesby £7 5s. They bound themselves and gave surety for the amount to William of all their lands in Great Creaton, to be deducted from a later payment by Catesby. Another document delivered was the principle bond[133] by John and Thomas Watford for £100 issued to William Catesby due at Christmas, 1478, if something went wrong. This was to ensure the Watfords performed all conditions of the sale including the passing of good title. An endorsement reads:

> Memorandum that ther is behynd to be contented 5 mark for the full contentacion for the bargene of all the landes in Creton. And that a feyn shall be takyn within viij. dayes after the xijth day nexst comyng by John Watford and Elizabeth his wif with a warent of hur and hur heires &c. Thomas his son and heire &c. Wherof is content to W. Newnham xxvjs. viijd. and to yong Watford att London vjs. viijd.

The memo appears to record that five marks (£3 6s 8d) of the full price of the sale was unpaid. And that John, Elizabeth and Thomas Watford would cooperate in the normal way with a fine to officially record the sale.

Recording the fine was the last requirement and the very important official record of conveyance to the Catesbys of the lands in Great Creaton and Watford. The fine summarised the lands passed to the Catesbys, and recorded that the Watfords had no further claim on the lands. The manor of Great Creaton included 14 messuages, 8 virgates of land, 70 acres of meadow, 2 acres of wood, and 15 shillings of rent in Great Creaton and Watford. The Watford component included messuages or crofts and 2 virgates and other land with common rights. The larger part of the deal was the manor of Creaton, originally of the Honor of Chokes, acquired by Robert de Watford as far back as 1310. For nearly a century and a half this branch of the de Watford family had lived here. The Catesbys paid 200 marks of silver for the entire package of lands.

After the sale, Nicholas Catesby promptly demised a watermill in Watford to Henry Boteler of Watford for 12 years at 23s annual rent. Thomas Walsh and William Moderey guaranteed Henry's end of the deal, essentially the payment of rents.

William Catesby: 1478–1485

The Catesbys had established their Watford manor late in the fourteenth century when a marriage brought Edmund de Watford's lands, and then, a century later, bolted on the lands of Thomas de Watford. The latter acquisition, in the late fifteenth century, was completed by William and John Catesby. Both were 'of Olthorpe' and sons of Sir William Catesby. The young William was fated to take his place in the annals of England's history after closely linking himself to the king, and with that and other alliances making substantial additions to the Catesby estates.

His father, Sir William, died about 1478. One of the last deeds he signed in 1476 concerned the manor of Yelvertoft, Northants, which his son William also signed, and another in December 1477, granted land in Coventry. He left a large family after two marriages, reputedly as many as 15 children, including William by his first wife and John by his second. John held 'Olthorpe' manor, 6 miles NW of Northampton, and often labelled himself 'of Olthorpe'. Olthorpe was a link from the Catesbys to the Spencer family, which became stronger over the course of the following years, as did the connection between the Spencers and Watford parish.

As a matter of course, manor lords kept track of tenants, rents and other dues owed. For this, they employed stewards or 'collectors' who kept records of the manor lands. These reports provide good insight into the tenants, rents, and other moneys received and paid in a working manor. The lord received rentals from his landholdings, whether small such as for a cottage, medium for pastures or for one or more virgates, or large for the lease of a manor, itself representing a collection of dwellings and farmlands.

The Catesby's steward prepared a report[134] on the Watford manor for the year October 1476 to the end of September 1477. At the top of the first page, John Sabyn is recorded as holding the manor and demesne lands. The tenancies total 8 ¾ virgates, not including anything for the demesne, but allowing for Sulby's virgate and the very recently purchased 2 virgates from the de Watfords called 'Osbournes'.

John Sabyn	manor, demesne, 1 virgate	60s
Henry Naseby	messuage and 1 ¼ virgates	23s 6d
Alexander Wryght	toft and 1 virgate	18s
William Lay	messuage and 1 virgate	16s
Richard Freman	messuage and 1 ½ virgates	27s
John Sabyn & William Wyllis1	½ enclosures {and half land & meadows }	23s 4d
Robert Yoman	1 ½ enclosures {formerly of Nich'as Walsh}	23s 4d
Robert Yoman	farm of the Abbot of Sulby	23s 4d
William Yong	the fishery	2s
Nicholas Kapell	a close and land	2s 7d
John Sabyn – Each	{ 1 enclosure and 1 virgate, }	18s
Jn Naseby and Wm Young – Each	{ lately of Osbournes }	20s

Under the details, total rents received is marked as £11 13s 2d. The actual total of rentals is more; the reason for the difference is not readily apparent. However, the excess may have been John Sabyn's to keep, once he had paid the fixed rent for the manor. The report records fixed rents paid out for lands, including 9d to the Burnebys, 6d to the Abbot of St James, and another 6d for a field called Dyngley. Fixed rents, as the name suggests, were agreed in advance and often remained unchanged for very long periods, even centuries. A good example in this case is the 6d per year payable in the past by the de Watfords and now the Catesbys for the right to hold the de Watford/Catesby manor of the Burneby manor chief lord.

Richard Horn held the Rectory of Watford with its farms for annual rent of £21 6s 8d, although only 40s was received ... but at least the rent of 12 hens was paid from another tenant.

Richard Horne, on account	40s	plus corn, barley, peas and oats given to the landlord
Richard Horne	30s	for a field called Kalender
Richard Horne	10s	for Abbots close
Burneby	6s 8d	
Land in Murcote	4s 2d	
Gosseford mill	12d	
Sub total	£4 11s 10d	
John Sabyn	£7 3s 9d	Fixed rental from tenancy of the manor
Thomas Mettley	44s	plus 'poultry rent' of 12 hens, all for 1½ messuages & 2½ virgates recently purchased from Thomas Mettley
Total receipts	£9 7s 9d and 12 hens	

The steward reported no fines had been received by the Manor Court, which made sure tenants followed the rules of the Manor and could fine tenants if they didn't. In this case, only warnings had been delivered to a few tenants for breaking rules by scattering straw around various dwellings and the 'kytlyn' house. The Steward went on to report payments out.

To Richard Freman	£1 2s 6d	Rent paid for a house and 1 virgate of land lying before the cross and another ¼ yardland. This was the land given to Elizabeth Hill in exchange for her land in Ashby Legers
To George Burneby	9s 3d	For tithes, 6d for Newcroft
	15d	For allowances
Net income	£8 3s 3d and 12 hens	

John Sabyn settled up with Sir William Catesby by paying him 32s 8d, after netting yet more expenses as recorded in an indented bill (see[135] Figure 55), written in Old English. Of John's 'allowances', 12d was because the fishery rent was short-paid, and the last 3d was 'quit' after recognizing John had indeed paid over the 12 hens to the Catesbys.

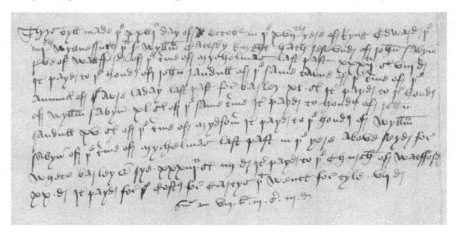

Figure 55: Indented Bill of account, 1477

Thys byll made the xxvj [ti] day of October in the xvij [th] yere of Kyng Edward the iiij [th] [26 Oct 1477] Wyttnessuth that Sir Wyllyam Catesby Knyght hath resevud of John Sabyn reve of Wattfford of the terme of Mychelmas last past xxxij [ti] s viij d [32s 8d] Item payd to the honds of John Randull of the same towne of the terme of the annunciation of owre laday last past for barley xl s [40s] Item payd to the honds of Wyllyam Sabyn xl s [40s] of the same terme Item payd to the honds of John

Randull xv s [15s] of the terme of Mydsomer Item payd to the honds of Wyllyam Sabyn of the terme of Mychelmas last past in the yere above seyd for whete barley & rye xxxiij ^{ti} s iiij d [33s 4d] Item payd to the Church of Watfford xx d [20d] Item payd for costes for cartys that wentt for tyle vij d [7d]

Summa – viij . £ . iij . s . iij . d [£8 3s 3d]

Silsworth and Watford had been home to the Freeman family since at least the middle of the 13th century. During the early and mid 15th century John Freeman accumulated more lands in Silsworth. The Freeman holdings caught the collective eyes of the Catesbys, who saw another opportunity to advance their interests in Watford parish. This time, in 1482, rather than buying they swapped lands to improve their position overall.

Even an exchange of lands was not simple. Richard Freman gave William and John Catesby and Henry Griffin 9 ½ acres of land and rights of pasture for three oxen in Silsworth field. This was probably one of the several small Hill/High fields bordering West Haddon. A few days later, John Freeman the younger gave the same trio 32 acres of land with rights of pasture for four oxen, as well as a meadow and croft in Silsworth, subject to the rent of two hens. In return, the Catesby trio gave John Freman the messuage, croft, land and meadow held by Alexander Wryght in Watford.

Thus, the Fremans swapped their long-held lands in Silsworth for a croft and land in Watford. The Watford land was probably the toft and virgate of land Alexander Wright occupied in the steward's report of 1477. This land was later known as Freeman's Croft and Bradwells Hays, lying immediately north of the manor park in Watford. And the Catesbys extended their holdings in Silsworth, with 32 acres of land with a meadow, which a century later may have become 'Sharrocks' located in the far north of Silsworth.

The same diligent steward of 1477-78 prepared a report on the Catesby manor in Watford for the first year of Richard III, which was 1483–84. The first item was the same 'fixed' rent mentioned in the report for 1477-78, but there was a different rent for the Rectory farm.

Fixed rents received	£11 13s 2d	
Rectory farm rents received	£25 18s 6d	
Total receipts	£37 11s 8d	
Expenses deducted		
Fixed rent paid	5d	For the land called Dyngley
To chaplain of chantry at Assheby	44s	Rents of lands formerly of Thomas Mettley
To Master John	£7 6s 8d	For the profits of his office
Total outgoings	£9 11s 1d	

Balance owed	£28 0s 7d		
Against this the 'accountant' was allowed:			
Paid to Richard Home	10s	For straw bought	
Paid for 7 ¼ virgates in Silworth	22d	Per ancient consignment	
Paid for glazing the steeple window	3s 4d		
Remaining net income	£27 5s 5d		

The reckoning continues with sundry receipts of 26s 11d from the farm and 39s 11d for the sale of wood in Silsworth. Both were paid to Master John in the presence of auditors. Even in the 15th century auditors were checking the books. The manor paid fixed rent for the land called Dyngley (or Dyngole) – the same house and virgate of land given to the husband-to-be of Margaret de Watford in 1348 for her marriage settlement.

Rentals arising from the separate Silsworth manor lands were set out without any total or indication of how the total rentals of £14 19s 6d were dealt with. The first item was 60s received for the land of John Comberford. This is further proof that the Catesbys rented, not owned, the Comberford lands in Silsworth, and then re-let them out again.

From land of John Comberford		60s	
Land lately of Freman		8s	6d
Messuage and 1 virgate		2s	
Messuage and 1 virgate of abbot of St James		12s	1d
Quartern of land of Richard Freman, paid 18d to B			12d
1 acre of John Naseby			6d
Croft called Gardyners, paid 12d to B			1d
2 acres lately of Sabyn his part of a farm in Watford			12d
2 acres lately of Nicholas Catesby			12d
½ year rent rent of the Rectory farm & meadows	£10	13s	4d

Another acquisition by the Catesbys, again by the brothers William and John, was the manor of Long Buckby, next door to Watford. In a seemingly normal deal the Catesbys paid 300 marks of silver for the manor, which among other assets included 13 virgates of land. Later, the truth about the deal is learnt from William Catesby himself.

The Catesby group acquiring lands in Watford had included Sir William Hastynges, but he vanishes from the party. He fell out of favour with the Catesbys as well as others high in the ranks of England's politics. The first Baron Hastings was executed in June 1483, with William Catesby potentially the key in Hastynges' fall from grace. At the same time, partly due to an advantageous marriage to Margaret, the daughter of the 6th Baron Zouche of Harringworth, Catesby rose to be among the highest ranked in the land. William was one of the first councillors to King Richard III, an allegiance that eventually cost Catesby his life.

William Catesby successfully pursued his interests in England through the favour of the king. He expanded the Catesby holdings beyond his inheritance from Sir William by acquiring various manors and lands. During this period, he was often referred to as 'of the king's body'. In one instance, he and the duke of Buckingham purchased the manor of Tylbroke for £200. In another, he secured from the Peytons the grant, release and feoffment of the manor of Welton in Northamptonshire, with warranty against the abbot of Westminster. An agreement dated a month before sets out the circumstances. Two bishops acknowledged a debt of 700 marks due by a Mr Haute to William Catesby. After the execution of the unfortunate Mr Haute among others, the bishops confiscated his property. They gave the manor of Welton to William Catesby and his brother, John of Olthorpe, in full satisfaction of the debt. The bishops gave two other manors in Kent to the former owner of Welton as compensation.

Such fame became attached to William and the other two of King Richard's advisors that William Collingbourne, an opponent of the king and therefore of Catesby, penned a little rhyme about the trio and tacked it onto the door of St Paul's Cathedral in London. The rhyme was one of the 'crimes' that triggered Collingbourne's execution in December, 1484.

The Cat, the Rat and Lovell our dog ruleth all England under a hog.

William Catesby was 'the cat', the 'rat' was Sir Richard Ratcliffe, and 'our dog' was Francis, 9th Baron Lovell. The reference to 'a hog' reflected King Richard's badge of the white boar. Ratcliffe died on the battlefield at Bosworth while Lovell escaped and died in obscurity. According to the victorious new king's own historian, 'King Richard, alone, was killed fighting manfully in the thickest press of his enemies.' He was the last English king killed in battle (see[136] Figure 56).

Figure 56: King Richard III, injured, Battle of Bosworth, 1485

William Catesby was himself executed on the 25 August 1485 as a traitor as ordered by the newly crowned King Henry VII just after the Battle of Bosworth. William had fought with Richard III, who lost the Battle. While a prisoner, and on the very day of his execution at Leicester, William had the courage to write a revealing will. He fondly remembered his wife and children and after admitting some wrongful property purchases, asked that they be returned to their rightful owners. The will appointed as his executor my 'dear and well-beloved wife to whom I have ever been true of my body'. William asked to be buried 'in the church of Saint Leger in Ashby' and his executor to 'restore all lands that I have wrongfully purchased'. What remained from his lands 'bought truly' should go to his children. He went on, 'I doubt not the king will be a good and gracious Lord to them for he is called a fully gracious prince, And I never offended him by my good and free will for god I take my judge I have ever loved him'. William then made a few specific bequests of land or small amounts of money. Among lands returned was Yelvertoft to the executors of 'Nicholas Cowley', and to 'Revell his land in Long Buckby'.

The new king, after literally battling his way to the Crown, wasted no time in firming his hold over England. The patent rolls are packed with hundreds of appointments of those loyal to Henry VII to various positions of authority around the country. On the other hand, the lands held by those on the losing side of the war were confiscated and re-granted by the king to others considered deserving in Henry's eyes, bringing many more entries to the patent rolls.

In five inquisitions held for William Catesby, the first paragraph read almost the same:

> By an Act of the Parliament held at Westminster on 7 November I Henry VII [1485], [William] was attainted and convicted of high treason for his traitorous offences against the king committed on 21 and 22 August of the same year.

William was 'attainted', which means executed. In one of the five inquisitions, the following was tacked on to the first paragraph:

> and all the castles, manors and lands &c whereof he was seized or possessed in fee on 21 August, I Henry VII [1485] are forfeit to the king by pretext of the said Act.

In each of the five county inquisitions, the escheator recorded the lands of which William had been seized on the date of his treason, and who had taken the profits from them since.

> Inquisition[137] 28 June 1486: Manors of Lapworth and Bushwood (Warwick) with rents from Lapworth; Bushwood hamlet included 440 acres, plus 150 acres of Henley in Arden, 240 acres in Beaudesert and 340 acres in Tanworth in Arden; all of which had been given to James Blount, knight.

Inquisition[138] 7 September 1486: In Lapworth (Warwick) 'Bromes Landes', which included 640 acres of lands of various kinds, had been possessed by John Brome since before August 1485. These lands had been the subject of dispute with the forbears of John Brome, so the escheator recorded Brome's heir had *expelled William therefrom, as well he might ... so that the said William was not seized of the premises on the said 22 August'*.

Inquisition[139] 26 November 1487: Yelvertoft (Northampton) which included 440 acres of lands of various kinds, benefits since taken by Messrs. Mermyn and Harper.

Inquisition[140] 14 January 1487: Manors of Bishopston, Ladbroke, Rodburne, lands in Corley, Ascote, Napton, and Hoddenhill including more than 1,139 acres, which were granted to John Rysley, knight.

Inquisition[141] 14 February 1494: (Northampton) 'seized of 300 acres of land and 490 acres of pasture in Syllesworth ... in his demesne as of fee', worth £10 beyond deductions. John Hallighwell had taken possession since August 1486.

One of the first to receive Catesby lands was James Blount, who had found favour of the king 'for services rendered at great bodily risk'. He was granted various manors and lands in Warwickshire, Leicestershire, Derby, and Blisworth in Northamptonshire from two disfavoured former landowners, one being William Catesby.

Sir John Risley, 'the king's servant', was granted lands formerly held by Viscount Lovell and William Catesby, two of the many attainted for high treason. Catesby's contribution to Risley's wealth included the manors of Ladbroke, Rodburn, and Bishopston. Rodburn came with 482 acres of land, and in Ascote there was 340 acres, plus 317 acres with Hodenhill. These three, together with one of the very large pastures in Southamwold, match the description of Rodburn Grange given in 1498, as detailed later.

The remaining Catesbys continued to encounter issues not always directly associated with their notorious relative, William Catesby. In 1488 the manor of Olthorpe was the subject of an internal family dispute over ownership. John Catesby, the son of Sir William Catesby and the brother of the attainted William Catesby, was challenged for ownership of Olthorpe. His challenger was his nephew, John Catesby, son of the attainted William Catesby and Margaret, his wife. The case was recorded in the Patent Rolls, and whereas entries in the Calendars are normally a paragraph long, one of many on a page, the recitation of this case took up more than three full pages of the Calendar.

Complicating matters, the two characters at odds were both named John Catesby and both were sons of a William Catesby. Even more, the deceased John Catesby who had held Olthorpe was uncle to the first mentioned John Catesby, who was uncle to the second John Catesby. What further muddled the case was the lack of a written will of the eldest John when he died in October 1486, without an heir to his estate including Olthorpe.

The middle Uncle John brought seven witnesses, saying his Uncle John (the eldest, and possessor of Olthorpe) meant him to be the heir. Several of the seven stated the eldest John of Olthorpe had given bedside testament to that desire, and his lawyer, Kebyll, and his nephew, yet another John Catesby, a judge, should carry out the transfer of title. (There really was another John Catesby, a Justice of the Common Pleas, who was a first cousin of the middle Uncle John. Justice John died between May 1485 and 1487.) One of the seven who heard the elder John's verbal testament was cousin Robert Catesby, a parson.

The nephew and youngest John, through his guardian – for he was a minor – brought five witnesses to speak for him. One of them backed up the minor John's claim with the story of the elder Uncle John Catesby, who upon 'perceiving' the soon-to-be mother Margaret 'big with child', brought her to Olthorpe to deliver her child there and promised to make the child an heir. Clearly, nephew John's witnesses were insufficient to convince the Chancellor of England, the archbishop of Canterbury.

The judgement issued in June 1488, in short, was in favour of the middle John Catesby, uncle to his challenger. By decree charter written by the Chancellor a month after the hearing, John received the manor of Olthorpe with 100 acres of land and 300 acres of pasture, held by gift of (his uncle) the elder John de Catesby, sergeant-at-arms. Quite some years later, a pardon was issued to (the middle) John Catesby of Olthorpe for alienations and entries relating to the manor and lands of Olthorpe done without the king's permission.

William Catesby's attainder caused his several land holdings in Watford's corner of Northamptonshire to take two separate and distinct paths. The two differently worded grants triggered opposite results. By a quirk of the king's pen, or perhaps by a carefully negotiated concession, the Silsworth manor lands, incorrectly said by the inquisition to be held by William 'in fee', would eventually return to a much reduced Catesby empire.

On the one hand, Sir John Halyghwell, a knight of Cornwall, was granted Catesby's holdings in Silsworth. The date of enrolment of the grant[142] was several years late, possibly to paper over a 'done deed' or to pursue other purposes.

> Grant in tail male to John Halyghwell, knight of the body, of 300 acres of land and 490 acres of pasture in Silesworth, co. Northampton, lately belonging to William Catesby, attainted, to hold by fealty only; with the issues and profits of the said lands from 21 August, I Henry VII [1485]. Ordered by the King.

Three years before the aforementioned 790 acre grant, Halliwell had also been given 40 acres of land and pasture in Silsworth to hold by fealty. It is not clear whether the later grant of 790 acres included the 40 acres given earlier. These 40 acres may be the lands held by the Catesbys by virtue of their exchange with the Freemans only a few years before. For the continuation of the Catesby's Silsworth story, see later pages following.

On the other hand, a different turn of phrase in the Act of Attainder sent Catesby's manor lands in Watford township to new owners, forever lost and never again part of a Catesby manor.

'The king's servant David Owen' was granted[143] in tail male by Letters Patent in 1489 a great many manors including lands in Watford, which were described thus:

> the maner of Watford in Watford *alias* 'Catesby maner' in Watford, 2 tofts, 2 closes and 56 acres of land called 'Watfordislondis', 2 tofts and 2 virgates of land called 'Osbournes' in Watford.

The Catesby's Watford Manor of Owen and Watkyn

David, John, and Henry Owen: 1489–1569

Davey Owen now held the Catesby Manor of Watford. Far from being a 'servant' in the modern sense, David Owen was born about 1459, some say the illegitimate son of Owen Tudor. He fought for Henry Tudor, later King Henry VII, at Bosworth for which he was richly rewarded.

The fortunate servant, 'Davey', received lands in Northamptonshire, Warwickshire and Leicestershire, formerly held by the less fortunate William Catesby, and other lands of the king in Norfolk. The lands in Northants other than Watford included: Peyton's manor in Welton, Gawgis manor in Wolde, Revells manor in Long Buckby, Watford's manor in Great Creaton (lands purchased from the de Watfords), part of the manor of Crick, as well as lands in Crick, Little Creaton, Ferthingston, and Shetlanger.

The Letters Patent had included a short description of the former Catesby holdings in Watford town that carried long into the future. The 'manor of Watford' was a reference to the lands of the several Edmunds de Watford, mostly in the west of Watford. The two smaller named parcels, one 'Osbornes' and the other, 'Watfordislondis', had been bought by Catesbys from the descendants of Thomas de Watford only a few years before.

Despite the Act of Attainder, a few properties within Watford remained occupied by the Catesbys after 1485. Any such lands may have been held by a widow or wife of one of the Catesbys according to her dower or marriage jointure. In any case, such lands were not held in fee and therefore not subject to confiscation when William was attained.

John Owen, the second son of Sir David Owen, knight, by Anne Devereaux, became David's heir after his eldest son died without an heir. John married Elizabeth, daughter of Richard Catesby of Ashby Legers. Their son, Henry Owen, plays a role in the ongoing story of the Catesby Manor in Watford. The Owens leased the 'capital messuage and land with a close called Watfordes close' to John Watkyn of Watford in 1543 for a 21 year term.

John, William, and Giffard Watkyn: 1569–1631

In the 11th year of Queen Elizabeth, the Catesby manor of Watford passed from the Owens into the hands of John Watkyn. John, not a Watford native, in 1530 had established himself in the parish at the age of 30. John came to hold the Catesby manor of Watford following a process that began in an unusual way.

First, in February 1569, Henry and Thomas Owen, seized in fee simple of the manor, sold the lands to Edward Andrewes of West Haddon for £105. The deal included a condition allowing Thomas and Henry to buy back the manor for the same amount in June of the same year. If they did not buy back the manor, then Edward would pay Thomas and Henry another £120 to keep the manor. The agreement also specified that Thomas and Henry would sell the premises to anyone named by Edward. It seems probable Thomas and Henry brought Edward Andrews into the deal as someone with local knowledge and broad influence in order to procure an advantageous sale to a third party. With two more documents also dated February, Thomas and Henry each appointed an attorney to grant possession, and confirmed he was a grandson or relative of David Owen. A Recovery[144] at the court spelt out the same extent of the manor as did the Final Concorde, which followed in May.

Second, on 2nd May 1569 the trio of Edward, Thomas, and Henry sold[145] for £266 the manor of Watford in the occupation of John Watkyn, to the same John Watkyn of Watford. The manor was described as:

those 3 messuages or tenements, 9 ¾ yardlands and all appurtenances scitnat lying and being in the towne and fyelds of Watford now being in the severall tenures & occupations of the said John Watkyns & of Henry Coxe John Welche & George Cosford

And also all the howses rooms edifices buyldynge tofts orchards gardyns dosshowses medowes leasnes pastures wooded underwoodde together with the grounde & soyle of the woodde and underwoodde moores marshes wastegrounde waters pooles fyshing courte seete liberties rente revercons comodities emoluments hereditaments whatsoever they be scitnat lying & being or to be within the towne fylde parysshe or hamlet of Watford ... and all the letters patente deeds evidences charters script of fine exemplifications records leases

And John was to have and hold the manor forever by right from the chief lords of the knight's fee of Watford (the Burnebys) at the cost of rent and other services as agreed long ago. Edward, Thomas, and Henry would, before next June 24th, make a fine in the form of the law to be levied of John Watkyn of the premises sold. The agreement and Final Concorde[146] then spelt out what the manor encompassed:

3 messuages, 6 tofts, 4 gardens, 300 acres of land, 100 acres of meadow, 200 acres of pasture, 4 acres of wood and 10 acres of brush and heath [a total of 614 acres]

The sellers gave John their warranty for the premises sold, holding him harmless against any of a long list of potential claims against him. Therefore, John should have uninterrupted and peaceful future use and possession of the premises. The warranty carefully listed all possible exceptions to the clear and free use of the manor. One was the rents and service remaining payable by John to the chief lord of the fee. Another was the rents due by John the tenant under the sellers' lease of all the premises to John Watkyn, which presumably meant John owed rent to himself. Finally, there were the important fixed rents for any of the manor lands not held of the manor lord but rented in from someone else. The manor's extent of 9 ¾ yardlands may tie in to the Steward's report of September 1477, which recorded rents on 8 ¾ yardlands, plus by this time another net 1 virgate after swapping 1 ½ virgates for the 2 ½ formerly held by Thomas Mettley.

Third and fourth, two separate agreements dated 13th of May 1569 were signed. In one, Thomas Owen and Henry Owen provided a recognisance for £500, sealed before a Justice of the Common Pleas, and their warranties. These assured the full performance of the bargain and sale of the manor of Watford as set out in the agreement of May 2, John's uninterrupted use of the premises, and no claims against John emanating from the sellers. If all went well, the recognisance would be null and void.

A key step in the process for John Watkyn in 1570 was to obtain an exemplification (see[147] Figure 57) of a key document written in 1495 – partly in Latin and partly in English. The Petition for Restitution included the terms of the original grant of lands in 1485, the repeal of the Act of Attainder, and the restitution of lands to George Catesby in 1495. Among other things, the restitution provided that any grant by the king's letters patent of lands formerly held by William Catesby to someone else could not be reversed, unless the beneficiary and holder of the lands died without male heirs. So John Watkyn succeeded in confirming that the Catesbys had no right to any claim over the lands, because the original grantee after the Act of Attainder, David Owen, had male heirs who therefore lawfully and currently held title to the lands.

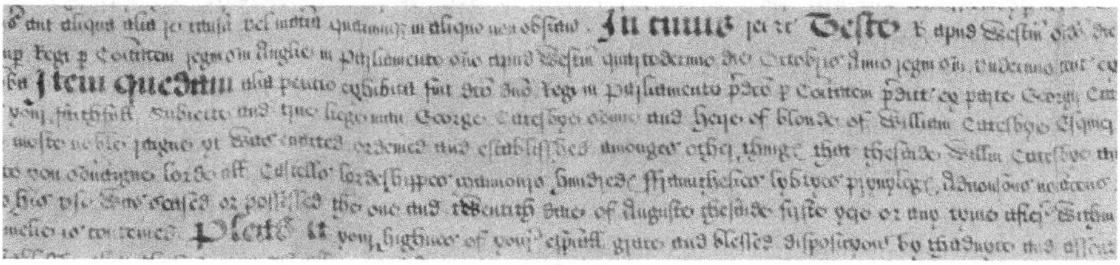

Figure 57: Extract from Exemplification of Petition for Restitution

At a court hearing,[148] John Watkin 'acknowledged that he held of the lord of Burneby manor 3 homesteads, 9 ¾ virgates of land, which he purchased from Thomas Owen & Henry Owen, by fealty, suit of court and annual rent at Michaelmas of 9d'. That appears to represent a rather large increase in rent of 3d, or 50%. John also acknowledged that he held of the lord 1 messuage and 2 virgates purchased from Thomas Haddon, by fealty, suit of court and 3d annual rent. This reveals that John had brought back into the family, so to speak, the 120 acres previously sold by the Catesbys to Thomas Haddon in 1533. That deal turns up in the pages to come.

From John Watkyn, who died and was buried at Watford in November 1583, the manor naturally passed to his eldest son, William Watkyn. John Watkin had lived in Watford with his wife Elizabeth and sons William, Giffard, Brian, and Thomas. One of Gifford's sons, John, was married twice, first to Katherine Cowley and then to Bridgett Fulnetby. The younger John and Bridgett maintained an interest in Watford lands, as will be seen. Another of Gifford's sons, also Gifford, born 1598 at Watford, was an another export by Watford to the New World – he died in Virginia in 1637.

In his will, John senior left cash bequests of £1,060 to his younger sons. His real estate had already been settled on William – John knew his holdings would descend to his heir by law.

After holding the manor for only 13 years, William Watkin died in February 1597, and his inquisition reported his 15-year-old son, Giffard, as his heir. Nine months later, William's brother, Brian, appeared before the Court of Wards and Liveries and made fine on behalf of his young nephew, Giffard. Brian provided the usual covenants not to undervalue the manor and agreed neither he nor Giffard would molest or disturb the manor's tenants. The extent of lands declared in the Court was precisely as found in William's inquisition, adding only that the annual value was £4. In the same month, writ of Livery[149] of the Catesby manor of Watford was delivered to Giffard Watkin, who by then had 'reached his full age of 16 years'.

The holdings inherited by Giffard Watkyn according to his father's inquisition were almost the same as those granted by Patent of 1489: *'manor of Watford in Watford, otherwise called Catesbie manor in Watford afsd with appurts and of 2 tofts, 2 closes & 26 acres of land called 'Watfordes Landes' and 2 tofts, 2 virgates of land called Osbornes in Watford afsd with appurts'*. The only difference was 'Watford's Lands', which had shrunk to 26 acres from 56. Worthy of note is the word 'and' inserted after the mention of the Catesby manor and before the two individual holdings. This distinguished between the manor lands on the one hand and the separate two closes and two virgates on the other. The 'loss' of 30 acres may have been caused by the Reformation, when a new owner nominated by the king rented that land to someone else.

Margery, William Watkin's widow, married again to Abraham Bowne and they lived in Margery's manor house at Boylonde. After reaching the age of 21, Giffard leased the Manor from Abraham, which he held in right of his wife. The manor included the capital messuage, 8 yardlands and all attached lands and tenements, but excluded all lands and tenements leased to them by the Rt Hon Robert Lord Spencer of Wormeleighton. Probably to clear any possible legal issues, ten days beforehand Gifford declared he had no claim on any profits and rents whatsoever previously received by Abraham and Margery. That covered any homesteads and lands in Watford, then occupied by John Naseby, George Cosford, Robert Haddock and Richard Smyth. The duration of the lease was 40 years or as long as Abraham and Margery should live, paying an annual rent of £50. Another exclusion from the lease, other than certain of Spencer's lands, was 1 ¾ yardlands originally held by Gifford's father and grandfather. These lands were likely located somewhere not contiguous with the grounds in west Watford and its manor house on Boylonde. They feature in later deeds.

Giffard Watkin and Elizabeth Ireton married in April 1608, and they became the last occupants of the old de Watford manor house at what became the modern-day Watford Gap in the western corner of the parish. As her marriage settlement Giffard gave her half the manor, which comprised the capital manor house and 9 ¾ yardlands. After living in the manor house for over 20 years, the Watkyns moved to neighbouring Long Buckby, where Elizabeth died – she was buried at Watford in 1634. Gifford died a year later at his home in Long Buckby, where he was buried. In his will, Giffard named several relatives, but there was no mention of any remaining holdings in Watford.

George Clerke bought[150] the Catesby manor from Giffard Watkin in 1631 for £460. Giffard gave warranty of himself, his father William, and John, his grandfather. According to the Final Concorde the manor of Watford encompassed one messuage, one cottage, three tofts, two gardens, 200 acres of land, 80 acres of meadow, 100 acres of pasture, 4 acres of woods, 40 acres of gorse and heath, and tithes with appurtenances in Watford. The sum of 424 acres is 190 less than the 614 acres purchased by Giffard's grandfather in 1569.

Before the sale to George Clerke, Giffard sold 1 ¾ yardlands, which appears to be the difference between the 9 ¾ yardlands inherited by the Watkyns and the 8 yardlands he leased out. For £300, William Naseby bought a homestead with 1 yardland in the Netherend Field of Watford and ¼ yardland in the Overende Field in Watford, or 50 acres of land. John Cattell paid £140 for a homestead and ½ a yardland, excluding a cottage occupied by John Rogers, or 41 acres. Cattell's land had been carved out of Giffard's inheritance of the whole manor descended from his father and grandfather. Giffard was therefore obliged to create a specific 'writing' as documentary evidence for Cattell that his lands had been properly separated from the manor.

The Catesby manor of de Watford lands seem to be located mostly in the west of the parish – partly those in the triangle southwest of the Watling Street, formed by the boundary with Ashby St Ledgers and Watling Street itself. This included the Manor House of Edmund de Watford later known as the Watford Gap, and the Boylonde Lordship including the 33 acres of Sulby Abbey. The other major part was the neighbouring lands just northeast of Watling Street. Another, smaller, parcel of the manor was in the northeast of Watford town.

The following is a reconstruction of the Catesby's Watford manor demonstrating the 637 acres of the earlier sale and 460 acres as declared in the later sale of the manor.

Lands	Acres	
The Triange lands (southwest of the Streete)	200	
Boyland lordship, including the Watford Gap		68
Boyland and Boyland meadow, later, the Railway lands		33
Boyland, later known as Larke and Mott		31
Burnhams and Lower Closes		68
Watford's West (northeast of the Streete)	260	
Middleton & Cringles		102
Overende		88
Cowpen/Cowley		70
Other de Watford lands	177	
Radmore field and meadow		86
Other Watford lands, 1 ¾ yardlands later sold		91

These 637 acres encompass 12 virgates as held in the sixteenth century. That includes 10 of Edmund de Watford's original 14 virgates, less the 4 virgates carved off for various de Watford descendants in the 14th century, plus 2 held by Thomas de Watford.

The several fields totalling nearly 70 acres known in modern times as Cowleys or Cowpen, are understood to be the two virgates of the descendants of Thomas de Watford, later known as Osbornes. The parcels known as Watfords Lands could be the closes totalling 50 acres at the western end of the Netherend field that were occupied by Lee and Gilbert as late as 1771.

The Catesby's Manors of Silsworth

Following the execution of William Catesby in 1485, the Catesbys lost forever their manor lands in Watford township. But the king's grant of their Silsworth lands after 1485 took a different tack. As a result, the rules laid down in 1495 for recovery of Catesby's lands allowed William's son the opportunity to once more hold the Silsworth manor lands. However, even that was lost to the Catesbys a little over a century later.

George and Sir Richard Catesby: 1495–1568

Ten years elapsed before the attainted William's son and heir, George Catesby, began the process of recovering some of the lost family holdings. This was an ambitious undertaking effectively requiring that an Act of Parliament be torn up. George needed help, including money, so he and his father-in-law, Richard Empson, borrowed 200 marks from John Spencer and his wife, Jane. They repaid most of the loan over the next five years.

In 1495, George petitioned the king in parliament requesting the 1485 Act of Attainder against his father be overturned. The young George and his worldlier father-in-law won that battle and the petition was granted – for some, but not all, of his former lands. For future proof of his newfound rights, George requested and obtained an endorsed certification of the new 1495 Act. This reversed the ten-year-old Act of Attainder making it null and void, but with an important exception – any grants already made by the king's letters patent would stand good if the grantee had an heir. On the other hand, any of Catesby's forfeited lands still held by the king because they had not been granted by license to another person could also be returned to George.

As an intervening measure, a threesome comprising the bishop of Ely, Richard Empson, and John Spencer were delegated to hold George's returned lands. From the income generated the trio should pay rent of £100 annually to the Crown for 7 years. George secured his right to 'enter' his re-found inheritance by obtaining license from the king to do so, without needing a 'proof of age' hearing. George had no proof of age on record – the inquisitions held for his father had no need to establish George's age, because he was disinherited at the time.

William Catesby's widow, Margaret, died in October 1494, and according to her inquisitions she was survived by her son and heir, George Catesby, aged 22. Margaret's father-in-law, Sir William, had given a healthy collection of lands to Margaret and William jointly, probably as a marriage settlement. Because the lands were not held in fee exclusively by William, they were not stripped from Margaret in 1485. She held the manor of Willicote in Glos, a fee-farm in Blysworth Northants, the manor of Wellesburn in Warw, and in Oxon, the manors of Walcote, Ipwell, and Chestelton. Margaret's inquisitions were held a few months before the Act to reverse the forfeiture of many of William's properties. When Margaret died, the manors fell into the king's hands. Under terms of the Act of 1495 the properties then descended from the king to George because they had not otherwise been granted by the king to anyone else. Many of these properties remained with the Catesbys and turn up again in later marriage settlements.

Sir John Halyghwell had been the favoured grantee of Catesby's Silsworth lands. On the strength of George's paperwork in 1495, Sir John demised and released all his right to 'certain lands in Silsworth' to George Catesby, son and heir of William Catesby. The paperwork refers to 300 acres of land and 490 acres of pasture in Silsworth as reported in 1494 by the second of William Catesby's two Northampton inquisitions. However, the quantification of the lands by the 1494 inquisition and the grant a year later do not quite reflect reality.

According to one historical record, the inquisition said the Catesby estate in Silsworth consisted of 300 acres of arable land and 400 acres of pasture … not clear why the 490 acres was rounded down to 400. A modern online report states, 'by 1485 the land of Silsworth was said to consist of 300 acres arable and 490 acres pasture' … not clear why the report implies the lands described by the inquisition encompass all of Silsworth. Neither description includes meadow.

Any inaccuracies introduced by the 1494 inquisition may be attributable to Richard Empson, who was known as 'one of the great oppressors in the reign of Henry VII', and a spy and key fundraiser for the king. Empson personally delivered the IPM for Silsworth to the Treasury. During its preparation, he may have been aware of the potential advantage to George Catesby, his son-in-law, of an official record overstating the Catesby holdings in Silsworth. Furthermore, William Catesby, by his own hand later admitted to some unfair acquisitions of certain premises.

Catesby cannot have directly 'held' most of Silsworth in fee, when two other manors each held a share of the township. This can be proven quite convincingly. The grantee of the supposed 790 acres recorded by the inquisition, Sir John Halyghwell, had at virtually the same time, separately leased from the Comberfords *their* holding of Silsworth lands. These were the former Parles lands and cannot have been held in fee simultaneously by the Catesbys. Similarly, the Burneby manor was found to hold at least 300 acres in Silsworth by special inquisition in the early 1500s. That large parcel was not 'bought' by the Catesbys until the late 1500s and therefore also cannot have been held in fee by the Catesbys in the late 1400s.

The Catesbys' claimed 790 acres in Silsworth, if accurate in area, probably consisted of leased lands, including for example the 'ancient consignment' of 7 ¼ virgates claimed in the Catesby steward's report. For example, 390 acres of Burneby manor lands, about 320 acres of the Comberford manor, plus 150 of Cooksfield and Viccars, less 70 acres of meadow (Hill 50, and 20 of Cooks, Viccars, & Middlefield). Otherwise put: the entire 915 acres of Silsworth, less 55 acres of Northingworth and 70 acres of meadow.

About a year after the passage of the 1495 Act of restitution, George Catesby and his wife Elizabeth obtained a Letter of Attorney that returned to them lands in West Haddon, Northampton, Silsworth, Gretton, and Houghton in Leicestershire. As a necessary first step in obtaining the grant back to himself, George gave two clerics all his lands in Silsworth. The lands were then officially given back to George from the same two clerics.

In yet another dispute over lands, trouble with the Catesby's part of the manor of Rodburn, called Rodburn Grange, caught up with them in 1498. The disputing parties came before the king and after a recitation of the agreed facts, and with a fine of £10, the king pardoned all the purchases, alienations, and entries made without his license. The court had been directed back to 1415, when the abbot of the convent of St Mary in Combe, who held the lands, let them out to Emma Catesby and John, her elder son and the father of Sir William Catesby. But there was a catch in the lease – should the rent be unpaid for six weeks, the abbot could re-enter the premises. Sir William Catesby, who inherited the property from Emma through John, carelessly left the rent unpaid for a year and so the abbot grabbed the property back. Sir William then went and built dykes at his own cost to accurately distinguish between the abbot's land and the adjoining land of Sir William's son, William Catesby.

Evidently this action had softened the abbot's position. On the 4th October 1481, he allowed a new lease of the lands to William Catesby, the son. Even so, other than raising the rent the wise abbot tagged another condition onto the lease. He could seize William junior's own Rodburn lands if rent on the abbot's Rodburn lands fell behind. Before closing the case, the court gave seisin of the premises to William, the son.

The abbot's new lease as granted to William jnr in 1481, was acknowledged by the king many years later. On the same day as the new lease was granted, the king issued a letter of attorney authorising the abbot to grant John Spencer seisin of the manor called Rodburn Grange, with lands and tenements in Rodburn, Hodenhulle, and Ascote. This transaction may have been the beginning of the Spencer family's special interest in the parish of Rodburn, which continued long into the future. Spencer may have discovered, seventeen years after obtaining seisin, that the appropriate licenses had not been obtained from the king. Acting on a warranty he almost certainly obtained in 1481 to ensure the effectiveness of the seisin, he required the Catesbys to legalise the transactions.

George Catesby's life ended on 27 November 1505, only a decade after the restitution of his lands. An escheator recorded his next heir to be his son, William, aged seven. Another said William's age was two or three in 1506 – that was more likely the age of William's younger brother, Richard, who plays an important role later on. All of the inquisitions noted:

At the Parliament held at Westminster on the 14 October 11 Henry VII [1495] it was ordained and enacted that the Act of attainder against William Catesby and his heirs should be of none effect, and George Catesby, his son and heir, should be restored and rehabilitated and have all the manors &c forfeited by the Act as fully as if it had never been passed.

The inquisitions held for George reported his extensive holdings, even after the loss of many lands stripped away after William Catesby's execution:

Inquisition[151] 26 January 1506: Northampton, Manor of Olthorpe, including 740 acres; John Catesby held the manor by virtue of a sale for £200 to him by William Catesby (the attainted brother of Ashby Leger) to hold for William's heirs. After the Act of 1495 the manor descended to George Catesby. Only one year after William's death in 1485, John Catesby also died. The manor had been held since then by a 'certain' John Catesby of Olthorpe.

Inquisition[152] 21 April 1506: Northampton, Manors of Gretton, Ashby Leger and lands in Silsworth. Gretton was held by George as a gift from Sir Richard Empson, father of Elizabeth Empson upon her marriage to George on 10 May 1496, and included 1280 acres of land, meadow and pasture and 1000 acres of wood. The manor of Ashby Leger included 572 acres held of the king and land in Yelvertoft of the abbot of Sulby by fealty and 3s rent. Northampton and West Haddon included 27 messuages, 10 gardens, 370 acres held as fee farm of Northampton worth £10 and of the king of the duchy of Lancaster worth £5 3s 4d. Last and not least, this inquisition reported 100 acres land and 200 acres pasture and 6s rent in Silsworth, worth £7, held of the abbot of St James by Northampton by fealty and 3s 4d rent yearly.

Inquisitions[153] 21 May 1506, 28 April 1506, 20 April 1506, 28 April 1506, 4 May 1506: Manor of Houghton, Leics with 480 acres held by the same marriage contract; Manors of Walcote, Ippewell, and Chestelton, Oxon, with 1270 acres, 730 acres, 1374 acres, all held of the king, and per his will all should go to his wife and family and brothers for their upkeep and the marriage of his sister Elizabeth; Manors of Willicote and Aliscote, Glos, including 812 acres held of the abbot of Evesham and 494 acres held of the abbot of Tewkesbury; in Warwick the manors of Lapworth, Bushwood, Bromesland and Kingswood, the first two included 1573 acres and the latter two, 792 acres, held of the king, the bishop of Worcester, and lands in Henley, Belledeserte, Wellesburn, Toneworth, summing to 1726 acres; and lastly the manors of Wareslegh and Bremerton in Worcs with 147 acres.

George Catesby's children, including his eventual heir, were minors at the time of his death. John Spencer had been knighted and became a guardian to the Catesby heirs – the grandchildren of William Catesby, one of King Richard's three favourites. The grandchildren included William, who died young in October of 1517, and Richard, eventually Sir Richard Catesby. Richard ultimately succeeded to the Catesby estates at Legers Ashby, Silsworth and elsewhere. He also did no harm to his station in life when he married Dorothy, the youngest daughter of Sir John Spencer.

Robert Gudale, abbot of St Mary's Sulby, in 1507, issued a receipt to Elizabeth, late the wife of George Catesby for 13s 4d rent and a 3s fine. This was for one very small part of the Catesby's holdings – a messuage in Watford and the 10 acre Cow Meadow, sitting in the far NE corner of Watford.

Figure 58: Althorpe, Home of the Spencers for 500 years

The Catesbys sold 'Oldthorpe' to the Spencers for £800 in 1508. The manor included 3 messuages, 2 mills, 1,000 acres of land, 10 acres of land covered with water, 21 acres of meadow, 60 acres of pasture, 20 acres of wood, and 10 shillings rent. The estate became known as 'Althorpe' and has remained in the family for more than 500 years (see[154] Figure 58).

The present stately home was built some time after 1508. One component of the Spencer development was allowed as follows:[155]

John Spencer of Olthorp. Licence to impark lands (extent given) in Olthorp and Wykehamond, Northt., and grant of free warren in all his lands and several fishery and vivary in all his waters in Olthorp, Brynketon Magna, Wykehamond, and Bodyngton Superior, Northt.; and licence to castellate the manors of Olthorp, Northt., and Wormeleighton, Warw.

A close and land called 'Lez Fythers' in Silsworth and a toft and croft in Watford were granted by William Harrison, a cleric. Four men received seisin in trust for Richard Catesby, son of George Catesby, because he was not yet of full age.

After the death of Sir John Risley in 1512 with no male heir, in accordance with the 1495 Act his lands returned to the care of the Catesbys. In 1515, John Spencer and an associate were issued a bond of £300 by the second husband of Joan, formerly the widow of Sir John Risley. This was to assure Joan would stand by the award of an arbitrator concerning her claim for dower rights in the lands previously held by her husband, and before that, by William Catesby. Lady Joan succeeded to some extent; in 1528 she recovered 40 marks rent of the dower lands in exchange for handing over all her rights in the lands to the Catesbys.

The Steward of Ashby Ledger filed a report on his disbursements in 1520, which was while the Catesby estates were in wardship, before Richard turned 21. One payment was to the abbot of St James near Northampton – £15 for five years for a farm in Silsworth. One wonders at the coincidence of the Comberford lands in Silsworth being leased at the same £3 per annum. Another payment was for 'diverse fifteenths', being taxes for the lordships of Ashby Ledger, Silsworth, Welton, Boylond, and Welicote – £11 7s 2d. While Silsworth was a 'town' in the north of Watford parish, 'Boylond' was a farm in the west of Watford township that had been the core holding of the de Watford family.

Watford parish was no less affected than others in the country when the King decided to make radical changes. From 1536, King Henry VIII carried out a plan to dissolve the Catholic monasteries, priories, convents and friaries in England, Wales, and Ireland and appropriated their income. Henry spearheaded the English attack on Catholicism that swept across Europe. The Catholic institutions held significant portions of landed wealth, which Henry's government desired, and their occupants were seen as lax, comfortably worldly, and wasteful.

One of the abbeys about to be closed was St Andrews of Northampton. The prior, facing the dire consequences of losing home and income, wrote a long and impassioned plea to the king. In a roundabout way he requested maintenance for the Priory's monks, about to be cast out onto the street. But not before admitting to 'many negligences, enormities and abuses of long time by us'. He was clever enough to know that complaining would probably result in a nasty backlash, so instead went to great length to declare how badly behaved he and his 11 followers had been and how they had wasted the priory's resources. He went on:

> *We revolving daily & continually pondering in our sorrowful hearts and thereby persevering the bottomless gulf of everlasting fire ready to devour us if persisting in this state of living ... do crave of your highness of your abundant mercy to grant unto us most grievous offenders against God ... your most gracious pardon*

The Abbey of Sulby was another facing extinction. Watford and Silsworth contributed £1 14s 6d towards the abbey's £305 income. This was 13s 4d from the 10 acre Cow Meadow in the north east of Watford, 14d for a cottage, and 20s from the 33 acre tenement sometimes described as 1 virgate in the far west corner of Watford, land held originally by the de Watford manor and now, the Catesby manor.

St Andrews Priory had been given 4 virgates by Alan de Watford. The priory's gross income of £334 included rent of 16s from this holding in Silsworth. All of the priory's lands were taken by the King himself rather than allowing the rents to be added to government revenues.

The lands of St Andrews in Silsworth were occupied by the Catesbys from the late medieval age through into early modern times. In 1551, the king's bailiff of the possessions of the late priory issued a receipt for 16s to Sir Richard Catesby for a year's rent paid for lands in Silsworth. The same 16s annual rent was regularly declared payable for part of the Burneby's fee-farm, a good indication that Athelina's quarter of the manor had held the 4 virgates.

Elizabeth Catesby, nee Empson, George's widow, lived much longer than he did. She re-married, her second husband being Sir Thomas Lucy. Her third husband was Richard Verney of London. In 1533, Elizabeth Verney and her husband sold 120½ acres in Watford 'for evermore' to Thomas Haddon, late of West Haddon. The holding included 7 measured closes and several houses and buildings. Elizabeth must have held a right to these lands under a dower or jointure, because William Catesby's own closes and lands had been stripped from the family. The lands sold were certified clear of all encumbrances such as mortgages, except for the rents and services due to the chief lord of the manor. The price for the entire precisely measured parcel was £140, of which £120 had been paid 'in hand', with the residue of £20, due on the 1st August following.

The premises Elizabeth sold included 'Boyelonde' in Watford, sometimes known as a 'lordship' in its own right. A meadow of that name had been a part of the holdings of Edmund de Watford in 1361. Decades later, when these lands were bought back into a Watford lordship by John Watkin, they were described simply as a messuage with 2 virgates.

The 'Boyelonde' name had a long life and can be identified as a number of fields at the western corner of the parish, stretching west from Watling Street across both sides of the modern railway. Boylonde included the manor house, originally the de Watford manor. Late in the 17th century the premises became a thriving Inn, known as the 'Watford Gap'. The Inn morphed into the steading of the Payne family who farmed 166 acres of the 'Watford Triangle'. In the present day, the Watford Gap is no more than a set of abandoned farm buildings at the western end of Watford, near Kilsby, a short distance northwest along the A5 from the modern Watford Gap M1 motorway services stop. Technically, when a well-known historian reported[156] 'Catesby an inclosed Manor with no house', he was correct. He wrote this around 1720, and by then the old de Watford family manor house, in medieval times a 'capital messuage', had long since ceased to be a manor house. The Catesbys had chosen to live in Ashby Legers.

Nearly ten years later (1542), for £47 Richard Catesby of Ashby Legers sold more land in Watford to Henry Wryght of Welton. £40 was paid upon sealing and £7 was due by Christmas. That was for two crofts, each with one yardland, two more crofts, and annual rents of 8s. The agreement then carefully excluded lands previously sold, being grounds called Boylonde. The lands were quit of all charges except the title of dower of his wife, at that time Elizabeth, and the chief rents and services due to the chief lord of the fee. The whole package held the yearly value of 47s 7d.

Once again, Catesby is a little puzzling. Apparently, he held these lands 60 years after his grandfather had been stripped of his Watford town manor. The evidence is George Catesby's widow held the lands under a jointure. As to which lands? The 2 virgates might be those formerly of Thomas de Watford. Or, the 2 virgates at the eastern end of 'Watford's Triangle', directly bordering the carefully excluded Boylonde lordship at the western end. Both parcels – one of Thomas de Watford and the other east of Boylond – contain just under 70 acres.

In 1546 Sir Richard leased for 41 years a Silsworth farm to Thomas Spencer, gentleman. Spencer paid Catesby £200 upon signing and agreed annual rents of 32 shillings for the first 10 years and £21 12s yearly thereafter. The premises were 'all that his pasture and field commonly called Silsworth'. The rent amount verifies the lands were the 320 acres of a Catesby Silsworth manor. In turn, this suggests the lease included the 170 acres of Silsworth Field, which swings across Silsworth's southwest boundary with Watford town, plus some 150 acres of The Oad Ground and Hill Meadow, both just north of Silsworth Field.

Sir Richard Catesby married three times. By his first wife, Dorothy Spencer, he had six children, of whom William was the eldest surviving. By his second wife, Elizabeth Astell, he had five more children, and by his last wife, Elizabeth Bray, he had a daughter. Known for his desire to improve his financial circumstances, he made the best of his right to grant or refuse his son in marriage. His eldest son and heir was William and for 630 marks Richard 'sold' his son to be married to Katherine Willington. But William, and possibly Katherine as well, was under age, so the marriage was 'frustrated' and could not be completed. Eventually the event took place a second time three years later, in 1544. Mixed blessings … young William died before his father, Sir Richard, but left a son, also William, as Sir Richard's grandson and heir.

Not much time went by before Sir Richard passed in March of 1553. At the time, his grandson and heir, William Catesby, was days short of his sixth birthday. Sir Richard was seized of the manors of Gretton, West Haddon, Silsworth and Ashby Leger. In addition, Sir Richard had granted William Lucie for the use of himself then his son and heir, William Catesby, upon his marriage to Kathryn Willington, lands and manors in Radburne, Ladbroke, Cheslington, and Warsley. The young grandson William became a ward of the king and consequently, the Court of Wards. The Court placed the minor, William, in the care of Sir Robert Throckmorton. For his trouble, Sir Robert was granted 40 marks per year from income derived at the Catesby seat, Ashby Legers. He was also granted rights to the marriage of William. No surprise when William married Anne Throckmorton, a daughter of Sir Robert, at Ashby St Legers on 9 June 1566, thus bringing the benefits of the Catesby estates to his daughter.

Sir William, Robert, and Robert Catesby: 1568–1625

William and his son Robert were the last of the Catesby estate lords. Their strict adherence to the Catholic faith would eventually be their undoing, and Robert's rebellion left a permanent stain on his family's name with its dark connection to events at England's Parliament. Sir William found the necessity to make many arrangements moving around the benefits of his lands, which usually featured the two central manors of Ashby Legers and Silsworth.

When his grandfather died William was a minor. At the appropriate time, June 1568, an escheator armed himself with a commission and conducted an inquisition to prove the king's ward had accomplished the full age of 21 in March of that year. A license to enter his lands followed. Queen Elizabeth granted William ceremonial livery which delivered possession of the lands descending to him from grandfather Sir Richard.

Manor of Gretton, 70 messuages, 2,400 acres land, meadow, pasture, wood

Manor of Ashby Ledgers, 12 messuages, 550 acres land, meadow, pasture, wood

Manor of Silsworth, 100 acres land and 200 acres pasture, and 6s rent

Manor of West Haddon, 27 messuages, 260 acres land

Manors of Lapworth, Bramham, Brisshophampton, Wellesbone, Walcot

Manors of Wilcot and Bushwood, Lordship of Rodborne, and Lapworth Park

Manors of Ludbroke, Chestlington, Waresley, Allescote, and a house in Warwick town

Catesby's manor of Silsworth, measured without meadow, was 'held of the Queen by fealty and 3s 10d rent' and was said to be worth £21 12s yearly. That was precisely the rental value of the lands leased to the Spencers. Altogether, William's inheritance was worth a total of £319 annually. Notably, the Catesbys' holdings in Watford parish consisted only of lands in Silsworth, with none in Watford township.

Three years after his marriage, and a year after reaching majority, Sir Robert Throckmorton and his protégé agreed terms for William's marriage settlement. Sir Robert would hand over 300 marks (£200) to William Catesby. For his part William made over five manors to Thomas Throckmorton, Thomas Tresham and two others, with instructions on their future uses. At the time, three of the five manors were held by Dame Elizabeth Catesby, the widow of grandfather Sir Richard, as her marriage settlement. First, the manors of Ashby Legers and Silsworth were to the use of William and Anne during the lifetime of Dame Elizabeth, and after her decease, they were to the use of William and his heirs, and if William had no heirs then to William's five uncles, George, Richard, Edmund, Edward and John Catesby. Second, the manors of Bushwood, part of the manor of Radburne, and the manor of 'Wyllycotes', except for Lapworth Park, was to the use of William alone during the life of Dame Elizabeth Catesby, and after her decease to the use of William, and after William's decease to the use of Anne during her lifetime for her jointure. After Anne's death, the premises should be to the uses specified in William's will, which included the right to make 21-year leases, and then, to the use of William's heirs, again with William's uncles last in line if William had no heirs.

Sir William and Anne were prominent recusant Catholics. In common with the majority of country gentry throughout England who resided at their estates disconnected from Queen Elizabeth's court, he threw in his lot with the many Catholics and suffered the consequences. William endured years of imprisonment for his faith, and in 1581 was tried in the Star Chamber alongside William Vaux, 3rd Baron Vaux of Harrowden, and his brother-in-law Sir Thomas Tresham, for harbouring the Jesuit Edmund Campion. On another occasion he suffered for the crime of not attending his parish church.

For whatever reason, but likely related to his financial difficulties, in 1582 Sir William desired to clarify the intentions of the leases he had made following his marriage settlement. There were three leases written to his trusted friends William Chibnall, Morris Myles, Thomas Ichens, William Brooks, and John Popson. One lease, to William Chibnall, was for the core family manor of Ashby Legers. The second lease was to Chibnall and John Popson for the manor and lands specified in the jointure for his mother, Kathryn Throckmorton, after her decease. The third, to Myles, Brookes, and Ichens, granted the manors and lands now assigned to Sir William's wife, Dame Anne Catesby (nee Throckmorton), after her death. Sir William's intentions were, first, the income from the leases should be for his own use – no surprise there. Second, after Sir William's decease, the income should be for purposes specified in his last will and testament including debts, legacies, and for the preferment of his daughters in marriage. Third, to the use and behoof of his son and heir Robert Catesby until he attained the age of 21, and upon reaching that age, he should have the lands delivered to him. Last, Sir William appointed his loving friend Sir Thomas Tresham and others to make account and take bonds to ensure all was properly carried out according to his stated intentions.

A few years later, and before refining his preferences for who might 'use' his income, Sir William was forced to pay as much as a fifth of his income as punishment for sticking to his faith. Consequently, financial difficulties continued to plague the family.

In 1587, Sir William Catesby made yet another agreement with John Popson and a new friend John Tomson. He instructed the pair to allow Thomas and John Spencer to take possession of two land estates. One should be the manors and lands of Ashby Legers and Silsworth. The other should be the manors and lands of Lapworth, Bushwood, Radburne, Stratford upon Avon, and Bowdsert in Warwickshire. A complex set of instructions for the use of the various premises followed. Most of the manors and lands including Silsworth were to be used by Sir William and his wife, Anne, for her jointure. Ashby Legers was the main exception, which was to Sir William's personal use only. After all other uses, Ashby Legers and Silsworth were to the use of Robert Catesby, Sir William's son. Many defaults were added – for Sir William's other sons, of which there were none, and his uncles, of which there were many, although now only five after one was deceased.

Accordingly, and coinciding with the end of the Spencer's Silsworth lease, Sir William Catesby obtained a license (see[157] Figure 59) from Queen Elizabeth to separate forever from his possessions the manor of Silsworth and grant it to John Popson and John Tomson. The cost of the license was £7 6s 8d. The manor of Silsworth comprised 100 acres of land, 200 acres of pasture, 20 acres of meadow, with 6 shillings rent in Silsworth. A few months later, Catesby obtained a plea of Recovery to use the force of the court to grant to Thomas and John Spencer the 'manors of Ashby & Silsworth' with 500 acres of land, 80 acres of meadow, 400 acres of pasture, 30 acres of wood, and 100 acres of heath and gorse, for a total of 1,110 acres. This is the exact measure given in 1568 for the total area of Catesby's manors of Ashby Legers, Silsworth, *and* West Haddon.

Figure 59: The Great Seal of Queen Elizabeth, 1587

Thus it may seem the former Parles and Comberford manor of Silsworth, including Silsworth Field, fell into the hands of the Spencer family. But not all was what it seemed when it came to the Catesbys. By 1592, the Catesbys had acquired from the Burnebys another manor of Silsworth. This is readily apparent from the arrangements made with the Burneby family late in the sixteenth century. Catesby's new manor included Middle Field, Hill/High Fields and Sharrocks Close. 'Sharrocks' had gained its name by this time from Giles Sharrock, the vicar of neighbouring Crick parish between 1561 and 1609.

Some of the arrangements made in 1587 were later cancelled and replaced on the occasion of Robert Catesby's marriage. Early in 1592, Sir William Catesby set up a marriage contract.[158] This was typical of the way the wealthier class of landed gentry took care of their eldest children.

They gave money and/or income-generating lands to the prospective newlyweds to set them up for the future. The other key party to the deal was Sir Thomas Leigh, father of the bride – his eldest daughter Katherine. Also present were the team of Sir John and Thomas Spencer. The parties agreed the settlements would be completed when the wedding took place, if each of Robert and Katherine consented to the marriage. At least the fathers agreed that their dear children had the right to give their consent or refuse the marriage.

On his side, Sir Thomas Leigh agreed to pay £2,000. For his turn, Sir William Catesby was to pay fines at Westminster earmarking which properties went to whose benefit. Two fines were to cover the manors and lands of Ladbroke and Chastleton as well as lands in the lordships of Radburne, Ladbroke and Brokend. One fine said the use of the manors of Chastleton and lands in Brokend were destined to Katherine for her jointure, then to the heirs of Katherine and Robert. The manor and lands in Ladbroke and Radburne were to the benefit of Sir William himself, then to Robert and his heirs. The second fine dealt with the manors or lands in Lapworth, Bromeham, Bushwood, Stratford upon Avon, and Bewdsart, which were for the use of Sir William and his wife, Anne, then Robert and his heirs.

The agreement continued to effectively specify the use of a third set of manors and lands that were more personal to the Catesby family. Sir William's rights contained in the 1587 agreement enabling him make a jointure for his wife and write leases for various lands were cancelled. Instead, Sir William gave the manors and lands of Ashby Legers and Silsworth, and other lands in Radburne not part of the first two fines, to Robert when he turned 21, with certain complex conditions.

> whereas Sir William and Dame Anne his wife are seized of lands in Radbourne in the possession of Morris Myles, parcel of the manor of Rodborne, and the manor and lands of Sillesworth, and Sir William is seized of the manor and lands of Ashby Legers, with remainder of all the aforesaid to Robert Catisby, with liberties for Sir William to make his wife a jointure and make leases of the premises, and whereas it is agreed the said liberties shall be extinguished, it is now agreed between Sir William Catisby and Sir Thomas Leigh that Sir William shall by deed in writing within one year after Robert Catisby shall accomplish the full age of 21 years surrender to Robert the manors of Ashby Legers and Sillesworth and all lands in Radborne and in Ashby Legers and Sillesworth in the occupation of Morrice Myles ... except such whereof Lady Katherine Throckmorton hath any estate for her life for jointure ... provided that the manor of Chestleton and Brockend assured to Katherine Leigh for her jointure, or lands in Watford and Sillesworth assured to Katherine for life by indenture 1st March, that upon recovery of the manor

of Ashby Legers after the decease of Sir William the capital messuage of Ashby Legers shall be to the use of Katherine for her life in recompense for the eviction of the capital messuage of Chastleton

One month later, yet another marriage contract was made, this time to provide for Robert Catesby's living expenses. The principal parties were Sir William Catesby of Ashby Ledgers, his son and heir apparent Robert Catesby, and of course the father of the bride Sir Thomas Leigh of Stonely, Warwickshire. Others brought into the contract were the Catesby's friends, the Spencers – Sir John of Oldthroppe, Thomas of Claverdon, William of Erdington, and Richard of Offley. Anyone wondering whether lawyers 400+ years ago had a hard time making a living need not be concerned after reading this lot.

The lucky couple, Robert Catesby and Katherine Leigh, were to receive payments of £300 each year for 'living' expenses. The annual amounts were to be taken from the Catesby estates in Radburne, Lapworth, and Bushwood, and were granted to the intervening parties of William and Richard Spencer. The payments were to commence in September 1595, after the marriage. However, the entire arrangement would be void if Robert Catesby after attaining the age of 21 did not, upon reasonable request, give Silsworth Manor to his father, Sir William, to hold from September 1595 for 50 years, at the notional rent of a peppercorn. That meant Middlefield, the High Field alias Hill Field with the meadows adjoining, and Sharrocks Close. The agreement was signed by Robert Catesby, endorsed and delivered by him in January 1593, which was a few months after the marriage in London on the 8th May 1592. Robert's 21st birthday would probably have been some time in 1594.

Sir William Catesby did complete at least one part of the bargain. In December 1592, he obtained a license from the Crown which allowed him to give the manor and lands of Silsworth to Robert Catesby, his son.

The Catesbys were more than a little financially stretched in the last few decades of the sixteenth century, largely due to their adherence to the Catholic faith and the fines imposed on them. They proceeded to sell properties and/or make other sometimes tangled arrangements to raise funds. As part of this process, in February 1596 Sir William and his son, Robert, sold a large number of messuages and land in Ladbroke for £2,800. The buyers were John Throckmorton and another. In November 1596, the twosome of Robert Catesby and John Throckmorton sold for £400 a messuage and a farm of 6 yardlands to a trio of Thomases, Messrs Leigh, Spencer, and Chamberlain. On the same day in November, Robert Catesby sold to the same three, as trustees, the manor of Ladbroke, together with Thomas Throckmorton's farm as well as a messuage and 8 ½ yardlands.

At the end of the sixteenth century, Robert Catesby and his sister Anne were both involved in legal actions concerning their inheritance. In one case, Anne laid a claim against her brother, Robert, and William Harris to decide who held title to lands in Silsworth. She said the lands had been purchased by Sir William Catesby from the Burnebys in November 1590, for a 'great sum of money'. The lands became subject to an elaborate scheme, perhaps to secure them from the hands of Sir William's creditors. He first passed the lands to a few reliable friends in trust, who then, on 17 December 1591, leased them for a term of 3,000 years at a notional or peppercorn rent to William Harris. Harris then made over the lease to William Cobb. Cobb, on 19 May 1593, sold the lease to Sir William and his son, Robert Catesby for £1,950. At which point the lands seemed to have completed a circle of ownership.

Cobb was to be paid the price of the lands over three years, i.e., in five small instalments each of £75, with the last payment of £1,575 due on 20 May 1596. The transfer of title was conditioned on full payment of all instalments. Sir William and Robert then decided to sell the lease for the highest possible value to pay some of Sir William's debts and provide a reasonable marriage portion to Anne, Robert's sister. Confusion arose concerning the five small payments and therefore who held title – meaning either William Cobb, if payment of the instalments had not been made, or Sir William and Robert, if due payments had been made.

Only a few days after the last and largest payment was due in 1596, William Cobb assigned the lease to four gentlemen including Sir Thomas Leigh (Robert Catesby's new father-in-law) and Thomas Spencer of Claverdon. They then assigned part of the lease to Sir Thomas Tresame, an acquaintance of the Catesbys. Tresame had other interests in common with the Catesbys and their

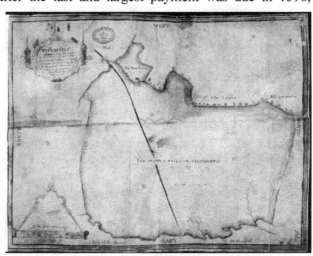

Figure 60: The Great Ground of Middlefield in Silsworth

Silsworth manor, for in or about 1595 he wrote a description of the Silsworth lands. All three ancient closes, as he called them, amounted to 390 acres. The grounds of Sharrocks and Hill/High field were not of a rich soil, but were very sound and bore reasonably good lamb. Middlefield (see[159] Figure 60) was of very rich soil, comparable to the best pasture grounds in the Shire of Northampton. He said rent should amount to £230 annually for all three closes. The next and last comment in his summary is confused. Tresame stated the usual selling price of such improved enclosures in Northamptonshire is twenty years' purchase, and continued by noting the value in sale amounted to £460, when arithmetically the value should have been £4,600.

Sir William Catesby, knight, died and was buried at Ashby St Legers in April 1598, leaving his only son, Robert, a daughter, Anne, and his widow, Dame Anne. However, in contrast to the large estates held by his ancestors, notwithstanding William Catesby of 1485, Sir William left an estate in severe financial stress. Almost immediately, Sir Randolph Brereton and Ralph Sheldon filed against the threesome of Sir Edward Greville, Anne Catesby and Robert Catesby claiming non-payment of longstanding debts to them of £280 and referring to many other large debts of Sir William. The pair claimed the Catesbys had 'confederated and plotted together to deceive' their many creditors. Furthermore, that Sir William's estate had been conveyed to Sir Edward Greville and had realised more than £20,000, and that Dame Anne had received funds since her husband's decease. And to top all that, they said Robert had inherited many manors which by law should be charged with Sir William's debts.

Sir Edward hotly denied the allegations. In particular, he said, there was no conveyance of manors to him. Instead he had paid many great debts for Sir William, who had undertaken to repay Sir Edward. Some repayment followed through the sale of the Lapworth, Bramham and Bushwood manors, supervised by Sir Edward. Then Sir William leased for nine years the core family manors of Ashby Legers, Silsworth and Radborne to Sir Edward for further recompense, but these manors were so indebted with former annuities that there was very little surplus. In the end, even after selling Sir William's goods and chattels Sir Edward lost a lot of money himself. As to what debts were owed, Sir Edward's own comment was he doubted Sir William himself was aware of exactly how much he owed or how much his estate was worth. That was because he was in 'so many ways so far indebted and had so greatly entangled his lands'. Lady Anne Catesby commented that Sir William's lands had long since been mortgaged to Sir Thomas Leigh – for Robert Catesby's marriage – and that she had not received any moneys since her widowhood. Robert added that he had not inherited any lands, although he did not know what moneys had been realised by Sir Edward.

Robert Catesby must have thought about the Brereton case. Only a few months later, he began legal proceedings against his 'kinsman' Sir Edward Greville. He claimed he had not been given an account of rents and profits for the manors of Ashby Legers, Silsworth, and Radburne conveyed by Sir William Catesby to Sir Edward in trust. Neither had he been advised how many of Sir William's debts had been paid. Sir Edward replied that there were many great Bonds and Statutes of unknown total value, but confirmed that about 1594 he had been leased the three manors. He knew of debts amounting to about £14,000, of which he had settled about £12,000. Further, he never agreed to settle *all* of Sir William's debts nor had he agreed to give any accounting and that in any case his Baylie who carried out the receipts and payments was dead and had not provided any account to him.

The extent of the financial plight of the Catesbys at the end of the sixteenth century is illustrated by a case[160] between Dame Anne Catesby and Robert, her son. Although undated, this was after Sir William's death in 1598 and probably before Robert sold their Radburne manor in 1600. Dame Anne asserted she had to her use, by fine and recovery, the manors of Ashby Leger and Silsworth. Robert replied – the claim 'upon truth is untrue and morally mistaken'. Robert provided reasons why her claim was untrue. In one instance, she had access to documents that plainly gave her the manors of Bushwood, Lapworth, Radburne and Willicots as her jointure, but which clearly excluded Ashby Legers. Also, Sir William, in his lifetime, 'finding the world troublesome' had leased Ashby Legers to friends, which would not have been allowed if the manor was part of her jointure. He adds that his mother was 'informed by an old lawyer of little wit & less learning'. Dame Anne was in debt herself, and had given her house in Lambeth as security to a pawnbroker for a loan of £300. Robert alleged she had tried to borrow £700 and then sell the house for £200 while still in hock to the pawnbroker. Robert added that 'in the middle of my late troubles', after his mother 'anihilated' his offer to buy the Lambeth house for £400, and with 'her debtors calling on her', she sold the house to someone else, rather than allow the house become forfeit to the pawnbroker. Robert advised that while there had been a great number of claims against Ashby by creditors, this was 'vain talk for I am greatly abused, but that all statutes [of the Staple] & recognizances are either cancelled or called in'.

By the year 1600, Anne Catesby had married Henry Browne. Her mother, Dame Anne Catesby, and her brother, Robert Catesby, were parties to her marriage contract, which to no one's surprise was rather complex. Henry Browne's brother, Sir George Browne, had entered into an obligation for £3,000 to Dame Anne, whereby if Henry produced lands of an annual value of £300 for Anne Browne, the obligation would be cancelled. However, all parties acknowledged Henry could not produce such lands without prejudicing his inheritance. Fortunately, various friends interceded and with the assignment of several statutes and leases by Henry Browne over to six men including Robert Catesby, all was agreed as satisfactory. Performance was guaranteed by Giles Sharrock, clerk of Crick, and Morris Miles, yeoman also of Crick, each for £600, sworn before Sir John Popham, chief justice. Should Henry Browne pay two sums of £300, the recognizances would be void. Also, the unexpired lease term of part of a close of pasture called Highfield in Silsworth containing about 60 acres would be assigned and conveyed to Henry Browne. These 60 acres, among other lands, in December 1591, had been demised and let to farm by the Catesbys to William Harris of London for the term of 3,000 years.

Also in the year 1600, in his continued effort to raise cash, Robert Catesby sold the moiety of the manor of Radburne to Sir Roger Wilbraham. Sir Roger held these lands until he died in 1616, and according to his will at PCC, he gave the manor to his daughter Elizabeth, who had married her cousin Thomas Wilbraham. Distinguishing between specific Radburne lands or fields comprising this or that 'manor' within the parish is rather problematic. But the Wilbraham parcel of Radburne lands, years later, was the manor moiety or lordship caused to be delivered to the Spencers in an exchange of lands engineered by George Clerke.

The inheritor of Silsworth and other lands, Robert Catesby (see[161] Figure 61) was a direct descendant of William Catesby, executed in 1485 after the Battle of Bosworth. Regrettably, Robert Catesby also found infamy. James I became king of England in 1603 and was less tolerant of Catholics such as Robert Catesby. Robert was a leader in the plot to kill the king by blowing up the House of Lords. Just before the planned explosion on the 4th November 1605, a tipoff alerted the authorities and Guy Fawkes was found with the gunpowder.

Figure 61: Robert Catesby

'Robert Catesby[162] was in London, and as soon as he heard of it took horse and rode hard to Ashby Legers with four other conspirators, viz. the two Wrights, Thomas Percy and Ambrose Rookwood. On the evening of November 7 they came to Holbeach in Staffordshire, being 60 in number. Here they were attacked next day by a force under Sir Richard Walsh.

They refused to lay down their arms and the fight began. Catesby and Percy, standing back to back and fighting furiously, were shot through the body with two bullets from the same musket. Catesby, crawling into the house upon his hands and knees, seized an image of the Virgin and dropped down dead with it clasped in his arms.'

Catesby's mother was Ann Throckmorton, daughter of Sir Robert Throckmorton. Another of Throckmorton's daughters was Muriel, who married Sir Thomas Tresham of Rushton, Northants, considered one of the Catholic elite. Their son, Francis Tresham, became an associate of Robert Catesby and was involved in the Gunpowder Plot. When the Plot was discovered, Francis was arrested but died in prison of natural causes only a month later. He was suspected of writing the letter tipping off the authorities about the plot, an accusation that was never proven.

Catesby's participation in the Powder Plot was vilified and provoked a flurry of claims and grants for the Catesby lands in the disarray that followed. In 1606, Sir William Lane appealed to the king for a lease of two parcels of 'the late traitor's' lands called Silsworth and Ashby. He partly succeeded, gaining the lease of the manor of Ashby Legers and other lands of Robert Catesby. The Silsworth lands, albeit misnamed as 'the manor of Watford', another part of Robert's possessions, were granted to Thomas Temple and John Rowse in June 1606.

All of the goods of eight named traitors, including Robert Catesby and Frances Tresham, were granted to Sir William Anstruther, who was attached to the court of King James. Messrs Marcus and Atee were granted 'the benefit of the recusancy of Lady Catesby of Ashby', and therefore the manors of Silsworth and Ashby Ledgers, part of the possessions of Ann Lady Catesby. Ashby Legers, the long-time home of the Catesbys, was taken from Robert's surviving family, then granted to Sir William Irving, Gentleman of the Prince's Privy Chamber, and later sold.

In 1612, a lawyer delivered to Sir William Irving the evidences of the lands of Robert Catesby, attainted for treason: 35 deeds, 6 cyrograf of fines, 12 sealed leases, 13 unsealed leases, 20 rentals of Ashby Legers, and accounts with Court Rolls at two years a book.

In 1610, Lord Arundel and Anne Catesby, widow, leased the pasture of Silsworth to Messrs. Shrimpton and Gregory of Harrington. A challenge to the Catesby's ownership was mounted in 1613, when the Commissioners for Defective Titles reached back into history and wrote to 'the pretended owner of the lands in Silsworth' forfeit by the attainder of William Catesby and accordingly granted by Henry VII to John Halliwell. The 'pretended owner' was required to rush to William Typper before April 1, to make good his defective title, 'as otherwise the course of law against him cannot be stayed'.

Lord Arundel in 1615 leased the Silsworth lands to John Lambe of Northampton. This explains the origin of Lambe's lands in Sir Richard Burneby's case against Lambe for Silsworth tithes totalling £600. Then, in 1618, the Attorney General exhibited a Bill against Sir Thomas Leigh (father of the deceased Robert's deceased wife, Katherine Leigh) of Stavely, Dame Anne Catesby (Catesby's mother), Robert Catesby (Catesby's son), and Dr. Lambe (presumably John Lambe). They should answer for fraudulently detaining from His Majesty the manor of Silsworth in Watford, formerly lands of Robert Catesby who was attainted for the Powder Plot, on the pretext of being settled on Anne Catesby, and for destroying, defacing, or antedating the evidences relating thereto.

Robert Catesby's only son, Robert, held the family's Silsworth manor as late as 1624, when the case over Silsworth tithes came alive once again. Now Sir John Lambe made the claim against all lands in Silsworth, including what he described as Robert Catesby's land of about 300 acres, even though Sir John himself was the occupant from 1615. Sir John's lands were situated immediately west of, and adjoining to, Middlefield. This was one of the manors included in Catesby inquisitions of the late 16th century. Lambe continued to hold the lease of the Catesby manor in Silsworth at least until the death of Robert Catesby jnr about 1625/6. And if the 1631 map (see Figure 60) showing the western boundary of Middlefield is accurate, after Robert jnr's death Lambe either still had the lease or he had obtained the land for himself in fee. To the west of Middlefield, the map is marked '*Part of Sir John Lambe His groundes*'.

The dispute with Sir John Lambe came to be resolved by Sir Thomas Leigh. Sir Thomas was the father-in-law of Robert Catesby, killed in 1605. By the resolution reached in 1632 Thomas Leigh agreed to manage the suit pending between, by then, Hastings Ingram and Richard Parker concerning the manor of Silsworth in the tenure of Sir John Lambe. As long as John Lambe held the manor by, from or under John Leigh he would pay John Leigh or his son, Thomas, the yearly rent of £150. Furthermore, John Lambe or the Leighs would give a year's notice to the other party to vacate the manor. Finally, Sir John Lambe was to be allowed against the rent an amount of £10 yearly which he would pay for 'St Andrews', and 4s for the 'Sharfes' (hard to read accurately) yield and 12d for 'Marstons Lea'. 'St Andrews' is almost certainly the land in Silsworth rented for centuries from St Andrews priory in Northampton until the dissolution. Both 'Marston's Lea' and 'Sharfes' remain unfamiliar, although 'Marstons Lea' could be a reference to a ley such as the ½ acre in Old Silsworth, later sold by the Marstons.

The only son of Robert Catesby, also named Robert, died about 1626, aged only 30, and without children. The death of Robert Catesby marked the effective end of the Catesby Manors in Watford parish, which since

1485 had been a story only of Silsworth. In all, from Agnes de Ardern, passing through the de Watfords to the Catesbys after marriage, the several Catesby manors in Watford parish lasted a little less than 500 years.

One of the Catesby's Silsworth manors, originally of the Burnebys, comprising Sharrocks, Hill/High Field and Middlefield was eventually broken into pieces after the fall in Catesby fortunes. George Clerke acquired Sharrocks along with many pieces of the former 200 acre Hill/High field and closes. Middlefield appears to have been leased by George Clerke, but never owned, a result possibly related to the early involvement of St Andrew's Priory in the field. Early in the 1600s, possibly around the time of Robert Catesby's death, the Great Ground of 150 acres (see Figure 60) came into the possession of a William Taylor of Banbury. His daughter carried the field to John Keyt through marriage in 1634, eventually inherited by his son, Sir William Keyt.

Some of the pastures, meadows, and lands of Silsworth were held by the abbeys of Northamptonshire, St James and St Andrews in particular, from the twelfth century until the Dissolution engineered by Henry VIII in the sixteenth century. There seems a high probability the various Silsworth 'Manors' were comprised in some part of church lands. This might explain why such lands were sometimes omitted from the official 'holdings' in fee of landed estates. Which also gave opportunity to the Catesbys to 'hold' large measures of land in the town that were in fact, leases.

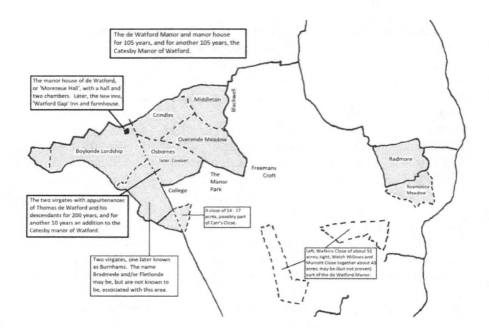

Figure 62: Lands of the de Watford & Catesby Manor in Watford, c 1480

PART 5: The End of the Watford Manors

Remarkably, after the Watford single manor of 1276 was split into four separate manors, 350 years later the many pieces were reassembled into a single manor. The modern age Clerkes became the only family other than the medieval Arderns to hold most of Watford parish. Their presence in Watford was built initially by Sir George Clerke and continued by his son, George Clerke, together lasting from about 1630 until late in the same century.

Sir George Clerke: 1625–1649

The Clerkes were descended from the ancient family of Willoughby in Warwickshire, originally carrying the name Hamund. One of them was Sir John Clerke, a military man of great valour, who had the good fortune to make prisoner the Duke of Longeville at the battle of Terouenne in 1513, gaining favour with the king, Henry VIII. Sir John was the sheriff of Northamptonshire three times; on the second occasion in 1529 he arrested and imprisoned Thomas Burneby for debt.

Robert Clerke, the elder brother of Sir John, and his wife had three sons. Clement, the youngest, became the father of George Clerke, born 1587. George married Barbara Palmer in 1617 at St Lawrence Jewry, in the City of London and was knighted in 1641. Their three sons were George of Watford, Robert of Long Buckby, and Clement of Laund Abbey in Leicester.

> [163][Sir George Clerke] was one of the leading City Royalists, serving as sheriff of London in 1641-42. 'The new, honest, stout sheriff' was chiefly responsible for the election of the loyal Richard Gurney as lord mayor. He was allegedly imprisoned as a delinquent in 1642-3 for refusal to pay his assessment. On his release he went to live on his country property, and at the height of the Civil war, it is stated, enclosed four-fifths of his manor of Watford. He was appointed to several commissions after the Civil War until a few months before his death, when he retired on grounds of ill-health, and suffered no further financial penalties for his loyalty.

Sir George Clerke's father-in-law, Robert Palmer, was of an affluent family. When Robert's brother died in 1636 he named George Clerke as one of his executors. Robert Palmer ran a flourishing retail business in London and also invested in property.

Something triggered (Sir) George Clerke's interest in the parish of Watford. Perhaps he became aware of the parish when observing difficulties experienced by two of its major landholders, the Burnebys and the Catesbys. The key event setting George Clerke in motion may have been the attempts by Sir Richard Burneby to sell his manor of Watford to pay debts and provide funds for his children.

Accumulating clear ownership of most of Watford parish and completing the necessary reorganisation took George Clerke almost 20 years. The process required many transactions, only a few of which brought him large tracts of grounds associated with the manors of the parish. Whether George understood before he embarked on the venture how difficult it would be to unwind the complexities formed through 500 years seems doubtful.

THE MANORS

George acquired all three manors of Watford, each previously discussed in detail:

The first and largest was Burneby's manor, purchased by an agreement signed in 1623 and completed in 1626. With that deal, he effectively obtained three of the four quarters of the Watford manor as split in 1276. While that included Court Leet and Court Baron for Watford, Burneby's large free tenancy of the Catesby's Watford manor was excluded.

Second, the de Watford manor of Watford, after passing through the hands of the Catesby, Owen, and Watkyn families, was purchased by George in 1631. This was the large free tenancy of the de Burneby manor.

In 1639, George acquired from the Spencers the Watford town lands of the Comberford and Parles manor – the fourth quarter of the 1276 split. This transaction specifically excluded the manor's lands in Murcott and no mention was made of any Silsworth lands.

A year after George took over the Burneby Manor, he held Manor Court. This was the medieval Court Leet and Court Baron with civil rights, not criminal, over serfs, tenants and free tenants living on manor land. The Court was a useful source of income to the lord because he was allowed to keep fines laid on any disobedient residents. A written record, called the 'Roll', was kept of proceedings by the Steward.

The Roll for the 1627 Court begins by excusing absentees – in this case, 10 of them. Next, 14 jurors were sworn in. The Court proceeded to fine a number of residents for washing animal skins in the common stream causing nuisance to other residents, and a 'foreign' baker for selling bread within the Watford baker's territory. Various tenant farmers were fined for leaving their sheep in the wrong places. All those who held a yardland were ordered to gather and carry a load of stones and lay them on the highways each year. Then the court made rules for laying down peas in the cornfields for the benefit of the poor of the parish. A number of appointments were made for the parish including the constable, tithingman, ale taster, and cattle counters. The beer taster was obliged to test the strength and quality of all locally-brewed ale and ensure it was good and wholesome and sold at a fair price. Watford, like most towns across England, had its own breweries because the product did not keep for long periods or travel well.

The last session was for the Court Baron, which considered the Free Tenants. Two free tenants were fined for skipping the Court and not making suit of court to the lord. Three more were fined for overstocking the commons of Watford. And the court noted that a ½ virgate of one free tenant had been sold to another, but no one knew what the rent should be.

THE LEASES

After he acquired the manors, which carried the right to *hold* such grounds in fee, George Clerke (see[164] Figure 63) found it necessary to address the many individual leases. These carried the right to *use* the same lands, which in Watford, was commonly for farming. When George purchased the manors, each farmer who occupied lands was usually described as the 'tenant or his assignee'.

Buying individual leases allowed George to avoid the potential for tenants to assign leases to their heirs long into the future. He also

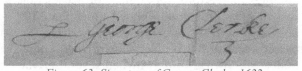

Figure 63: Signature of George Clerke, 1632

acquired the right to lease lands to any farmer he chose, and to some extent operate the farms in the manner he preferred. He could also ease his way towards reorganising the remaining open fields of Watford by inclosure. This was a process beginning in the late 1500s and continuing especially in the 17th and 18th centuries involving raising fences (hence, 'inclosing') around common lands making 'closes'. Once open land with grazing rights became enclosed, use of the land was restricted to one farmer only, ending communal use.

The process was very unpopular among farm workers because it deprived them of a livelihood – although did provide displaced workers for an industrial revolution. While Silsworth had been entirely enclosed by the early 1600s,

Murcott and a large part of Watford town remained open common land when George commenced his buying spree. Any land described or denominated in yardlands was a sure sign that the land referred to was open and carried rights to graze on common grounds. In contrast, a 'close' was a closed off field, unavailable to other farmers' animals.

George Clerke began buying leases shortly after he agreed to buy the Burneby manor. The first was for 243 acres under Sir Richard Burneby's own occupation – the fields he listed separately in the sale agreement. This included his Watford fields stretching north and east from the manor house, excluding Cookes and Viccars in Silsworth, and cost George £160.

In a string of smaller deals after finalizing the Burneby manor purchase, George bought about 5 ½ yardlands for a total of £1,140, plus barns and leyes for another £40. A few of these were formerly of one or another abbey, since passed through several hands from the Crown. In another example, the lease had been handed down through two generations.

There were a number of larger tracts of land George needed to get his hands on, at least one of them technically not part of a manor he had purchased. The first of these deals concluded early in 1632 – he bought the messuage, two closes and 2 yardlands specifically excluded from the Burneby manor purchase. Just before George bought the Burneby manor, these lands had been plucked out of the manor and sold to a relative of the manor family. George paid £900 to purchase about 128 acres in this holding from Sir Richard's nephew.

A second large transaction closed in March 1641. George bought a homestead with 2 ½ yardlands, formerly one of the St James Monastery holdings in Watford, for £640. For decades the land had been held by the Crown after Dissolution ended more than 300 years of the Monastery's possession. King James granted the lands to two gents of London who passed them to Sir William Gar(ra)way, knight. Sir William was a major trader who owned or part-owned several privateering ships, with which he amassed a fortune. Some of his ships took part in fighting the Spanish in 1598. He sold the land in 1622, still valued at the same 49s 8d yearly, which directly links them to one of the abbey's leases when dissolved. The holding was sold to George in socage, not knight's service, with fealty to the king's own manor, and so as a purchase in fee was different to George's purchases of leaseholds.

After the purchase in fee of the St James premises from a scion of the Watkin family, George saw the necessity to purchase the lease of the same lands. In September 1641, George paid another £280 to Henry Willies for the lease. These lands may be those lying 'in the south fields of Watford' referred to as far back as 1303. On the 1771 new inclosures map, lots 1 through 8 mark off a farm of 131 acres, or 143 after adding roads, a dovecot, and a second homestead.

The third significant transaction, in May 1641, sees George Clerke buying premises in Watford, which according to the fine encompassed 4 homesteads and 186 acres. The total price paid to the Eyre family was £1,560, described as two homesteads ('now used as one'), a close of pasture used with the two homesteads, a cottage with 2 yardlands, another ½ yardland, and a separate 1 yardland including a cottage. The several pieces of this holding appear to be located in the Upperend of Watford.

This package had a complex background. The Eyres paid £800 to the Marstons of Farndon, Northamptonshire for the parcel – so the Eyres made a tidy profit. Some years before, the Marstons had involved Richard Braybrooke with the same parcel. Separately, two cottages, a ½ acre in Old Silsworth, rent from a ½ yardland and a cottage, were purchased by George Clerke from the Marstons and Braybrookes for another £36 in 1630. At some point, the Baselys of Everdon must have held the lands because they were required to add their warranty along with the Eyres' for George's good title.

George Clerke completed a number of other lease purchases for which documentation is not readily available. However, wills and other evidence indicates George bought a 2 yardland parcel from longstanding residents, the Gilberts, and another 2 ¾ yardlands including 20 odd lands associated with the Wrights.

GEORGE CLERKE MAKES NEW LEASES

Subsequent to establishing a firm hold of the many and varied Watford lands throughout the parish, George then wrote new leases to his chosen farmers. He took care to include covenants preventing the lessees assigning the lease to anyone else. He also forbade the cutting and otherwise harvesting of any 'great trees' – Ash, Oak, or Elm – growing on the premises. Each lease also included provisions specific to the individual farmer and in some cases, continued long-established practices whereby some farmers were required to perform services to the manor lord.

The fields of Silsworth were already enclosed when George bought them. So almost immediately he leased about 210 acres in the South Field of Silsworth to Edward Shuckburgh in September 1627. However, this was at the time a certain Sir John Lambe had launched a suit in Chancery, claiming tythes from all occupants of Silsworth, of which Edward was one. So Edward built in a covenant protecting himself from any suit brought by Sir John Lambe for tithes on any lands in Silsworth.

One farmer was granted a lease in September of 1633 for a homestead, a little attached close, and a patchwork of leyes amounting to one quartern. To assist the farmer, he was granted 'four beasts commons' with 21 more leyes, roods, and pasture grounds. This was the first lease in which

George reserved his right to begin the process of inclosing the common fields of Watford, which the farmer agreed not to oppose.

Another farmer was rewarded with the let of a homestead, an orchard, a garden, close, and a 2 yardland farm formerly occupied by the long-established Gilbert family. This agreement again records George's desire to enclose his Watford lands. The farmer agreed not to obstruct George doing any reasonable act to bring to pass and perfection the inclosure. That could include laying together any of the lands in the lease, or as specified by George, the lands of any other owner or occupier of the common fields in Watford. Upon inclosure, George acknowledged he would make a new lease in respect of the same demised premises at a rent to be agreed by indifferent parties appointed by each of them.

William Rogers was one of the family whose now famous son, Thomas, had sailed to the New World of America in 1620 while William remained at home. William was granted the lease of a close and 1 yardland in the netherend. His farm was part of the Comberford manor being acquired by George. If George requested, William would exchange his own land in the Upperend field for another ½ yardland in the Netherend field of the same goodness and quality as set forth by four indifferent men. William also agreed to provide his workmen, a team and cart for four days at harvest time to carry anything for George Clerke within the parish of Watford.

William Sabine was a descendant of the long-established tenant farmers of the Comberfords and Spencers. In October 1639, when he signed a new lease for 21 years with George Clerke, part of the consideration was his surrender of the lease signed with William Lord Spencer, nine years before. Sabine's new lease took in a homestead, an adjoining close and 2 yardlands. The annual rent payable was directly proportional to the yardlands rented in the old lease, that is, whereas under Spencer, Sabine paid £15 annually for 2 ½ yardlands, now he paid £12 for 2 yardlands. As part of his plan to reorganise Watford's farmlands, George prised William Sabine off the former Comberford lands mixed into the Hay and Barley Piece north of the capital messuage and replaced them with lands in the south of Watford. William already occupied one of the yardlands, the other was in two halves, both in the netherend. In addition, William agreed to perform about 5 days' carriage work for George every year and prune and care for the willow, fruit trees and great thorne growing on the premises. George also lifted two tasks directly out of William's former lease with Spencer and wrote them into his own lease with Sabine. William should deliver annually 15 hundredweight of pitt coal suitable for burning to George's manor house (rather than Spencer's mansion), and within three years he should plant and care for 80 trees – Oak, Ash, and Elm – on the premises ready for George at the end of the lease.

Immediately after Henry Willies sold the lease of the St James lands to George, he took on a new 21 year lease of 2 yardlands at £10 9s 8d per year. Both yardlands were in the Netherend of Watford, one of them was part of Henry's former St James lands. Henry was another tenant required to provide a cartage service to his landlord's mansion house, in his case a cartload containing 20 hundredweight of pitt coal. Clearly, the manor house needed lots of heating.

Six months later, the same farmer took on a second lease for 10 years at £20 per annum – four closes amounting to 20 acres right beside the manor house. Henry agreed with George, now Sir George Clerke, that the premises would be rated at one yardland for the purposes of taxes, duties, or tenths whether levied by the king, church, or the poor.

Thomas Paybody[165] may have been George's most trusted farmer. George placed a large area of farmland into Thomas's care for ten years, from May 1642. He even advanced £195 to stock the farms with sheep, cattle and other 'beasts'. Thomas became the leasehold farmer of 500 acres of pasture in Watford town, in return for rent of £500 per annum. The fields formed an arc over (and not including) the manor park estate, extending from the east or Upperend fields, north of the manor park, to the west fields of Watford town:

Barley Piece (both of the former 'peeces' together)	50 acres
Nayesborough, including a little meadow	80 acres
Thorney close	20 acres
Upper Hayes	60 acres
Great Ground (alias Great Hayes)	80 acres
Blackwell	30 acres
Middleton Hill	50 acres
Cringles	50 acres
Watfurlong (alias Overende)	80 acres

The parties agreed that the last three of the fields named were to be rated in total as 6 yardlands for the purposes of church and other taxes. Thomas's lease also granted him a place to live – a messuage with a 'little close of pasture' belonging in Watford and now in his own occupation.

SIR GEORGE CLERKE RETIRES

Beginning in 1623, buying most of Watford took Sir George until 1642, ending about when the English Civil War was warming up. The only other major landholder remaining in Watford was Earl Spencer. Sir George was either satisfied with his re-organization of Watford's farms or discouraged from making further changes due to the Civil War (see[166] Figure 64). In any event, the parish continued life as best could be managed. Regardless of politics Sir George conducted Manor Court, possibly the last for Watford, in October 1648. In the same year George Clerke the younger was married and given the Watford estate as his settlement. Sir George died on the 30th January 1648/9, the same day King Charles I was beheaded in London.

Sir George Clerke's will was relatively straightforward, written after the grant of his real estate in Watford as a marriage settlement for his son, George. His will was drawn up less than a year before he died in the context of England's civil war. He tactfully described himself as an Alderman of the City of London. Personal estate of goods and chattels and ready money was divided into three parts 'according to the Custom of the City of London'. One part was for his wife, Barbara, a second was to be shared among his surviving children, and the third part was, as tradition allowed, 'his' share to do with as he wanted.

Barbara, Sir George's wife, died and left a will proved in February 1655/6. Her children, other than George junior, were given various sums totalling £6,000. George was bequeathed the remainder and was sole executor. With a codicil, Barbara gave many small sums to her servants as well as the poor of Watford and many other local parishes. Barbara wished to be buried beside her husband, Sir George, in Watford church.

Figure 64: Parliamentary trooper

Sir George and Lady Barbara Clerke, part of the well-heeled landed gentry of Northamptonshire, left their family well provided for. They were unaware that George, their eldest son, would not reach the end of his life in the same circumstances.

George Clerke, son of Sir George Clerke: 1649–1689

George Clerke the younger enjoyed his inheritance in Watford with no need for significant reorganisation, although he did buy a few fields in Silsworth. George held the manor of Watford during the term of the republican Commonwealth under Oliver Cromwell, which ended with the Restoration of King Charles II in 1660, and for another three decades afterwards. However, he appears to have spent beyond his income, requiring at least two mortgage loans, and what was effectively another loan in 1668 by selling, for £520, the annual £40 rental income from Radmore farm, for as long as the purchasers might live.

Mary Holman, the only daughter of Philip Holman of Warkworth, Northants, married George Clerke, the eldest son and heir of Sir George in 1648 and died 20 years later. Their only two sons died young at Watford and of five daughters, only the two eldest married in good time, which George was not afraid to declare a disappointment. George himself married a second time to Susan Turnour in 1678 bringing no further children. Though not to forget, George was paid £8,000 in two instalments by his new father-in-law. For his side, George settled lands on Sarah for her jointure with an initial dower of £900 per year. Ten years later, George topped up the dower to £1,200 per year.

George was elected an MP for Northamptonshire in 1661. He travelled in Europe extensively before taking any appointments in England. With a substantial estate said to be worth £3,000 per annum in 1660, he was proposed for a knighthood of the Royal Oak. This was at the time of the Restoration of King Charles II, in appreciation of those who had supported Charles during his exile in France. The knighthoods were abandoned as too reminiscent of the old order. During George's lifetime the old medieval system of 'holding' lands by service of knight's fee officially ended, so George was safe to say he 'owned' his lands.

THE ESTATE OF GEORGE CLERKE

George Clerke the younger was buried at Watford in May 1689. He left a long and comprehensive will[167] detailing his substantial land holdings in Watford, Silsworth, and Murcott. See the Appendix with a Table summarising the properties and other rights given to the various beneficiaries. In the Table, any text in [brackets] was added by the author.

After lamenting his 'many daughters unmarried', George's main bequests were:

(a) to the heir of the Manor of Watford, his nephew Sir Robert Clerke, the Manor House, cottages and lands of the Park with surrounding houses and lands. With that, he inherited two intailed leases of farms located in Watford town, but none in Silsworth or Murcott. What turned out to be a devastating condition was laid on Sir Robert before he could take the two leases of land. He had to pay cash legacies to George's three unmarried daughters of £2,000 each. And he had to allow George's widow to live in the manor house of Watford during her lifetime;

(b) to his daughter and executor, Dorothy Clerke, about 25 identified tracts of lands of various extents in all three towns, plus tithes in Watford, but only when George's second wife died, which didn't happen until 1722. Dorothy was given most of the Netherend, the lion's share of Silsworth, Watford tithes, Radmore in the Upperend, and George's only parcel of land in Murcott;

(c) to his daughter, Jane Clerke, about 13 named closes or grounds in Watford and Silsworth plus tithes in Murcott, but only after George's second wife died. Jane's grants included a trio of closes in the north of Watford. She also found herself the beneficiary of the New Inne with its three closes, which in medieval times was part of the Boylonde Lordship;

(d) to his daughter, Elizabeth Clerke, about 4 named lands plus rights to the moiety of a few minor tithes, all in Silsworth, but only after George's second wife died; and

(e) sundry small legacies of money and personal effects to various legatees including his two sons-in-law, married to his two eldest daughters.

At the beginning of 1689, George owned virtually all of Watford town. He owned the larger part of Silsworth, about 565 acres, which excluded Middle Field, Silsworth Field, and three small closes in the Highfield. In Murcott town he possessed only 2 ¼ yardlands. Pretty much the only other significant landowner in the parish was Earl Spencer, who held a large tract in Murcott.

After probate, the Clerke's Watford manor was substantially diminished. The manor's lands were located only in Watford town, but the manor didn't include all of Watford town. Sadly, the manor held no land at all in Murcott or Silsworth. The lands peeled away from George's former manor by probate had been and given to George's three unmarried daughters.

The already shrunken manor quickly lost more lands creating a new landowner in Watford, the Bretons, as described later. Another parcel of not dissimilar extent was also eventually sold by the Clerkes. And at the end of its life, the residual of the Clerke legacy manor was sold to another new landowner, the Henley-Edens, also described later.

GEORGE CLERKE'S DAUGHTERS

Only two of George Clerke's daughters, Mary and Barbara, were married before he died. Although they received nothing from George, they were far from destitute. Mary in particular married very well, to Sir William Craven who left her a wealthy widow in Winwick. Second daughter, Barbara, married Sir Gilbert Clarke and lived at Chilcott, Derbyshire. On the other side of George's Balance Sheet were his unmarried daughters – Dorothy, Jane, and Elizabeth.

George's third daughter, Dorothy, became the second wife of Sir John Francklin less than a year after George died. In 1695 Dame Dorothy Franklin sold 19 of her properties and Watford tithes to Thomas Cartwright, keeping a few properties to herself. Before the sale could be completed, she had to use some of the proceeds to pay off George's two mortgages and another of his debts. In the Table in the Appendix, the inherited lands Dorothy sold are marked in italic. The Cartwrights became significant landowners in Watford, and are discussed below.

When she died in 1727, Dame Dorothy gave her remaining properties in Watford including Radmore to her sister Elizabeth. She also left £400 to each of Jane and Elizabeth. Dorothy had not given Jane more, she said, because she had paid 'a considerable sum' to discharge an annuity of £50 charged on one of Jane's inherited lands.

Jane Clerke married William Becher and their daughter, Jane Rachel Becher, married Thomas Lewis in 1719. When Jane died she gave her daughter, Jane Rachel Lewis, all her real and personal estate. Part of Jane's legacy was the 'New Inne' in Watford, now known as 'Watford Gapp', with the three closes lying nearby. Additionally, Jane had 56 acres lying just north of the manor estate all cared for by George's faithful servant Samuel Theede at the time of his death. The family sold the lands in 1719, and by 1771, they were in the hands of H.B. Harrison, a lawyer of Daventry. He died and left his children two homesteads and 240 acres in Watford, which were most of the 'Triangle' lands in the west of Watford and the northern 56 acre bloc.

Two fields in Silsworth were also part of Jane Clerke's legacy to Jane Rachel Lewis. Craven Lewis Esq., son of Thomas and Jane Rachel Lewis, owned the two closes in Silsworth in 1771. The larger of the two, called Adams of about 30 acres, appears to have been bought by the Cartwrights between 1760 and 1778, and joins the Oad Ground in Silsworth, part of Silsworth Lodge farm.

George's youngest daughter, Elizabeth Clerke, married Thomas Hanbury of Kelmarsh, a barrister. Their son, William, was one of those involved in bringing Bridges' History of Northamptonshire to publication. Elizabeth Hanbury had been given Radmore farm by her sister, Dorothy. She gave the property to her son subject to paying an annuity of £40 to her daughter. Radmore has remained with the Hanburys ever since. Elizabeth also inherited lands in Silsworth, most or all of which by 1760 came into the hands of Earl Spencer.

The Legacy of Watford Manor, 1689 - 1700

Consequent to George's death, there were a number of problems to be addressed. As an urgent matter, only two months after George died, his widow Sarah made an agreement with all the tenants of her jointure lands. They banded together and agreed to pay to her the quarter's rents then due to the deceased George Clerke, and to continue with weekly payments for rents thereafter. In return, she agreed that the tenants would remain as tenants of the lands they now held according to terms previously fixed with George Clerke.

Next, Sarah questioned the sufficiency of the real estate in the dower to provide the promised income to her of £1,200 per year. Someone, presumably a lawyer, wrote up undated summaries of the rents generated from lands and rights listed in George's various deeds, whether yardlands, acres, dwellings, or tithes. For example, the first dower for £900 per year when granted produced an ample £926 per year. However, about half of the many leases in the dower suffered reductions in rents, totalling £142 p.a., and rentals now amounted to only £784. Sarah also claimed shortages in the second and third dowers of £21 and £100, respectively. Adding to Sarah's claim was the fact that some of her dower was to be augmented if she did not have use of the manor house, as George had instructed in his will. In the event, Sir Robert Clerke did take occupancy of the manor house himself, presumably ejecting Sarah in the process, and increasing her claim against him as a result.

Apparently the latter part of the seventeenth century was a difficult time for farmers, resulting in lower rents for the landlords. The greatest rent reductions in Watford were for the largest fields, such as £45 p.a. for Cooksfield, or £28 p.a. for the Oad Ground, both in Silsworth. In general, rents for the farms appeared to be set at about £1 per acre, or £9 per yardland, more or less. Presumably, the lower relative rate for a yardland was due to additional church and various service fees traditionally payable for yardlands, but not for enclosed fields.

The lawyers also listed the encumbrances on the estate, which needed to be cleared. There was the annual payment to Samuel Adams of £50, which became Dorothy's problem. The two annual fee-farm rents remained payable, one was £20 for the third part of the Burneby manor, paid since the early 14th century, and the other was £23 for the Rectory of Watford, which held, among other things, the land upon which the manor house stood. Two faithful servants of George Clerke were to be paid £23 annually between them. The vicar of Watford was to be paid £10 from lands in Silsworth, and another £4 went to other persons.

Another matter needing attention was the debt left by George. He appears to have run short of ready cash and borrowed against the security of a selection of his lands in the parish. Two mortgages and another debt secured mostly on Dorothy's legacies needed to be cleared before she could sell her lands.

Worst of all though, was the debt of £6,000 left dangling over the head of Sir Robert Clerke. Before Sir Robert could take his large inheritance he was obliged to pay £2,000 to each of George's three unmarried daughters. The estate had no money to pay this; it seems George junior had spent the £8,000 given to him for his second marriage as well as all his income, leaving nothing for the manor estate. Sir Robert had no alternative – in 1690 he was forced to mortgage his entire manor estate for the £6,000. He was at risk of losing everything.

In 1694 when he could not repay the mortgage, Sir Robert persuaded a friend in neighbouring Norton to help out. Elizabeth Breton agreed to pay £9,000 for a large chunk of Robert's remaining manor estate in Watford town – of which £6,000 should repay the mortgage. So the Watford manor, already smaller after George's bequests of real estate to his daughters, was depleted even further by the sale of more land. These were all enclosed fields – two in the west of Watford town and many more making several farms in the Upperend of Watford town.

Sir Robert's financial woes were not over. He borrowed several smaller amounts from Elizabeth Breton, eventually adding up to another £2,000. He tried to sell Elizabeth another parcel of lands for £2,000, but she refused because they were unenclosed open common lands. That led to a long dispute between them not resolved until 1716, and not to Sir Robert's satisfaction. However, the family must have sold another 400-plus acres of his common lands to extricate himself from the predicament, as many decades later the manor estate does not include such lands.

Let alone the problems of debt, George left certain inconsistencies in his will that prompted dispute among the beneficiaries. Dorothy Clerke had been given certain lands situated within the manor house grounds and garden, meant for his nephew Sir Robert Clerke. Conversely, Sir Robert became possessed of certain lands which Dorothy evidently regarded as her territory. The situation became embroiled in suits between the parties and accusations of trespass. The widow Sarah Clerke was also involved, with similar claims pertaining to what was included in her jointure.

The disputes were finally resolved a few years after Dorothy married Sir John Francklin in 1691, when they were looking to monetise her inheritance. Agreement was secured in September 1695 for Thomas Cartwright to pay £7,270 for most of Dorothy's inherited real estate. Her lands were released from the 200 year trust designed to repay the mortgages of £1,000 and £1,200, plus interest, so they could be sold clear of encumbrances.

To tidy their various counterclaims of land, in January 1696 the parties swapped the offending properties. Dorothy gave to Sir Robert her lands in the Park and the garden of the Park, while Sir Robert gave Dorothy certain lands in the open and common fields of Watford and a few other parcels, such as two identified homestalls.

For the main event – selling lands to Cartwright – the parties executed several agreements in February 1696. For one, the northernmost field in Silsworth was brought into the deal by reciting the Catesby's complex dealings with the former Burneby manor lands in Silsworth. In two more, the Francklins gave to Cartwright possession of and title to Dorothy's lands. The properties sold and exceptions listed in the various agreements were almost the same, with a few minor differences probably identified when lawyers got busy after the initial agreement was signed. Added, due to omission from the earlier agreement and apparently forgotten in George's will, were the Hindmill closes and a few small closes in Silsworth.

The lands sold to Cartwright were subject to the life use of Sarah Clerke. Presumably Sarah maintained her composure whilst observing several legal agreements with one of many terms reading, 'after the decease of Sarah Clerke'. From the total price of £7,270, the two mortgages plus interest were deducted, also payment for the remaining £580 due to Samuel Adams for Sharrocks and Viccars in Silsworth, leaving the Francklins with £3,799. Of that amount, Dorothy directed £2,348 be paid to her husband, Sir John Francklin.

According to the final concord, Dorothy's sale of 13 ½ yardlands and many inclosed grounds to Cartwright amounted to over 1,100 acres plus five each of homesteads, gardens and orchards. Four of the five homesteads stood in the village lined up against Watford Park, with the fifth lying on the west boundary of the Oad Ground in Silsworth. Uncertain wording in the final concord appears to suggest 242 acres of Cartwright's newly acquired lands did not carry tithes, including 154 acres in Silsworth and 66 belonging to Watford church. The Cartwrights listed about 950 acres for sale in 1802, which seemed to include at least 30 acres purchased in Silsworth. Therefore, the Cartwrights either sold about 200 acres in the intervening century or so, or the inclosures within the same time frame effectively reduced the holding by that amount.

After including words in the agreement to sell 'all' of Dorothy's lands, the lawyers then listed the eight exceptions. Six of these are listed in the Table in the Appendix showing Dorothy's inherited lands – the ones not in italics – and include one yardland and several homesteads and tenements. The other two of the eight had been 'created' when Dorothy and Sir Robert swapped properties – the homestalls and a homestead, both in or around Watford village.

Also excepted from the sale were tithes on Old or Great Silsworth and a number of small closes in Silsworth. These tithes had been granted under several trusts for the benefit of the Vicar of Watford and his successors. Further excepted out of the premises sold were the tithes given to Jane Clerke arising from the eleven yardlands in the common fields of Murcott, being the lands of the right honourable Robert, Earl of Sutherland. And finally excepted, were all tithes arising within the parish of Watford belonging to the vicar of the Church of Watford and his successors.

Watford Landowners after 1700

Bridges' published History of Northants provided a description of the parish as it was about 1720. The more detailed text in his working volumes[168] reads in part:

There is one hamlett, one part (also) the one half of Murcott, viz 5 houses that belong to this parish. Inn-ships, or, odd houses, are 6, viz: 1 the house at Sellesworth, which is reported to have been formerly an Hamblett, and that there were several houses there, and a causey pitched with stone from the Town of Watford thither. The said place, no doubt, has been disinhabited for very many years. 2 is Pilson Mawbey's house. 3 Thomas Andrew's house. 4 William Slynn's house. 5 William Muscott's house. 6 John Archer's house. All the said 6 houses stand up and down in the Grounds. To these we shall add a seventh, which is Watford Gap. A very noted well-accustomed Inn, upon the Great Road. At the perfecting of the building of which, Sir Rob Clerke, to make the place more signal, ordered a large pudding to be drawn on a timber carriage from the town of Watford hither, and being partly to their journey's end, the sawed axle-tree alined in sunder that upon the least motion the pudding might break the carriage, which accordingly it did. And the artificers, using no further ceremony, fell to work with it with their spades and trowels. The number of houses in this town is 3. Houses erected for the poor are 4. [Under Long Buckby]:[169] Their hamblett is Murcott [which used to be in Watford] ... the number of houses in Murcott aforesaid belonging to this parish is 6; Inn-ships or odd houses standing out of their town are 4 viz, 1 the Lodge, 2 the Folly, both these stand on Buckby Heath, 3 is their Water Mill near Murcott, 4 their other Water Mill, standing about 300 yards below their Town.

Sir Robert Clerke is the sole lord of the manor for this town. The living is the king's gift and is a vicarage, worth about £80 per annum. The Revd. Mr John Dudley is the present incumbent. The said Mrs Sarah Clerke, Widow of the late George Clerke Esq. (and aunt to the present Sir Robert Clerke), besides the set of communion plate, mentioned at the end of the register, gave a pulpit cushion, and a communion table-cloth. And ordered a place to be taken out of the church, which is made fit for receiving their town-born, towards whose education she has for several years past allowed a master £12 per annum for officiating therein; tis indeed at the present continued on at her pleasure, but tis said she will settle the same forever by her last will and testament. The said Sir Robert Clerke's Court for the Town is Court Leet and Baron, when he calls the same, which is but very rarely, is held at this Town. The greatest part of this lordship belongs to the said Sir Robert Clerke. And the following have Estates in this lordship, viz the late squire Breton of Norton juxta Daventry has about £400 per annum; The Earl of Sunderland has in Murcott about £150 per annum, part of which is in this parish, as aforesaid; Mr Thomas Clerke (brother to Sir Robert Clerke) has about £50 per annum; The Revd. Mr Watkin of West Haddon about £30 per annum. Mr George Clerke of London has some small estate here. And when the said Sir Robert Clerke's aunt dyes, tis said several persons of distinction will lay claim to some estate in this lordship. Their Constable is putt on by the justices at any of their settings, and in their own court, when holden. They have two overseers of the poor, who are chosen by the majority of the Town on Easter Monday. Rocks - They have several of stone, but none reputed very good for building, excepting one in Burnham's Close. Crosses – There were formerly 2 in this town in the times of superstition.

One of historian John Bridges' workbooks[170] contains further comments recorded after a visit in Watford and a meeting with Sir Robert Clerke on September 12, 1722. A selection of these comments found their way, via Bridges' editors, into his work published decades later. An early note is that four parts in five of the Lordship was enclosed in four manors under the single Court of Sir Robert Clarke: Watford, Silsworth, Catesby, and Comberford. The enclosures, Sir Robert reported, were made in the year 1644, which is more likely the year Sir George completed the process, commenced as much as a decade before that date. The recorder adds, 'Of the manor mentioned on the other side [of the page], Silsworth, formerly belonged to the Prior of St John of Jerusalem.' This may be another inaccuracy by Sir Robert. He probably should have referred to the Prior of St James, near Northampton, although his statement may not have been totally erroneous. In her brief reign 20 years after the dissolution, Queen Mary did attempt to re-establish the abbeys as they were by re-giving many lands to St John of Jerusalem, including some in Watford. Then, a clearly incorrect statement, which found its way into the published work: 'Sir George Clerke had Comberford from the Lord Spencer by exchange for an estate in Boddington.' The exchanged estate was in Radbourne, co. Warwick, not Boddington. There follows a useful statement taken into the final published volume: 'The old manor house of Comberford is now the Crown Ale house and has on the outside and on a chimney above stairs these arms viz: a fret [a voided diamond with diagonal bands running through it]. Continuing on another topic: 'In the Chester road from Watford Gap, near Sir Robert Clerke's grounds, is a water called Calendar [aka Kalendre / Kalender], supposed to come from Calendar house about 1 mile north of Guilsborough.' After a comment about gravel appearing visibly on the top of the banks, we read: 'about ¾ mile south of Flore in the fields are deep pits of gravel of the same nature and one furlong distant from the Watlingstreeteway'. The remaining comments in the notebook refer to the church, describing its form, dimensions and many of the inscriptions in the chancel and elsewhere.

THE CLERKES, THE LEGACY WATFORD MANOR

George's widow, Sarah, lived until 1722. She was known for her benevolence towards the parish and left funds as a legacy for a school there. Her gift to the church in 1720 was a silver flagon, a chalice with a cover, paten and a table-cloth to be used at communion, and cushion for the pulpit. Sarah had also, at her own expense, caused a place to be taken out of the north aisle of the church as a school for the children of the town as well as provide for a master.

The Manor estate, albeit markedly reduced by probate and by claims of mortgagees, remained with Clerke descendants. Initially this was through George's nephew, Sir Robert Clerke, who was the son of Robert, George Clerke's younger brother. He was the third generation of Clerkes beginning with Sir George. Sir Robert Clerke's inheritance was the manor house adjacent to Watford village known as Watford Court, Watford Park, and two leases of intailed lands. The Watford Park estate comprised primarily fields later known as Top Park, Middle Park, and Home Park, stretching westwards from the manor house.

From Sir Robert Clerke, the manor passed through two more generations of the Clerke family: Edward C. T. Clerke and Charles W. Clerke. The last Clerke was Charles' younger brother, George Clerke, inheriting in 1764. George married Ann Pilkington two years later.

Evidently George and Ann came to live elsewhere, as they advertise the let, or re-let, of the manor and park in 1779 (see[171] Figure 65). The advertisement serves to

NORTHAMPTONSHIRE.
TO be LETT, and Entered upon at Lady-Day next (or sooner if required, by agreeing with the present Tenant)

A large commodious MANSION-HOUSE, situate at Watford, in the County of Northampton: Consisting of a very good Kitchen, three Parlours, a Drawing-Room, two Halls, a Butler's-Pantry, three large Cellars, seven Chambers with good Garrets over them, and three Closets; a very good Brewhouse, Bakehouse, Laundry, Larder, and Dairy; a Coach-House, Stables, and Barns; a large Kitchen-Garden walled in, well planted with Wall Fruit-Trees, &c. with the extensive Manor of Watford aforesaid, together with (or without, or with Part of) upwards of 120 Acres of very good Feeding, Pasture, and Meadow Land, commonly called Watford-Park, fenced in with a Stone Wall; with an exceeding good Cold Bath on the Premises.

Note. Watford is a small Country Village, about twelve Miles from Northampton, five from Daventry, and seven from Rugby, all good Market Towns; and about six Miles from Althorp, the Seat of the Right Hon. Earl Spencer.— There are several Packs of Hounds kept in the Neighbourhood of Watford.

Any Gentleman inclined to take the House, Gardens, Manor, &c. is requested to enquire for Particulars of Mr. Edwards, Attorney at Law, in Daventry.

. Edward Welch, of Watford, will shew the Premises. December 17, 1779.

Figure 65: Watford Park to Lett: Northants Mercury, 20 Dec 1779

describe the manor house and park as it was 100 years after the occupation of George Clerke in the 1680s. A similar advertisement was run again in 1783. Both advertisements refer to Watford Park, without the extended Estate. Edward Welch, who in 1779 would show the estate, was a descendant of long-time residents and tenants of Watford. In 1783 it is the descendant of another long-resident family, Mr Joseph Butlin of the Star and Garter, who shows the premises.

George Clerke died in 1787 without any children. Ann Clerke married again to John Bennett in 1793. The estate was held in trust, following the death of the last of the Clerkes.

In 1796, it is Ann and John Bennett who advertise the let of

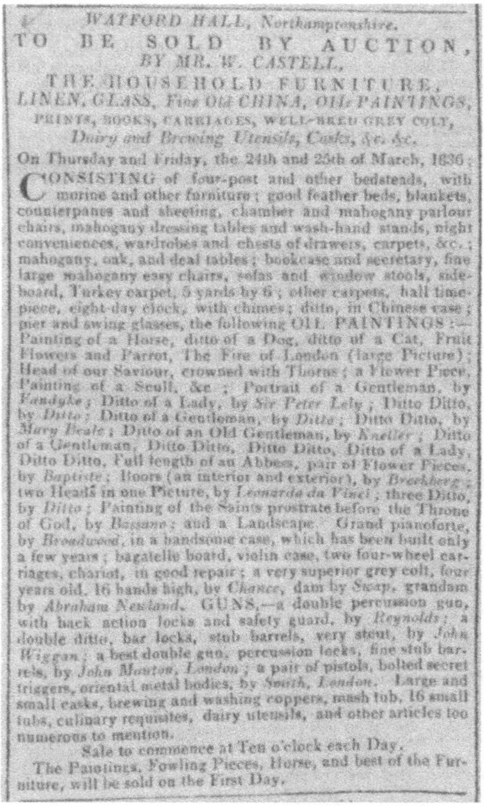

WATFORD HALL, Northamptonshire.
TO BE SOLD BY AUCTION, BY MR. W. CASTELL,
THE HOUSEHOLD FURNITURE, LINEN, GLASS, Fine Old CHINA, OIL PAINTINGS, PRINTS, BOOKS, CARRIAGES, WELL-BRED GREY COLT, Dairy and Brewing Utensils, Casks, &c. &c.

On Thursday and Friday, the 24th and 25th of March, 1836; CONSISTING of four-post and other bedsteads, with morine and other furniture; good feather beds, blankets, counterpanes and sheeting, chamber and mahogany parlour chairs, mahogany dressing tables and wash-hand stands, night conveniences, wardrobes and chests of drawers, carpets, &c.; mahogany, oak, and deal tables; bookcase and secretary, fine large mahogany easy chairs, sofas and window stools, sideboard, Turkey carpet, 5 yards by 6; other carpets, hall timepiece, eight-day clock, with chimes; ditto, in Chinese case; pier and swing glasses, the following OIL PAINTINGS:— Painting of a Horse, ditto of a Dog, ditto of a Cat, Fruit Flowers and Parrot, The Fire of London (large Picture); Head of our Saviour, crowned with Thorns; a Flower Piece, Painting of a Scull, &c.; Portrait of a Gentleman, by Vandyke; Ditto of a Lady, by Sir Peter Lely; Ditto Ditto, by Ditto; Ditto of a Gentleman, by Ditto; Ditto Ditto, by Mary Beale; Ditto of an Old Gentleman, by Kneller; Ditto of a Gentleman, Ditto Ditto, Ditto, Ditto of a Lady, Ditto Ditto, Full length of an Abbess, pair of Flower Pieces, by Baptiste; Hoots (an interior and exterior), by Brockberg; two Heads in one Picture, by Leonardo da Vinci; three Ditto, by Ditto; Painting of the Saints prostrate before the Throne of God, by Bassano; and a Landscape. Grand pianoforte, by Broadwood, in a handsome case, which has been built only a few years; bagatelle board, violin case, two four-wheel carriages, chariot, in good repair; a very superior grey colt, four years old, 16 hands high, by Chance, dam by Swap, grandam by Abraham Newland. GUNS,—a double percussion gun, with back action locks and safety guard, by Reynolds; a double ditto, bar locks, stub barrels, very stout, by John Wiggan, a best double gun, percussion locks, fine stub barrels, by John Manton, London; a pair of pistols, bolted secret triggers, oriental metal bodies, by Smith, London. Large and small casks, brewing and washing coppers, mash tub, 16 small tubs, culinary requisites, dairy utensils, and other articles too numerous to mention.

Sale to commence at Ten o'clock each Day.

The Paintings, Fowling Pieces, Horse, and best of the Furniture, will be sold on the First Day.

Figure 66: Watford Hall contents: Northants Mercury, 19 March 1836

Watford Hall, Manor, and Lands. The owners described the Estate in three components, and prospective tenants could take any one or all of the parts. First, the mansion house and surrounding gardens, stables, coach-house, and other offices, which occupied about 5 acres. Second, up to 120 acres of 'Watford Park', and third, another 260 acres of farmland. Initial attempts at letting the entire estate may not have succeeded, as another, similar, advertisement appears 18 months after the first, except the 260 acres of farmland was no longer on offer.

John Bennett died in 1808 at Chapel Brampton, aged 53. Ann Bennet, nee Clerke, nee Pilkington followed in December 1834, aged 92. Soon after, the trustees put the estate and contents up for sale. First to be sold were the trees on the estate – 34 prime Elm, containing upward of 100 feet in each tree. Shortly after, the brewing utensils of the late Mrs Bennett went under the auctioneer's hammer.

A month later, 25 March 1836, the contents of Watford Hall were sold (see[172] Figure 66). Other than many pieces of furniture, Mrs Bennett's possessions in the manor included collections of oil paintings and guns. Evidently, the artwork included a portrait by Vandyke, a picture of two heads by Leonardo da Vinci, and another by him of three heads. The guns included pistols and a number of weapons fired by percussion.

The estate itself with manor house was sold separately. The buyer was the Rt. Hon Lord Henley. The purchase date of Watford Park Estate, 23 March 1836, was virtually the same as the date of the auction of the mansion contents, and the completion date was some 10 months later. These dates were written by hand on a Plan[173] of 'Watford Park Estate', probably drawn up at the behest of Henry Pilkington in preparation for a sale.

That Plan indicates there was only 415 acres remaining in the Manor Estate, including 125 acres of Watford Park and another 290 acres of farm land. The extent of Watford Park is consistent with a map[174] dated 1740, drawn up for Edward Clerke, Esq. The inclusion of spinneys, woods, coppice, ponds, brooks, waters, canals, in each accounts for the additional 30 acres in the Estate Plan.

THE CARTWRIGHTS OF AYNHO

Richard Cartwright was a successful lawyer who first purchased the manor of Aynho, Northamptonshire, in 1616. His son John supported Parliament and his mansion was burnt down in 1645 by the Royalists. He died in 1676 and his grandson was Thomas, born 1671. This was the Thomas Cartwright who, in 1695, bought about 1,100 acres, being most of the lands inherited by Dorothy Clerke.

Thomas's son, William Cartwright was one of a group who obtained Bridges' manuscript of *The History … of Northamptonshire* and eventually brought part to publication. In his will, William left to his son, Thomas Cartwright, 'all my manors messuages lands tenements and appurtenances in Watford and Murcott'. Not satisfied with his original will, he proceeded to write ten codicils, the effect of one lasting a very long time. In the 1765 codicil he created a rent charge of £200 a year payable out of all his freehold in Silsworth in the parish of Watford, to last forever.

His grandson was William Ralph Cartwright. The lessee of Ralph's lands in Silsworth refers to certain of his lands in Silsworth rented from 'Mr. Cartwright'. This was a reference either to the estate of Thomas Cartwright or William Ralph Cartwright acting through his guardians, as Ralph was only four years old at the time. The lessee eventually bought the Silsworth farm called Silsworth Lodge, taking on the obligation of the £200 annuity as part of the price paid.

In the first years of the 1800s, the Cartwrights remodelled their Manor at Aynho. The need for funds for this purpose and the accumulated debt of past decades are likely the reasons William Ralph Cartwright in 1802 decided to sell the Cartwright estates in Watford parish (see[175] Figure 67), originally acquired by his great grandfather. Six years on, Cartwright succeeded in selling the estate. This required the Dorset-based Henley-Eden family to team up with Richard Abbey, the farmer of Silsworth Lodge. Together, they provided sufficient buying power to repay and

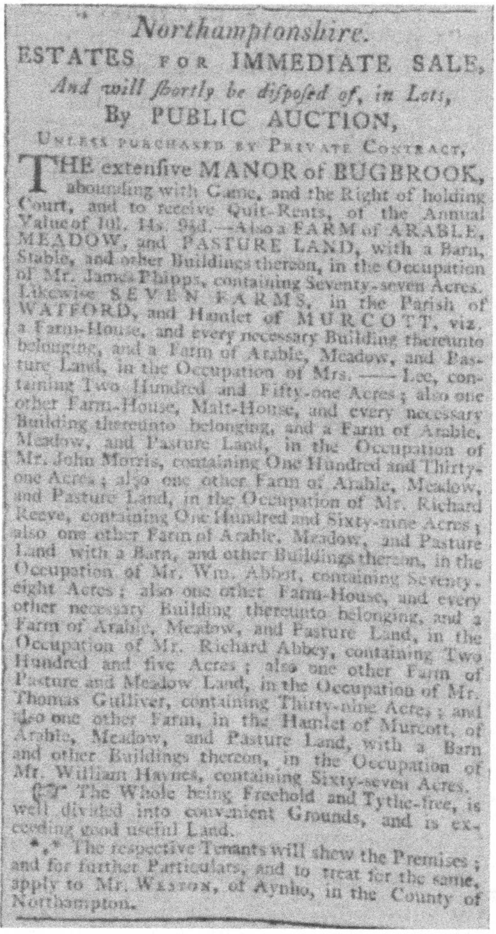

Northamptonshire.

ESTATES FOR IMMEDIATE SALE,

And will shortly be disposed of, in Lots,

By PUBLIC AUCTION,

UNLESS PURCHASED BY PRIVATE CONTRACT,

THE extensive MANOR of BUGBROOK, abounding with Game, and the Right of holding Court, and to receive Quit-Rents, of the Annual Value of 10l. 1s. 9½d.—Also a FARM of ARABLE, MEADOW, and PASTURE LAND, with a Barn, Stable, and other Buildings thereon, in the Occupation of Mr. James Phipps, containing Seventy-seven Acres. Likewise SEVEN FARMS, in the Parish of WATFORD, and Hamlet of MURCOTT, viz. a Farm-House, and every necessary Building thereunto belonging, and a Farm of Arable, Meadow, and Pasture Land, in the Occupation of Mrs. —— Lee, containing Two Hundred and Fifty-one Acres; also one other Farm-House, Malt-House, and every necessary Building thereunto belonging, and a Farm of Arable, Meadow, and Pasture Land, in the Occupation of Mr. John Morris, containing One Hundred and Thirty-one Acres; also one other Farm of Arable, Meadow, and Pasture Land, in the Occupation of Mr. Richard Reeve, containing One Hundred and Sixty-nine Acres; also one other Farm of Arable, Meadow, and Pasture Land with a Barn, and other Buildings thereon, in the Occupation of Mr. Wm. Abbot, containing Seventy-eight Acres; also one other Farm-House, and every other necessary Building thereunto belonging, and a Farm of Arable, Meadow, and Pasture Land, in the Occupation of Mr. Richard Abbey, containing Two Hundred and five Acres; also one other Farm of Pasture and Meadow Land, in the Occupation of Mr. Thomas Gulliver, containing Thirty-nine Acres; and also one other Farm, in the Hamlet of Murcott, of Arable, Meadow, and Pasture Land, with a Barn and other Buildings thereon, in the Occupation of Mr. William Haynes, containing Sixty-seven Acres.

☞ The Whole being Freehold and Tythe-free, is well divided into convenient Grounds, and is exceeding good useful Land.

, The respective Tenants will shew the Premises; and for further Particulars, and to treat for the same, apply to Mr. WESTON, of Aynho, in the County of Northampton.

Figure 67: Cartwright sells Estate: Northants Mercury 18 Dec 1802

release the mortgage on Cartwright's estate in Watford and Silsworth and take on the annuity of £200. While Lord Henley-Eden bought over 600 acres of the Cartwright lands, Richard Abbey took on nearly 300 acres in Silsworth along with the £200 annuity, leaving some 78 acres apparently going elsewhere.

THE BRETONS IN WATFORD

The Breton family of Norton, near Watford, in the 1690s was headed by Elizabeth Breton, who had been left a healthy estate after her husband died. Her neighbour, Sir Robert Clerke, had found himself in a quandary when not being able to repay a mortgage of £6,000 he took out in 1690 to pay debts forced onto him. In 1694 Elizabeth was persuaded to buy a large parcel of Watford manor's enclosures from Sir Robert for £9,000. Sir Robert continued to borrow smaller sums until he owed Elizabeth £2,000. By 1702, thinking to repay the debt, Sir Robert tried to sell Elizabeth more of his estate in Watford – this time 6 yardlands for £2,000. She refused, saying she had no intention of buying unenclosed open grounds. There ensued a back-and-forth between them as to whether or not there had been an agreement to sell, which if so, was unperformed. Several local farmers were called upon in 1716 to give evidence in Watford for the High Court of Chancery, who ended up on Elizabeth's side.

The late 'Squire Breton' of Norton next Daventry, as he was described about 1720, had an estate in Watford worth about £400 per annum, which was a considerable amount at that time. The 'squire' was Nicholas Breton, who died in 1716. He gave his widowed mother, Elizabeth, his entire estate of lands, manors, and mortgages to distribute as she saw fit, along with the custody of his children.

From Nicholas Breton, the Watford estate descended to Eliab Breton, born in 1710 at Norton. Eliab died in December 1785, with estate in several parts of England. His Estate was assessed for land tax in Watford in an undated document, but probably late in the 18th century after he died. The following lists his fields in Watford. The next owners in about 1805 and 1849 are also noted. All in all, this land amounted to about 460 acres.

Breton's fields in the 18th century	Owner, 1805 / 1849
Haygate and Naseborough Meadow	Martin Lucas / John J Ashby
Naseborow Ground	Martin Lucas / John J Ashby
Thorney Close	Martin Lucas / John J Ashby
Archers Ground	Earl Spencer / Earl Spencer
Hollandsides	Earl Spencer / Earl Spencer
Radmorend (not Radmore farm)	Earl Spencer / Earl Spencer

New River Grounds	Earl Spencer / Earl Spencer
Barfurlong (Barn & Wad)	Earl Spencer / Earl Spencer
Little Meadow	Ann Bennett / Lord Henley
Middleton	John Brooks / Lord Henley
Crindle	John Brooks / Mrs Freer

THE SPENCERS IN WATFORD

By the mid 20th century, the Spencer family had been present in Watford for over 400 years. As discussed towards the end of the Parles/Comberford chapter, the Spencer's holdings in Watford parish in the eighteenth century amounted to over 500 acres. The family owned properties in Watford both before and after the Clerkes arrived in the parish.

By the mid nineteenth century the family's holdings had increased, much of which can be attributed to a farm of nearly 150 acres. This farm lies in NE Watford, between Lord Bateman's Radmore and Spencer's other lands in Murcott. The Bretons owned the land in the late 18th century and in or around 1787, some or all of their estate was sold. At the turn of the century, this farm was under the occupancy of the Tebbetts, and by 1805, the land was in the hands of Earl Spencer.

THE HENLEY-EDENS IN WATFORD

In the 19th century, the Henley Eden family were the largest single landowner in modern Watford. The Right Honourable Lord Robert Henley, 2nd Baron Henley, acquired the Watford Manor Estate in 1836, comprising 415 acres of the Manor House, the manor Park, the large northern fields of the Hay and Barley Piece, and the western ends of New River and Little Meadow in the upper and east end of Watford town.

His father, the Rt. Hon. Morton Eden and 1st Baron Henley, had first purchased lands in Watford well before 1836. Morton Eden had taken the Henley name after marriage, and had retired from the diplomatic corps in 1799.

Lord Henley held no lands in Watford when a survey of the parish was completed about 1805. His initial acquisitions in the parish can be dated to 1808, when the Rt. Hon. Morton Lord Henley purchased over 600 acres from the Cartwrights. His purchases comprised the two farms in the netherend of Watford totalling some 290 acres, 205 acres in the southeast of Silsworth, 70 acres in the western corner of Murcott, and another 44 acres in Watford township.

Baron Henley's will was probated in 1831, in which he named his seat as Chardstock, Dorset. His son, the Hon. Robert Henley Eden, and his wife-to-be, Harriet Peel, were party to a lease and release dated March 1824. The agreement was a marriage settlement on Robert and Harriet of the 'Manor and Estate in the parish of Watford Northamptonshire'. As demonstrated by various maps, other than the manor estate and Cartwright lands, over time approximately another 300 acres was added to the family's estate in Watford town.

The family's presence in Watford continues to the present day.

Give a Manor Take a Manor

Appendix 1: Descendants of Agnes de Ardern

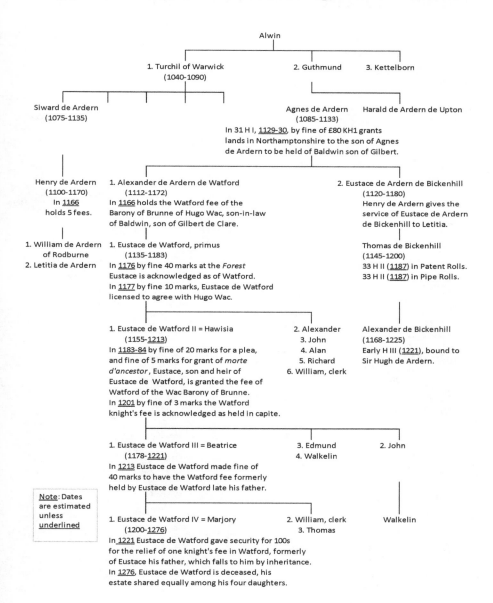

Alwin

1. Turchil of Warwick
(1040-1090)

2. Guthmund

3. Kettelborn

Siward de Ardern
(1075-1135)

Agnes de Ardern
(1085-1133)
In 31 H I, 1129-30, by fine of £80 KH1 grants
lands in Northamptonshire to the son of Agnes
de Ardern to be held of Baldwin son of Gilbert.

Harald de Ardern de Upton

Henry de Ardern
(1100-1170)
In 1166
holds 5 fees.

1. Alexander de Ardern de Watford
(1112-1172)
In 1166 holds the Watford fee of the
Barony of Brunne of Hugo Wac, son-in-law
of Baldwin, son of Gilbert de Clare.

2. Eustace de Ardern de Bickenhill
(1120-1180)
Henry de Ardern gives the
service of Eustace de Ardern
de Bickenhill to Letitia.

1. William de Ardern
of Rodburne
2. Letitia de Ardern

1. Eustace de Watford, primus
(1135-1183)
In 1176 by fine 40 marks at the *Forest*
Eustace is acknowledged as of Watford.
In 1177 by fine 10 marks, Eustace de Watford
licensed to agree with Hugo Wac.

Thomas de Bickenhill
(1145-1200)
33 H II (1187) in Patent Rolls.
33 H II (1187) in Pipe Rolls.

1. Eustace de Watford II = Hawisia
(1155-1213)
In 1183-84 by fine of 20 marks for a plea,
and fine of 5 marks for grant of *morte
d'ancestor*, Eustace, son and heir of
Eustace de Watford, is granted the fee of
Watford of the Wac Barony of Brunne.
In 1201 by fine of 3 marks the Watford
knight's fee is acknowledged as held in capite.

2. Alexander
3. John
4. Alan
5. Richard
6. William, clerk

Alexander de Bickenhill
(1168-1225)
Early H III (1221), bound to
Sir Hugh de Ardern.

1. Eustace de Watford III = Beatrice
(1178-1221)
In 1213 Eustace de Watford made fine of
40 marks to have the Watford fee formerly
held by Eustace de Watford late his father.

3. Edmund
4. Walkelin

2. John

Walkelin

1. Eustace de Watford IV = Marjory
(1200-1276)
In 1221 Eustace de Watford gave security for 100s
for the relief of one knight's fee in Watford, formerly
of Eustace his father, which falls to him by inheritance.
In 1276, Eustace de Watford is deceased, his
estate shared equally among his four daughters.

2. William, clerk
3. Thomas

Appendix 2: Descendants of Eustace de Watford

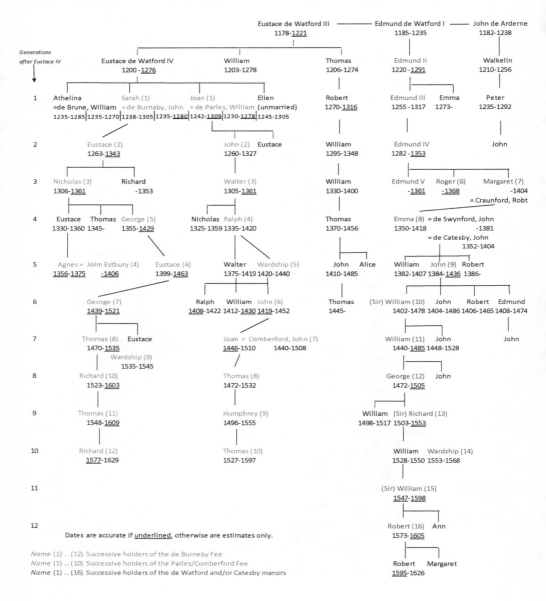

Eustace de Watford III 1178-<u>1221</u> ——— Edmund de Watford I 1185-1235 ——— John de Arderne 1182-1238

Generations after Eustace IV ↓

Generation 1

Eustace de Watford IV 1200-<u>1276</u> | William 1203-1278 | Thomas 1206-1274 | Edmund II 1220-<u>1291</u> | Walkelin 1210-1256

1
Athelina =de Brune, William 1235-1285 | Sarah (1) = de Burnaby, John 1235-1270 | Joan (1) = de Parles, William 1238-<u>1305</u> | Ellen (unmarried) 1242-<u>1309</u> 1230-<u>1278</u> | 1245-1305 | Robert 1270-<u>1316</u> | Edmund III 1255-1317 Emma 1273- | Peter 1235-1292

2
Eustace (2) 1263-<u>1343</u> | John (2) Eustace 1260-1327 | William 1295-1348 | Edmund IV 1282-<u>1353</u> | John

3
Nicholas (3) 1306-<u>1361</u> Richard -1353 | Walter (3) 1305-<u>1361</u> | William 1330-1400 | Edmund V -<u>1361</u> Roger (6) -<u>1368</u> Margaret (7) -1404 = Craunford, Robt

4
Eustace 1330-1360 Thomas 1345- George (5) 1355-<u>1429</u> | Nicholas 1325-1359 Ralph (4) 1335-1420 | Thomas 1370-1456 | Emma (8) = de Swynford, John 1350-1418 -1381 = de Catesby, John 1352-1404

5
Agnes = John Estbury (4) <u>1356-1375</u> -<u>1406</u> Eustace (6) 1399-<u>1463</u> | Walter 1375-1419 Wardship (5) 1420-1440 | John 1410-1485 Alice | William 1382-1407 John (9) 1384-<u>1436</u> Robert 1386-

6
George (7) <u>1439-1521</u> | Ralph 1408-1422 William 1412-<u>1430</u> John (6) <u>1419</u>-1452 | Thomas 1445- | (Sir) William (10) 1402-1478 John 1404-1486 Robert 1406-1465 Edmund 1408-1474

7
Thomas (8) 1470-<u>1535</u> Eustace Wardship (9) 1535-1545 | Joan = Comberford, John (7) <u>1446</u>-1510 1440-1508 | William (11) 1440-<u>1485</u> John 1448-1528 | John

8
Richard (10) 1523-<u>1603</u> | Thomas (8) 1472-1532 | George (12) 1472-<u>1505</u> John

9
Thomas (11) 1548-<u>1609</u> | Humphrey (9) 1496-1555 | William 1498-1517 (Sir) Richard (13) 1503-<u>1553</u>

10
Richard (12) <u>1577</u>-1629 | Thomas (10) 1527-1597 | William 1528-1550 Wardship (14) 1553-1568

11
(Sir) William (15) <u>1547</u>-<u>1598</u>

12
Robert (16) Ann 1573-<u>1605</u>

Robert Margaret <u>1595</u>-1626

Dates are accurate if <u>underlined</u>, otherwise are estimates only.

Name (1) ... (12) Successive holders of the de Burneby Fee
Name (1) ... (10) Successive holders of the Parles/Comberford Fee
Name (1) ... (16) Successive holders of the de Watford and/or Catesby manors

Appendix 3: Summary of George Clerke's Will

<u>Given to Dorothy Clarke*</u>:
- *one yard land in the common fields of Watford bought from [John & William] Capell*
- *one close in Watford called Murcutt Close*
- *Balys Close in Silesworth*
- *Two closes in Silesworth bought from _____ Gutteridge*
- *two yard lands and a quartern in the common fields of Murcutt*
- *Vicars Close in [Watford Silesworth]*
- the Close called Radmore in Watford
- *two yard lands and a quarterne in Watford common fields and the house and homestead rented by Thomas Reeve Senior*
- *a house homestead and three yard lands rented by John Lee*
- *Edward Reeves house homestead and yard land [and the] one yard land bought from William Gilbert*
- *three roods in Fardals nine odd lands and two leas [and] two yard lands and nine more odd lands in common fields of Watford bought from Thomas Welsh*
- *a house and Close in the tenure of John Griffin*
- another house and close bought from John Welsh [in 2 tenements]
- one yard land bought from [the widow] Wills [William] Burgess and [John] Herbert
- *Northingworth ground in Watford*
- *the impropriate Tithes of the Common fields of Watford*
- *the close called Sturges his close in Silesworth in Watford*
- *half a yard land lying in the common fields of Watford bought from [John & William] Capell*
- *a close called by the name of Forty Acres in Silesworth bought of [Fitzherbert, DD] Adams*
- a house and close bought from Newell Browne

<u>Given to Jane Clarke:</u>
- the New Inne and grounds thereto belonging in the parish of Watford after the life of William Chambers
- and the several Closes and the meadows thereto belonging lying near thereto called by the names of
  - Gilberts Close
  - Wills's Close and
  - Maycocks Close
- two Closes called Brodwells Hays
- the ground called Freeman Croft in Watford
- Car[r]s house and Close
- widow Roberts house & close in the Tenure of Newell Browne
- Townsend
- Poole Close
- Lucas's Close in the tenure of Widow Segly
- the Tithe of eleven yard lands in Murcott in the parish of Watford
- a Close in Silesworth called Adam's Forty acres [s/be Adams Lesser Cl]
- a close called Carters close

Obligation to pay £50 p.a. to Samuel Adams for his lifetime secured on the New Inne and Gilberts, Wills's, and Maycocks closes

<u>Given to Elizabeth Clarke:</u>
- all the several grounds in Silesworth bought of Mr Flint
- Barkers two Closes
- Cross's Close
- Bucknolds two closes in Silesworth
- half the Tithe of some small closes there [in Silesworth]

<u>Given to Sir Robert Clarke:</u>
- the Park of Watford and the Capital Messuage gardens orchards and Courts thereunto belonging
- Intailed lands of a £200 lease in Watford of the grounds called:
  - Great Hayes
  - Upper Hayes

- a tenancy bought from Thomas Youngbone
- a new house in which widow [Priscilla] Sedgley lives in and the homestead thereto belonging
- *the ground called Cookesfield in Silesworth and the Meadow thereto belonging*
- *the Horse Close in Silesworth*
- *the several closes in Silesworth bought from Mr [Thomas] Duncumb ['the Oad Ground']*
- *the remainder of all real estate [i.e. HindMills & Carters closes]*

Obligation to pay £40 p.a. for two Lives charged on Radmore
Mortgage to one Palmer
Mortgage to one Rathbone

Given to Sir William Craven and his wife Mary, nee Clarke:
- £100
- All such money as she has disbursed for her sister Elizabeth

Given to Sir Gilbert Clarke widower of Barbara, nee Clarke:
- £100

Given to Barbara Clarke, a 'Goddaughter' (daughter of Barbara Clarke, who married Thomas Kinnersley)
- The Chamber in Lincoln's Inne bought in the name of her brother Sir Robert Clarke
- The perpetual right of Patronage of the church of Guilsborough

- o Barley peice
- o Thorny Close
- o Blackwell Close
- o Chrindals
- o Middleton
- o Overend Meadow
- o Navesborough
- o Barfurlong
- o Penclose
- o Little meadows
- o Vicars Close in Watford
- Intailed other lands (not named in will) in a £150 Lease (messuages & closes named in 1688 lease):
  - o Msg Cls 1 ½ YL occ L Adson
  - o Msg Cls 2 YL occ H Wills
  - o Msg 2 Cls 1 ½ YL occ W Rogers
  - o Msg Cls 1 YL occ R Reeve
  - o Msg Cls 2 YL occ Jn Justin
  - o Haygate Close occ T Kertland
  - o Lynes Meadow occ T Sly
  - o Wrights Close occ Jos Welch
  - o Two Broadwell Closes & New England Close occ Geo Clerke
  - o Bretts Close occ T Slinn
  - o Msg occ Paybody/Coleman
  - o 15 Cottages all occupied
  - o Tithes of above closes & of Smythes Boyland
- Obligation to pay £1,000 from the intailed leased lands to his widow Sarah for his unmarried daughters
- Obligation to pay £2,000 to each of three unmarried daughters Dorothy, Jane and Elizabeth

* Dorothy's bequests in italics, she later sold to the Cartwrights; those in plain type, she retained.

Appendix 4: Lands of Watford Parish

Summary of handwritten survey[176] of Watford, taken about 1805.

Proprietor	Occupier	Name of close or field	Acres
Central Watford			
Ann Bennett	Herself	Manor House and Park	124
Ann Bennett	Villagers (eight)	Houses, barn, smithy, pub	7
Vicarage	Gilbert, Gilbert, Butlin	Churchyard, house, orchd	1.5
Vicarage	Joseph Butlin	Top & Bottom closes	17
Samuel Butlin	Himself	House & orchard & close	9
James Green	Himself	Valentines close	7
Thomas Abbott	Himself	House	0.5
			166
North Watford			
Ann Bennett	James Neal	Upper Hay	51
Ann Bennett	James Butlin	Lines & Slye	17
Ann Bennett	Herself	Barley Piece	21
Ann Bennett	William Gilbert	Gilberts Barley Piece	32
Ann Bennett	Thomas Poole	Great Hay (5 closes)	59
George Arnold	William Gilbert	Blackwell & Bretts	53
Harrison & Paine	Thomas Payne	Freemans Croft/Wht/Bank	56
			289
East Watford (aka the Upperend)			
Earl Spencer	Mrs Tebbett	Archers/Bar/Holland	145
Ralph Cartwright	William Abbott	Behind Mill & Horse	77
John Wadsworth	Himself	Cow Meadow	9
Ann Bennett	James Neal	Little Meadow, New River	108
William Hanbury	John Abbey	Radmore	66
Lucas Martin	Stephen Watson	Heygate/Naseboro/Thorney	157
			562
West Watford (the WestEnd)			
Ann Bennett	James Gilbert	Cowpen / Cowley	69
John Brooks, snr	Mr Brooks, jnr	Crindle & Middleton	98
John Harper	Mrs Wedding	Overend / Upperend	87
George Arnold	Thomas Abbott	College	25
George Arnold	Thomas Moore	Boyland (beyond railway)	33
Harrison & Paine	Thomas Payne	House grounds & Boyland	47
Harrison & Paine	Thomas Payne	Mott & Larkhill	52
Harrison & Paine	Thomas Payne	Burnhams & Wills	68
			479
South Watford (aka the Netherend)			
William Gilbert	Himself	Chitty/Street close (lot 34)	20
Alice Lee	Herself	Leek/Drove/Meadow (lot 35)	27
James Gilbert	Himself	What/Far Close (lot 36)	17
Mary Reeve	Herself	Close & home (lots 32 & m)	20
Esther Gilbert	Herself	Close & home (lots 31 & c)	41
Vicarage & Prsh Clerk	J Butlin, T Butlin	Goodfellows (lot 28 & 29)	16

Samuel Harrison	Wm Abbott, Th Paine	Barn & Brockhall (lot 26)	59
King & Freeman	Nathaniel Gilbert	8 closes (lots 22-25 & 27)	88
William Morris	Himself	Closes (lots 33 & g)	49
Ralph Cartwright	Mary Reeve	Willows (lot 21) & Mrct Cls	42
Ralph Cartwright	Thomas Pool	11 cls's Strtflong (lots 1-8)	135
Ralph Cartwright	John Pell	12 cls's Langbro (lots 9-20)	149
			663
	Sub-total Watford Town		2,159
Silsworth Town			
Ralph Cartwright	Richd Abbey	Northingworth & Viccars	98
Ralph Cartwright	Alice Lee	Cooksfield & meadow	107
Ralph Cartwright	Richd Gulliver-Th'ly	Sharrocks	41
Ralph Cartwright	Mary Reeve	Palmers/Over/Highway	31
Ralph Cartwright	Richard Abbey	Hill/Oad/Thorne/Dunkleys	206
Mr Godfrey	Thomas Lovell	Great Ground	152
Earl Spencer	Robert Heygate	Silsworth Field	170
Earl Spencer	John Heygate	40 acre & 20 acre	58
Earl Spencer	John Heygate	Crosses/Hovel/Kitts	9
Six various	Six various	Earls/Wills/Bos/Undw/WH	31
Vicarage	Thomas Pool	Three Meadows	11
			914
Murcott Town			
Not in survey R. Cartwright	William Haynes	Six lots (at The Wash Brook)	70
Earl Spencer	Mr Collis	12 closes Townsend/Butts	136
Earl Spencer	Mr Wiggins	15 closes Grnshill/Twinney	147
William Clark	Himself	Rush close on Kingsham	22
(Not in Survey - some in Watford parish some given to Long Buckby parish)			305
			680
Total towns of Watford, Silsworth and Murcott			3,753

Notes to Appendix 4:

1. The Survey totalled 3,357 acres + 21 for minor adjustments + 375 omitted from Murcott = 3,753.

2. Total Watford Town as above 2,159 acres, whereas Watford per Atlas of Northants p18 includes 2,249 acres. The Atlas seems to include in Watford 70 acres formerly of Cartwright in Murcott, 54 acres of Northingworth in Watford, and excludes 34 acres of the Horse & Cowe closes from Watford. The Ordinance Survey declares Watford as 1278.4 hectares, or 3,159 acres. This seems to be 3,753 without all Murcott 680 acres but adding back the 70 acres of old Murcott adjacent to Watford Town, making 3,143 acres. BHO states Watford is 'more than 1400 hectares', which at more than 3,460 acres appears to exclude only about 305 acres given to Long Buckby.

3. The 305 acres 'Not in Survey', can be identified in the 1771 map: Lots 7, 9, 12, 14, 15, 17, 18, 19 of, respectively, Tomkins 55a, Revd Fox 17a, Craven 16a, Freeman 8a, Hanwell 7a, Lichfield 61a, total 164 acres probably in Long Buckby; Lots 13, 16, 20, 21, 22, 23 of respectively Craven 2a, Hanwell 35a, Watts 52a, Coleman 40a, Clarke 5a, Murcott village 7a, total 141 acres probably in Watford.

Works Cited

archive.org The Internet Archive, a digital library of Internet sites in digital form.

Blaauw, William Henry. *The Baron's War.* London, 1871.

Blount, Thomas. *Ancient Tenures of Land.* 1815. Butterworth.

Bodleian *Libraries*, Oxford University, The Bridges Collection, MS. Top. Northants. c. 1 to c. 39, e. 1 to e. 8, f. 1 to f. 5 [52 volumes].

Bridges, John. *The history and antiquities of Northamptonshire*, in 2 vols, compiled by the Rev. Peter Whalley, Oxford and Northampton, 1755 & 1791.

British History Online, Version 5.0 <www.british-history.ac.uk> especially Ancient Deeds, inquisitions post mortem (E-CIPM), and early-modern state and parliamentary documents. [accessed 2016-18].

British Library, The. London. (BL)

Camden, William. *Visitation of the County of Warwick, 1619.* London, Harleian Society, 1877.

Cassidy, Richard. *The 1259 Pipe Roll.* Kings College, University of London, PhD, 2012.

Collingwood, James. *Royal finances in the period of baronial reform and rebellion, 1255-1270.* University of London, PhD, 1995.

Comerford, Patrick. *comerfordfamily.blogspot.ca*

Coss, Peter. *Lordship, knighthood and locality.* Cambridge University Press, 1991.

Dugdale, William. *The Antiquities of Warwickshire.* Thomas Warren, London, 1656;

Dugdale, William. *Monasticon Anglicanum.* Originally 1693. Revised and updated in 8 volumes 1817 – 1846, by Caley, Ellis, and Bulkeley. Longman, Hurst, Rees, Orme & Brown.

Emery, Anthony. *Greater Medieval Houses of England and Wales, 1300-1500, Volume 2.* Cambridge University Press, 2000.

Fernandes, Mario Joseph. *The role of the Midland knights in the period of reform and rebellion 1258-67.* Kings College, University of London, PhD, 2000.

Field, P.J.C. *The Life and Times of Sir Thomas Mallory.* D S Brewer, 1993.

French, George Russel. *Shakespereana Genealogica.* MacMillan & Co, 1869.

Hall, David. *The Open Fields of Northamptonshire.* © Northamptonshire Record Society, 1995.

Harvey, William & Vincent, Augustine. Visitations of Northamptonshire, 1564 & 1619. Mitchell and Hughes. 1887.

Hervey, Sydenham (S.H.A.H.). *Ladbroke and its Owners*. Paul & Mathew, Bury St. Edmonds, 1914.

HMSO. *List of the Lands of Dissolved Religious Houses, No III, Vol 3*. Kraus reprint, 1964.

Keats-Rohan, Katherine. *The COEL Database (The Continental Origins of English Landowners 1066-1166)*, 1999, 2002.

medievalgenealogy.org.uk maintained by Chris Phillips. for medieval English genealogy, especially the many Rolls, Inquisitions, and the Feet of Fines.

National Archives, The. London. (TNA). *www.nationalarchives.gov.uk.*

Nichols, John Gough. *The Topographer and Genealogist vol. 1*, John Bowyer Nichols and son, London, 1846.

Northamptonshire Record Office (NRO), Northampton. *northamptonshire.gov.uk/councilservices/archives-and-heritage/northamptonshire-archives/Pages/default.aspx.*

Partida, Hall and Foard. *An Atlas of Northamptonshire*. Oxbow Books, 2013.

Richardson, Douglas. *Plantagenet Ancestry*, Second Edition, v. 1. 2011.

Staffordshire Record Society. *Collections for a History of Stafforshire, v. 8.* Harrison & Sons. 1887

Watford Church Parish Registers; births, deaths & marriages.

Wikimedia Commons contributors, "Main Page," Wikimedia Commons, the free media repository, *commons.wikimedia.org/w/index.php?title=Main_Page.*

Wilbraham, Sir Roger. *The Journal of Sir Roger Wilbraham*. 1902.

Wilson, George. *The Constitutional Right to a Revision of the Land Tax*. National Anti-Corn-Law League. 1842.

Citations

[1] Map from Wikimedia Commons, customisation by author.

[2] Wikimedia Commons.

[3] Image by permission TNA, E 31/2/2/1000/fol 229r.

[4] K.S.B Keats-Rohan, 1999, Domesday People, Appendix II The Northamptonshire Survey, pp 98, 105. Also, VCH vol1 p 379.

[5] Ancient Tenures of Land, Thomas Blount, 1815, pp 143-144.

[6] Wikimedia Commons.

[7] Pipe Roll Society, vol 95, original editor Joseph Hunter, 1833; Pipe Roll, 31 Henry I, p 84. New edition, 2012, p66.

[8] College of Arms, Vincent MS 10 f. 9v; and, John Gough Nichols, v1, p 214, iii, Arms of Watford.

[9] Arms from author's collection.

[10] College of Arms MS 2H5/111v.

[11] Luffield Priory Charters, vol 2, Hugh: no 294A, p3; Richard: vol 2, no 294, pp 2&3. Pipe Rolls, 31 Henry I, Hugo p83.

[12] Wikimedia Commons.

[13] Liber Rubeus de Scaccario, or The Red Book of the Exchequer, vol 1, p 378-9; translation partly from: The History of the Borough of Chesterfield … Reprinted from the Feudal History of Derbyshire, 1840, p 120-121.

[14] The Red Book, vol 1, p 290.

[15] College of Arms, Vincent MS 10 f. 9v; NRO OK 231, dated 1412.

[16] College of Arms MS Vincent 88 p4. Reproduced by permission of the Kings, Heralds and Pursuivants of Arms.

[17] Ancient Deeds, A.8730. Ref also A.6266 for 'Walter son of Turstan Coc', and A.6267 for Adam son of Turstan.

[18] Charter rolls, 18 Edward I, vol 2, 28 August 1290, p 371.

[19] Lands of Dissolved Religious Houses, No 3 Vol III, ref 374(a), p 48.

[20] Pipe Rolls: 22 Henry II p52/3, 23 Henry II p 91, 23 Henry II p 95, 24 Henry II p 53.

[21] Henry II of England from Cassell's History of England - Century Edition - published circa 1902.

[22] Bridges' Northants: vol 1, p 453, his ref Reg Priorat folio 104 b; Dugdale's Monasticom Anglicanum: vol 5, p 186.

[23] Bodl. MS. Top. Northants, C. 5 fol 546.

[24] College of Arms, Vincent MS 10 f. 9v; and, loosely, John Gough Nichols, v1, p 214, ii, Arden of Watford

[25] Arms from author's collection.

[26] Patent Rolls, 9 Edw II, p 491, 14 March 1316.

[27] Dugdale's Monasticon Anglicanum, 1846, vol 6 part 2, pp 903, 904, 905.

[28] Dugdale's Monasticon Anglicanum, 1825, vol 5, Roll 27 'Genealogia de Braybrok', p 183.

[29] Close Rolls, 15 John, 7th November 1213, p 155, Woodstock. (Thomas Duffus Hardy edition).
[30] Fine Rolls, 15 John, p 509, 24 November 1213.
[31] Fine Rolls, 15 John, p 510, 14 January 1214. Fine Rolls, 15 John, p 517, 18 January 1214.
[32] Close Rolls, 18 John, 17 August 1216, p 281 & 282, (sequential entries) at Worcester (Thomas Duffus Hardy).
[33] Wikimedia Commons. Matthew Paris, Chronica Majora, volume II, folio 51v (55v).
[34] Close Rolls, 1 Henry III, 15 June 1217, p 311, Stanwell (Thomas Duffus Hardy).
[35] Testa de Nevill, vol 1, p 324.
[36] Bodl. MS. Top. Northants., C. 5 fol 325.
[37] Image by permission TNA, C 60/15/m7.
[38] Fine Rolls 5 Henry III, no. 118, p 63; Henry III Fine Rolls Project, King's College London.
[39] Mario J Fernandes, Midland knights, pp 85 & 335, his ref: Pipe Rolls 6 Henry III, p 82.
[40] Arms from the collection of Priscilla Carney.
[41] From: 'The 1259 Pipe Roll', by Richard Cassidy, p 92.
[42] From: 'Royal finances in the period of baronial reform and rebellion, 1255-1270' by James Alexander Collingwood, pp 169 & 253.
[43] Rotuli Selecti Ad Res Anglicas et Hibernicas, 1834, Part III Rege Henrico III, p 91&95.
[44] Wikimedia Commons.
[45] Paragraph compiled from Midland knights, by Mario J Fernandes, pp 91, 120, 330, 331.
[46] Patent Rolls, 50 Henry III, 25 August 1266, p 631, Kennilworth.
[47] Patent Rolls, 52 Henry III, 2 July 1268, p 248, Northampton.
[48] Image used by permission NRO, NRO OK 139.
[49] Cal of (Ancient) Inq vol 1, p58, #32, 4 Edw I; and Cal (Modern) Inq vol 2, p111, #182, 4 Edw 1, March 1276.
[50] Close Rolls, 4 Edward I, vol 1, Feb 1276, pp 326 – 331, C 54 / 93.
[51] Fine Rolls, 5 Edward I part II, vol 1, p 86 (both entries): 7 July 1277 at Stourton and 6 September 1277 at Chester.
[52] NRO map 3158.
[53] BL MS and map 78141 A, dated 1778.
[54] David Hall, The Open Fields of Northamptonshire, pp 77 – 79.
[55] Image supplied and used by permission of Swyrich Corporation. Arms feature a red leopard and two red bars.
[56] Image by license Florida Centre for Instructional Technology.
[57] Patent Rolls, 5 June 1314, at Newminster, a parliamentary writ, 7 Edward II part II, p 122-123
[58] Calendar of Scutage Rolls, p 395, 23 August 1319, Fenham.

[59] Patent Rolls, 1 March 1322, Coventry.

[60] Close Rolls, Edward II: March 1322, Derby.

[61] Fine Rolls, 15 Edward II, part I, vol 3, March 1322, Doncaster.

[62] Image by permission and © of Northamptonshire County Council.

[63] Patent Rolls, Edw III, vol 8, p 88, 11 April 1348.

[64] Image by permission TNA, CP 25/1/177/76, no 218, 14 Edw III, 3 November 1340. Image from medievalgenealogy.org.uk..

[65] Patent Rolls, 27 Edw III, part 1, vol 9, p 430, 24 April 1353.

[66] Image of his original artwork © and by kind permission of Paul Hitchin, warriorsfortheworkingday@gmail.com.

[67] Image of his original artwork © and by kind permission of Paul Hitchin, warriorsfortheworkingday@gmail.com.

[68] History of Market Harborough, by J H Hill, 1875, chapter on Baggrave (a branch of the Burneby family), p 333.

[69] Wikimedia Commons.

[70] By permission Hamline University, St Paul MN, Brass Rubbing item b_lam_1406, from St. Michael and All Angels church, Lambourne, Berks.

[71] Wikimedia Commons.

[72] E-CIPM 23-212, July 1429; also Calendar (Ancient) Inquisitions vol 4, p 120, no 29, 7 Henry VI

[73] E-CIPM 23-665, October 1431; also Calendar (Ancient) Inquisitions vol 4, p 136, no 34, 10 Henry VI

[74] Drawing by Paul Davies, 2013.

[75] Testament Vetusta, 1826, vol 1, p 255.

[76] Field, The Life and Times of Sir Thomas Mallory, p 87, his reference: G.L. Kittredge; also 'Last Years of T.M.' by same author.

[77] Wikimedia Commons.

[78] Wikimedia Commons.

[79] Bridges History of Northamptonshire, vol 1, p 585

[80] Image used by kind permission of Daniel White, Watford.

[81] Wikimedia Commons.

[82] College of Arms MS 2H5 f 111v. Reproduced by permission of the Kings, Heralds and Pursuivants of Arms.

[83] Dugdale's Monasticon Anglicanum, 1830, vol 6 issue 1, p 116.

[84] State Papers Queen Elizabeth – Volume 240: 1591, item 137

[85] NRO OK 4, dated 2 February 1591; and NRO OK 137, dated 3 February 1592.

[86] PCC Wills: PROB 11: Will Registers 1599-1623 Piece 101: Bolein, Quire Numbers 1-56 (1603).

[87] House of Commons Journal Volume 1: 23 April 1624, and 07 May 1624.

[88] NRO OK 64.

[89] Image used by permission NRO, from NRO OK 223.

[90] Image supplied and used by permission of Swyrich Corporation. Arms feature ermine and two silver barry wavy.

[91] Feet of Fines: Henry III 1218-1245.

[92] 'Houses of the Benedictine monks: The priory of Sandwell', by BHO. Also Peter Coss, Lordship, knighthood and locality, p 279.
[93] Parliament Rolls, 18 Edward I [1290], Roll 2, no 88; SC 8/256/12795.
[94] NRO OK 202, 18 October 1315.
[95] Image used by permission NRO, NRO OK 202.
[96] Wikimedia Commons.
[97] Patent Rolls, 22 Edward III, p 96, 28 May 1348, Westminster.
[98] David Hall, The Open Fields of Northamptonshire, p 358.
[99] A History of Northamptonshire: Vol 5, the Hundred of Cleley (BHO).
[100] Greater Medieval Houses of England and Wales, Volume 2, p 293.
[101] Timeline for Stoke Bruerne and Shutlanger History: © The Friends of the Canal Museum.
[102] Greater Medieval Houses of England and Wales, Volume 2, p 294.
[103] Patent Rolls, 8 Henry V, 16 November 1420, p 308.
[104] Image used by kind permission of Daniel White, Watford.
[105] C 139/102/24 mm. 1–2 or E-CIPM 25-475; courtesy http://www.inquisitionspostmortem.ac.uk
[106] NRO OK 55, 14 July, 14 Henry VII, 1499. Image used by permission NRO.
[107] Calendar of Patent Rolls, Eliz I, vol 3, HMSO, Deputy Keeper of the Records, 1950. 6 April, 5 Eliz [1563], p 550.
[108] Image used by permission NRO, from NRO OK 229.
[109] Indent b&s: NRO OK 463, 20 Sep 1569; Grant: NRO OK 114, 27 Sep1569; Final Concorde: NRO OK 460, Sept 1570; Indent recov: NRO OK 121 & NRO OK 167, both 20 March 1571; Exemp Recov: NRO OK 18, 30 Oct 1571.
[110] Bridges' History … of Northamptonshire, vol 1, p 587.
[111] NRO OK 48.
[112] NRO OK 338.
[113] NRO OK 49.
[114] John Gough Nichols, The Topographer and Genealogist, p 212; from College of Arms, Vincent MS, 10 f. 9v.
[115] Ancient Deeds, A.8228, 13 October 1315.
[116] Image by permission TNA, CP 25/1/177/76, no 218. Image from medievalgenealogy.org.uk.
[117] Watermill from Luttrell Psalter, c1335, by permission © British Library Board (Add. MS 42130 f181r).
[118] Ancient Deeds, A.10083, written at Watford 2 October 1348 (in French).
[119] William Camden, Visitation Co. Warwick, 1619, p 129.
[120] Wikimedia Commons
[121] William Camden, Visitation Co. Warwick, 1619, p 129.
[122] http://www.historyofparliamentonline.org/volume/1386-1421/member/catesby-john
[123] Dugdale's Antiquities of Warwickshire, p 223.
[124] College of Arms, Vincent MS 10 f. 9v.
[125] Arms from author's collection.

[126] Image by permission of the Parochial Church Council, Ashby St Ledgers.
[127] From illustration by F W Fairhall, c 1862; author's collection.
[128] Calendar of Charter Rolls, vol 5, 1412, 13-14 Henry IV, p 447
[129] Ancient Deeds, A.8448, 6 August 1464.
[130] Wikimedia Commons.
[131] Patent Rolls, 38 Henry VI, part I, p 551, 20 March 1460, Westminster.
[132] Bodl. MS. Top. Northants., C. 6, fol 427; 28 July 15 Henry VI, 1437.
[133] Ancient Deeds, A.9892, 12 December 1478
[134] TNA E 36/178.
[135] Image by permission TNA, E 36/178.
[136] Image of his original artwork © and by kind permission of Paul Hitchin, warriorsfortheworkingday@gmail.com.
[137] Calendar Inquisitions Henry VII Vol III, 28 June I Henry VII [1486], p 574, no 1143.
[138] Calendar Inquisitions Henry VII Vol III, 7 September 2 Henry VII [1486], p 361, no 615.
[139] Calendar Inquisitions Henry VII Vol III, 26 November 3 Henry VII [1487], p 368, no 639.
[140] IPM, 14 January 1487; the latter IPM recorded by another IPM at Warwick 18 May 1512 held after the death of Risley; Sydenham Hervey, Ladbroke and its Owners, p 78-79. That 1487 IPM is not in the Calendar Henry VII Vol III.
[141] Calendar Inquisitions Henry VII Vol III, 14 February 9 Henry VII [1494], p 511, no 998; also TNA E 150_673. The dorse has endorsement: the inquisition had been delivered to the Treasury by the hand of Richard Empson.
[142] Patent Rolls, 10 Henry VII, p 11; 5 December 1494, Westminster.
[143] Patent Rolls, 4 Henry VII, p 276; 2 July 1489, Westminster.
[144] NRO OK 117.
[145] NRO OK 169.
[146] NRO OK 135.
[147] Image used by permission NRO, from NRO OK 120.
[148] Bodl. MS. Top. Northants., C. 6, fol 427; per Bridges: Fine Rolls 11 Eliz, MS Hatton.
[149] NRO OK 243.
[150] NRO OK 457.
[151] Calendar Inquisitions Henry VII Vol III, p 513, no 1003, 26 January 21 Henry VII [1506].
[152] Calendar Inquisitions Henry VII Vol III, p 56, no 101, 21 April 21 Henry VII [1506].
[153] Calendar Inquisitions Henry VII Vol III, p 55 no 99 21 May 21 Henry VII, p 55 no 100 28 April 21 Henry VII, p 57 no 102 20 April 21 Henry VII, p 57 no 103 28 April 21 Henry VII, p 58 no 104 4 May 21 Henry VII.
[154] Wikimedia Commons.
[155] Close Rolls, P.S. Pat. 4 Hen. VIII. p. 2, m. 2. [3524.] 8 Nov. 1512, delivered Westminster 13 Nov.
[156] Bridges' History ... of Northants, v 1, p 585.

[157] TNA E 41/401, 2 Dec. 30 Eliz [1587]. Image by permission TNA.

[158] Sydenham Hervey, Ladbroke and its Owners, p 80/81, from Indenture dated 2 March, 34 Eliz, 1592; also NRO ASL 74.

[159] Image by permission TNA, MPF 1/34.

[160] NRO ASL 1178/1.

[161] Wikimedia Commons.

[162] Sydenham Hervey, Ladbroke and its Owners, p 76; also Hervey's ref, the DNB.

[163] http://www.historyofparliamentonline.org/volume/1660-1690

[164] Image used by permission NRO, NRO OK 250.

[165] NRO OK 43.

[166] Image of his original artwork © and by kind permission of Paul Hitchin, warriorsfortheworkingday@gmail.com.

[167] PCC Wills: PROB 11: Will Registers 1688-1696 Piece 395: Ent, Quire Numbers 47-90 (1689)

[168] Bodl. MS. Top. Northants., C. 32 folios 169 – 173.

[169] Bodl. MS. Top. Northants., C. 32 fol 154.

[170] Bodl. MS. Top. Northants., F. 4 folios 63 – 65.

[171] Newspaper image © British Newspaper Archive. All rights reserved. With thanks to the British Newspaper Archive (www.britishnewspaperarchive.co.uk).

[172] Newspaper image © British Newspaper Archive. All rights reserved. With thanks to the British Newspaper Archive (www.britishnewspaperarchive.co.uk).

[173] NRO map 3162.

[174] NRO map 3161.

[175] Newspaper image © British Newspaper Archive. All rights reserved. With thanks to the British Newspaper Archive (www.britishnewspaperarchive.co.uk).

[176] NRO ZA 901. Cartwright lands include those put on sale before 1805 and sold after 1805. Includes changes folllowing the deaths of John Lee 1802 and Richard Reeve in 1804. See also NRO ZA 903.